The People and the Faith of the Bible

The People and the Faith of the Bible

André Chouraqui

Translated by William V. Gugli

University of Massachusetts Press   Amherst   1975

Originally published in French as
La Vie quotidienne des Hébreux au temps de la Bible
Copyright © 1971 by Librairie Hachette
Translation copyright © 1975 by
The University of Massachusetts Press
All rights reserved
Library of Congress Catalog Card Number 74-21237
ISBN 0-87023-172-3
Printed in the United States of America

Library of Congress Cataloging in Publication Data

Chouraqui, André, 1917–
    The people and the faith of the Bible.

    Translation of La vie quotidienne des Hébreux au
temps de la Bible.
    Bibliography: p.
    1. Jews—Civilization. I. Title.
DS112.C4813   220.9′5   74–21237
ISBN 0–87023–172–3

Contents

Contents

Prologue The Sustaining Roots

The year is 1031 B.C.; the city is Gilgal near Jericho, in the land of the tribe of Benjamin. The Hebrews are gathered together to crown their first King, Saul—the son of Kish—who is easily recognized by his imposing figure. In the sanctuary the priests offer holocausts and communion sacrifices to their God, whose ineffable name is YHWH. The rejoicing is great; wine is flowing, and there is dancing and singing on this mystical and joyful day, the first of a new era, that of the Kings of Israel.

Four hundred and forty-five years later, in 586 B.C., blood flows, that important historical symbol—this time in the streets of Jerusalem, and the sacrificers are the soldiers of Nebuchadnezzar, the conqueror. In the fires of the city and the Temple the victims of this new holocaust, which marks the fall of the Hebrew monarchy, are human beings, the soldiers of a defeated and enslaved Israel.

Between these two dates the Holy Land has been the site of extraordinary events. The traditions handed down from the Patriarchs, Abraham, Isaac, and Jacob, and the laws and teachings of Moses inspired the Kings and Prophets. We have, as it were, been witness to the founding of a new civilization in the history of mankind, that of the monotheistic ethic, whose principles challenge and destroy not only the religious but the political, moral, and social bases of pagan antiquity.

There will be successive additions to the nucleus of the new world, but the essential parts of the thirty-nine books of the Bible are conceived and written at this time. They dominate Israel's thinking almost exclusively during the centuries when the canon of Holy Scrip-

1

ture is defined, and when the new religions, Judaism and Christianity, for which the Pentateuch, the Prophets, and the Hagiographers are a revealed authority, are founded. Consequently, the daily life of the Hebrews in the time of the Prophets becomes an incomparable and exemplary source of inspiration for many nations.

Throughout the ancient world, in Egypt, Mesopotamia, India, China, Greece, and Rome, man attempts to save everything he can from the general erosion of time. Through architecture, sculpture, and painting the fleeting realities of daily life are preserved. The bas-reliefs and paintings in an Egyptian tomb show a man with his wife and children, his household. They tell that he liked to cover his domain on foot, or on a litter, or in a boat; whether he preferred fishing to hunting, and what equipment he used for his favorite sport. One may see his manicurist and chiropodist at work and observe their clothes, their jewels, and their faces. The whole gamut of the trades is shown as if in a film—the peasant who plows, sows, reaps, ties, and stores his grain. One sees the production of flour, bread, wine. Artists work with their clay, stone, metals, wood, and precious stones, which adorn lovely people whose faces are as familiar to us as those of our contemporaries. From the beginning of the Fourth Dynasty, Egyptian artists refined the extensive collection of pictures and sculptures that represent life and its tasks. The evolution of their techniques, arts, manners, and customs is presented through the centuries. What is true of Egypt for three thousand years applies in the same way to all the great civilizations that have escaped the destruction of time.

We know the faces of Seti I, of Ramses, of Ur-Nanshe, the King of Lagash, of Naram-Sin, King of Agade, of Meli-Shipak II, King of Babylon. We know Assur-bani-pal's expression as he stood in his chariot and we are familiar with the extraordinary beauty of the Priest-King of Knossos. We have a bust of Aristophanes, Caesar, and a thousand others, dating from every era and representing every country.

This is not the case for Israel, however, whose Prophets, in the name of the Almighty, wage a victorious battle against all images, which are forever excluded from the Hebraic city in the name of YHWH, creator of heaven and earth, whose law forbids the reproduction of forms. The faces of Abraham, Moses, David, Isaiah, Ezekiel are forever lost to us because of a transcendental will that aims at erasing the contingent—even the most exceptional—for the sake of the eternal. As soon as man, or his creation, or even the idea of duration tends to move from the Hebraic obsession of seeing everything in relation to God, a mental process works to put them back in their places in the divine transcendental order. The sky, the earth, the situations and activities of daily life, birth, marriage, international relations, war, peace, life and death have no reality other than the one conferred by the divine plan.

All ancient civilizations are awed by the sacred, which for the Hebrew conscience takes traumatic proportions, to the point that the realities of daily life—be they political, social, religious, national, artistic, literary, or poetic—acquire dimensions and characteristics unprecedented in the history of mankind. It is within this framework, and nowhere else, where the increate eternal insinuates itself into creation, that the key to the existence and permanence of Israel must be sought. Because of this, the natural conditions of Hebrew life undergo a transcendentalization in order to conform to a social organization that subordinates the individual and the people to an order determined by religious revelation. This revelation is all the more obvious in that all sources of knowledge of the Hebraic world have disappeared. If they ever existed, they have been censored, either voluntarily by the guardians of national orthodoxy or naturally by the drifts of time, so that they cannot be uncovered. If there is mystery in a people's acceptance of a religion that imposes the severest restraints, it lies in the various levels of the definition of the new religious message, in its reception and its uninterrupted transmission from generation to generation, and in its universal dimensions, stemming from the development of the three monotheistic religions, Judaism, Christianity, and Mohammedanism.

A priori, it would seem that the task of describing the daily life of the Hebrews in such a far-off time might be difficult. The Prophets predict and in a sense provoke the absorption of the temporal into the eternal. To make matters worse, their country is at the crossroads of the principal communication routes of antiquity. It is coveted, and conquered, by all the great empires. In every era and in its every corner it is pillaged by the Egyptians, the Assyrians, and the Babylonians. Successively, the Persians, the Greeks, the Romans, the

Byzantines, the Arabs, the Crusaders, the Seleucidae, the Turks, and the English occupy the Holy Land, destroying any traces that might have escaped the vigilance of the Prophets and given some direct and specific clue about everyday life. Nowhere else have vestiges of the past been so eradicated—sometimes with good intentions—as in this inspired country.

What remains of this prestigious past? A few archeological sites where rare treasures can be dug up, and a few books, very limited in content and wholly tendentious. What would we know about the West if, in describing its 2,000-year history after Christ, we had only the Justinian Code, Saint Thomas Aquinas' *Summa Theologica,* a few medieval tales, and a history of the Church written four centuries ago —all in the form of extracts not exceeding a thousand pages? Yet this is the situation when we attempt to establish the daily realities of the biblical people—with the additional problem that time has almost completely destroyed the extra-biblical sources in Israel and among the neighboring peoples.

The East, beginning with the most ancient legends of Egypt and Mesopotamia and up to the writing of the Gospels, the Talmuds, and the Koran, has devoted its genius almost completely to assimilating holy scriptures. This general trait shows itself most strongly in the Hebrews, no doubt because they have been so intent upon seeing everything in relation to God, *sub specie aeternitatis,* and because their most humble daily realities have been viewed as a reflection of heaven.

We do not know what Abraham looked like, yet we know the principal episodes of his life intimately. We see him tear himself from his family and cross the Asian deserts in order to launch the great adventure that begins a new era in the history of man. We see Jephthah's expression as he plunges his knife into his daughter's throat. Her blood gushes out, to be burned with her young flesh in the sacrificial flames. We detect the psychology of desire, of murder, and of salvation in the drama of David and Bathsheba's love. Solomon displays all the ostentation of the East in his court and his harem. As we read the Bible the details of the daily life of the Kings, the princes, the notables, the priests, the Levites, the Prophets, the men and women of the people unroll before our eyes as in a moving picture. Not only are the externals described with the refinement and care of a memorialist, but the psychology of history's players is exposed in the light of a deeper science, the knowledge of God, with nothing left to guesswork.

The thirty-nine books of the Bible, written between the second half of the second millennium and the second half of the first millennium B.C., describe a period that stretches from the call of Abraham to the post-exilic era and tries to encompass the story of mankind since the creation of the world. The most intense coverage, however, is that of the monarchical period. The Bible addresses itself to this period primarily, but not without an occasional examination of earlier and later periods. In any case, after the introduction of iron into this part of the world, at the beginning of the first millennium, the fundamental techniques of the Hebrew way of life remain almost unchanged during the 445 years that form the core of this study. Then, in the post-exilic era, the political, religious, social, and intellectual structures will be deeply shaken.

Thus the Bible is an amazing storehouse of knowledge. In its laws and historical accounts it does not neglect any detail, neither the price of a cart or horse in Solomon's time, nor the intrigues of the court or harem, nor the manner of sacrificial offering or the waging of war.

In the past hundred years biblical criticism has defined precise methods that allow a scientific utilization of the essential data of the book. A large body of literature, patiently developed in Israel and elsewhere, throws new light on biblical texts whose age and fundamental historic value are constantly reconfirmed by contemporary research and discoveries. These studies have extended into neighboring empires (Mesopotamia and Egypt) for the same period, as well as to the people of Canaan, renewing and broadening our field of knowledge.

Finally, archeology provides an ever-increasing flow of varied and positive information. Hundreds of excavation areas yield tangible traces of the life of the Hebrews to the teams of scholars who work them. Here the contact with the past is immediate, presenting us with undeniable realities in its objects and inscriptions. "The earth has recognized us; it has started to talk to us," a shepherd in a Galilee kibbutz told me recently.

Epigraphic documents, in Hebrew, in Aramaic, in Phoenician; the stele of Mesha, King of Moab, the Siloam Inscription, the numerous tablets found in Samaria, in Lachish; the stele of Shishak of Egypt, the inscriptions in the sanctuary at Karnak, the numerous Assyrian and Babylonian inscriptions—the royal annals of Shalmaneser, of Tiglath-Pileser III, of Sennacherib—provide copious material, to be dealt with circumspectly. The neo-Babylonian chronicles that report the history of the years 745 to 538, primarily those of Nebuchadnezzar, strikingly confirm biblical information.

Here is a jug that could have contained Abraham's oil or wine; these walls, this palace, were built by and for Solomon. This trepanned skull, which dates from the ninth century, proves the existence of knowledgeable surgeons in Lachish—though the Bible does not mention them. The patient, probably an important figure of the period, survived his operation for years, as the state of the skull testifies. Here are some chairs, some tables, some instruments, some art objects of the times. Bit by bit secrets are revealed. While I am writing these lines, the Israeli radio announces the discovery of a treasure of silver and jewels in Eshtemoh, near Hebron—the most important one to date for the royal era whose portrait appears with ever-increasing precision.

Thus the historian is faced with a considerable volume of all sorts of documents that, in their richness and variety, impose the strictest critical caution.

The Bible is the primary source. It presents the history of a few Semitic people who lived in Asia three millennia ago and brings it —paradoxically—close to us. By its diffusion, the Bible, a catechism for a great segment of mankind, becomes a book of *contemporary* history for many others. This is true even in France, where the Book of Books is absent from the university originally created to be its interpreter. This deficiency in French education, which may be explained historically, calls for satisfaction elsewhere. Each year numerous translations and commentaries appear, and widely circulated periodicals and films distribute them.

In thousands of ways the biblical past haunts us—in Israel as a revival; in Christian countries as a renewal in theology, catechisms, philosophy, literature, art, and liturgy. Even the revolutionary protest of our times is informed, consciously or unconsciously, by the perspectives and message of the Prophets of Israel. We are tempted to project our current realities into the biblical past, as the Renaissance painters used Florentine faces and scenes to evoke those of the Holy

Land. So Kierkegaard in *Fear and Trembling* projects his personal fate as that of Abraham leading Isaac to the sacrificial site. Another example is Darmesteter, or, even closer to our time, Henri Pirenne describing biblical society while introducing our contemporary concerns. Errors of this sort have risks or consequences, which are all the more serious because research is rarely divorced from the need to prove something—in support of classical Judeo-Christian apologetics, or to its detriment.

The permanent conflict that we find in Israel between the business of daily living and the eternal, between nature and revelation, between the world and God, has this essential fact as a result and a corrective: from its origin, and increasingly so, Hebrew religion has been "historic," in contrast to the natural religions of antiquity. Hence the extreme complexity of the realities that must be understood. The histories of Egypt, Mesopotamia, Greece, Italy, or Gaul exist *in themselves,* without being essentially dependent on a religious credo, a credo that may vary—ranging from polytheism to Christian or Moslem monotheism to contemporary nonbelief—without threatening the existence of the nation.

In the case of the Hebrews, on the contrary, there is a relatively late and simultaneous birth of a religion and a people established on the land where their destiny is to be fulfilled. From the beginning, there has been a fusion of the God of Sinai, the people of Israel, and the country, the Holy Land. The daily life of the Hebrews will be animated by three indissociable realities: a God, a people, a land. The message cannot be separated from the people who receives it, and this people can conceive of itself only in relation to its land—an alliance all the more restrictive because it is indissoluble. The infidelities of the people may cause it to be expelled from its land and alienated from its God; yet it will be no less tied to its double adherence, celestial and terrestrial.

This global intuition of God, man, and the land places us in the concreteness of history, and perhaps confers a parcel of truth to Dubnov's thesis that the history of Israel has to be understood as "co-extensive to the totality of history."

These assertions explain the profound meaning of our presentation. In the process of divine incarnation, which biblical Israel is, the ultimate goal of human and social life consists in the temporal order's being informed by the eternal so as to make the presence and the will of the creator a reality. We shall see how the organization of social and religious life is oriented toward these transcendental ends. If Israel's size saves it from imperialistic ambitions—which neither Egypt, Mesopotamia, Greece, nor Rome could resist—it pushes Israel, by the thrust of faith, to aspire not only to the unity of the world but, further, to its reshaping and rebirth in the splendor of the kingdom of God in the day of the Lord. The historical character of the revelation made to the people of the Bible comprises a very precise view of the world's future. Its golden age lies in the past, in the Garden of Eden, but also in the ever-imminent future of Messianic victory. The people of Israel are chosen only to the extent that they fulfill the desired mediation and work for the coming of the Messiah by their conformity to the revealed order. The Messiah will ensure the triumph of light over darkness and the spirit over matter by accomplishing a true change of the natural order. Then "the wolf will lie with the lamb" (Isaiah 11:6). Israel will live in peace with its neighbors and warfare will be no more. All creation has a beginning, and aims toward one goal—the establishment of the kingdom of God. The various orders of the Covenant mark Israel and humanity's progress toward this supreme end. The choice of the "elect," in the biblical perspective, does not constitute a belittling of God, as a prisoner of a tribe and its customs, but is an act necessary to the process of universal salvation. It is no doubt in this sense that Jesus' bold declaration, "Salvation comes from the Jews" (John 4:22), must be heard. God has chosen Israel as his people, the messenger of a historic and ethical monotheism that transmits his revelation to all nations. Not only is the daily life of the Hebrews sacred in content, but history itself is conceived as a rite whose stage is the entire universe and whose mission is the fulfillment and liberation of man. This is the plot that was devised and acted out in the days of the Bible, on occasion crucifying people who played their roles. Its drama has given its true eternal meaning to the daily life of a great many men.

In contrast to the vast territories of Egypt, India, Mesopotamia, Elam, Iran, Syria, Canaan, Anatolia, and the Aegean world, since the fourth millennium B.C. the Hebraic people occupied one of the tiniest spaces—a few thousand, sometimes only a few hundred, square kilometers—before all geographical support was denied it in its exile. It is antedated by Egypt, whose calendar goes as far back as the end of the fifth millennium B.C.; Mesopotamia's civilization can be dated to the early fourth millennium; Susa developed some eight hundred years before Abraham left Ur; Byblos goes back to the beginning of the third millennium; Crete was in the metal age at the time; and the civilizations of the Indus or the Chinese Shia dynasty go back to the middle of the third millennium.

Unlike Egypt, Mesopotamia, or Persia, Israel's size forces it to dissociate the civilizing factor from imperialism. There is a special situation in the Near East, for a long time characteristic of the shores of the Mediterranean: the birth of great civilizations is soon followed by the appearance of empires that rather quickly show a tendency toward world domination—which often leads to their downfall.

Israel's size has saved it from such undertakings. Small, and poor as well, it has nothing to compare with the Nile, the Tigris, or the Euphrates. The crossroads of Africa, Asia, and Greece, it has constantly had to defend itself from greedy conquerors, thereby wasting its resources and worsening its poverty. No acropolis, no pyramids, no dazzling art or architecture, no original science or new techniques worked in favor of the Hebrews. In all these accomplishments, which enhance the neighboring civilizations, Israel's share is negligible.

Such are the days of the Bible: a peasant gets up at dawn, prepares his tools and goes to the fields, while his wife, in their modest house, goes about raising the children, doing the cooking, and feeding the animals; an artist finishes a sculpture in ivory for the sacred prostitute of a sanctuary at Dor; a village is pillaged by men from Moab; a child is born—the parents are joyful as they prepare for his circumcision; a priest plunges his knife into the throat of a lamb—he offers YHWH its life and Israel's as the sacrificial blood runs; a leper shrieks with pain; at Lachish, a surgeon, a contemporary of Solomon, successfully performs a trepanation; an adulterous woman is stoned; a thief is beaten; a parricide is stoned; hundreds of slaves build a palace; a dignitary embraces the seven women of his harem, leaves his luxurious home, and in a gift-laden chariot goes to visit his King. The King, in Jerusalem or Samaria, is surrounded by a court and an administration that make it possible for him to keep up to date on the internal affairs of his domain; he receives the nobles, administers justice to the poor, welcomes ambassadors from Mesopotamia, Egypt, and Damascus, and even from distant Sheba, on occasion; he offers his sacrifices in the Temple, where the priests, who it is said have rather bad characters, eat a great deal of meat—that of the animals sacrificed to YHWH's glory. True, they have the thankless job of teaching their people. Overcoming the tumult of business and war, transcending time and space, the ever-relevant voice of the Prophets is raised— seers, madmen of God—who dare defy all the paganisms of antiquity, including that of their own brothers, to announce a new message, yet unheard, a message of justice, brotherhood, unity, love, and peace.

Henceforth Israel, echoing that voice, concentrates on expressing a new conception of man, God, the universe, and history. Herein lies its absolute originality and endless significance—so great, Saint Paul has said, that it constitutes a mystery whose roots sustain us.

A mystery is stated, it is not explained. This book intends to help the reader cross the five thresholds of the daily universe of the Hebrews: the gates of the land, of the people, of the days, of the temporal and the eternal, and finally of heaven.

The First Gate The Land

The Land Is a Living Person

Historical studies of ancient civilizations limit themselves to a few generalizations on the countries of their origins. Fustel de Coulanges does even less: he treats the ancient city without any reference to the geographical realities of Greece or Italy that allowed its development. Such an omission is impossible in this work. The most naive Hebrew knows that his land is a pivotal reality in the universal order and that his own life is an integral part of that reality. Both are creatures of Elohim and, as such, are subject to the Law. The land is the essential reality of his existence, not only as it relates to being, from birth to death, but, more mysteriously, as it relates to spiritual destiny. There is a mystical union between Elohim, man, and the sod: the man-earth relationship is never separate from God. The fertility of the fields or their barrenness, rain or drought, and the sea's rage or calm are not dependent on the play of natural laws but are the obvious result of man's conformity with, or revolt from, the divine order.

More than any other people of antiquity, Israel preserves and cherishes the memories of its past. Subjectively, its historic memory goes back to the creation of the world. The entire universe is a totality and the people, created in the image of Elohim, are integral and essential to it. The dialogue both with God and the elements, which depend on his will for global harmony or collapse, is inescapable. A Hebrew who invokes the heavens and the earth, who huddles in a circle, or who offers a sacrifice to end a drought accomplishes an efficacious act. Not a single listener who hears the story of Jonah doubts for a moment the obvious link between the fleeing Prophet's misdeed and the terrible storm that threatens the boat on which he has taken refuge.

The nations know that their countries belong to them by virtue of the nature of things. The Hebrew feels that he has a land by the grace of God and the strength of the promise that allowed the conquest and occupation of Canaan. The land of Israel does not belong to its people in the same way as Egypt does to the Egyptians, Canaan to the Canaanites, Aram to the Arameans.

A divine order has determined the natural order of things. Elohim spoke to Abraham one day: "Go forth out of thy country, and from thy kindred, and out of thy father's house, and come into the land which I shall show thee" (Gen. 12:1). That is how it happened. Elohim makes everything complicated, and it is difficult to fathom his plan. But one thing is sure for the Hebrews: God exists, and it is absolutely impossible to escape his omnipotent will. Abraham's call, Jacob's election, Moses' mission, the exodus from Egypt, the revelation of the Torah, the conquest of Canaan, the Bible insists, are departures from the natural order, mutations caused by the free intrusion of the transcendental will of God.

God tears Abraham from Ur of the Chaldees, from the tranquillity of his home, and sends him into the solitude of the great Asian deserts. Toward what? The text states it well: toward a land continually in the future, promised in a vision and unknown at the start. Land of the revelation. Such it is for Abraham, such it remains for the Hebrews. Land of the promise, but one that man must earn by his rectitude, his faith, and his strength. Every Hebrew knows by heart the trials of Abraham, Isaac, and Jacob as they go toward the continually promised but continually refused land. He knows what this struggle has cost his people: Abraham reduced to accepting the sacrifice of his son, Moses confronting Pharaoh in the prodigious combat by which he delivers the people from slavery, Joshua becoming a military leader to wrest the land from its natural occupants.

The Desert and the Land of Men

"In the beginning God created the heavens and the earth" (Gen. 1:1). The Hebrew vision places the land in the center of his universe.

Above are the heavens, inhabited by God. All around are the mountains, the stars, the sea, and, farther down, the place of the dead, Sheol. The entirety is a huge tent, a gigantic palace with God as its King (Isaiah 40:22; Job 26:11; Gen. 7:11; II Kings 7:2). For the Hebrews, the land is basically the country "flowing with milk and honey," wheat, oil, wine, fruits, which God has given to them (Deut. 11:9). It is the chosen and blessed place. Its blessing is the true source of fertility, happiness, the fulfillment of the promise, the vision and the Law.

The Hebrew is horrified at the possibility of being expelled from his land. Away from it there is nothingness, or, worse still, the desert, the cursed place where there are "neither plants, nor figs, nor pomegranates, nor even water to drink (Joel 1:12; Num. 20:5; Isaiah 5:6, 7:24; Deut. 8:15). Only demons inhabit it and even animals flee from it (Lev. 16:10, 21). We are far from the romantic concept of the desert held during the patriarchal age, or that of a later period when the Rechabites reacted against the sedentary city life. There is no doubt that desert life is terrifying.

The supreme punishment inflicted upon the land soiled by man's sin is to be transformed into a desert. The land, a living person, is part of the humanity inhabiting it. When the latter is unworthy, the former is ravaged by flood and made desolate. If the sky turns to brass and the land to lead, the fault lies with the sin of man, transgressor of the Covenant. Isaiah describes the sad process in these terms:

> Their land shall be soaked with blood ... And the streams thereof shall be turned into pitch, and the ground thereof into brimstone: and the land thereof shall become burning pitch ... from generation to generation it shall lie waste, none shall pass through it for ever and ever. The bittern and hedgehog shall possess it: and the ibis and the raven shall dwell in it: and a line shall be stretched out upon it, to bring it to nothing ... it shall be the habitation of dragons, and the pasture of ostriches. And demons and monsters shall meet, and the hairy ones shall cry out one to another (Isaiah 34:7–14).

Thus the boundary that divides the fertile land from the desert is none other than that which separates benediction from curse, life from death. Nobody can live in Sodom and Gomorrah, not because of the climatic conditions of these desolate places but because of the corruption and sin of their inhabitants (Gen. 18, 19).

The desert, the curse, and death are consequences of the fearsome power by which man is free to say no to the will of God. If man is worthy of being blessed, he inherits the land of men with its pastures and flocks, its fields and harvests, its orchards and fruits. The people and the land form a living couple. The relationship is intimate and mutual. If man is good, he becomes established on the land. If he falls prey to sin, the land vomits him (Ex. 20:12; Lev. 18:25, 19:29; Jer. 12:4; Hos. 9:3; Amos 7:17). It is up to man alone to make of earth a heaven or a hell.

Land of YHWH, Land of Ancestors

All man's earth was made by God, but its heart is the Holy Land, where YHWH has led Israel. YHWH is present where man can be in communion with his holiness, which is given exclusively to Israel until the Gentile is converted. Israel is YHWH's base, the place chosen for his revelation and his presence. The country is the land of YHWH; its cities are Elohim's, who is master of all. Its sanctuaries—the Temple of Jerusalem is the most important of them—are the earthly abodes of him who dwells in heaven. YHWH himself and Israel are partners, working together to conquer the country. Elohim has the best share in the conquest, and he is the more extreme in his plans for he desires the destruction of its natural occupants, the seven peoples of Canaan.

There is an intimate relationship between Elohim, the "God of the mountains," and his mountain people, Israel (I Kings 20:28). That is why the people will not be able to remain in its country unless it obeys YHWH's law (Lev. 20:22). The land of Israel is the land of the Covenant. Without it the relation of the people to its God would be jeopardized. The life of each family of Israel depends on the land of its heritage. YHWH's omnipotent will and history manifest Israel's title over its land.

Canaan is constantly referred to by the Hebrews as the land of the ancestors (Gen. 48:21, 50:24; Deut. 1:8, 6:23, 31:20). This historical reference is linked to the very essence of Israel's vision of the world. The people, like the land, is a person whose face is renewed by each generation and whose every act engages the future. Merits and demerits shape its destiny. Repeatedly the Prophets return to this idea: the history of Israel in its land is the result of the virtues and shortcomings of its forefathers. In this sense the past informs the present, whose nature it determines by shaping the soul of the people. Throughout the ages the people are joined to the land, and both to YHWH, creator of all life, of every living soul.

The land of man and those who inhabit it are in some way inextricably united. The people comes into being at the time of its exodus from Egypt, the country of slavery. To free them, God had to crush the dragon, and had to dry up the waters to make a path through the sea. It is this miracle that prepares the way for Zion and allows the people to take possession of the Promised Land (Isaiah 51:9–12; Ezek. 29:3, 32:2). The crossing of the Red Sea is pivotal, a leap from the darkness of slavery toward the freedom of the land redeemed by the victory of the people. Their deliverance transforms the desert into the land of man, a pool, a fountain, and gives it the vocation of salvation (Isaiah 41:18, 43:16–19). The monster whose name is Rahab, the dragon, is conquered (Isaiah 51:9–11).

The Land of the Covenant: Its Sabbath and Its Jubilee

The Hebrew does not make a clear-cut distinction between the soul and the body, mind and matter, the thought and the nature it informs. He has an intuitive and synthetic global view of reality. For him, the earth and stones are living beings that participate in the soul of the people who inhabit the earth and in the spirit of YHWH who creates them; a Covenant, a result of the creative act itself, is the basis of the relationship between the people and the land, understood and accepted as a living person. This Covenant, formally sealed by Noah, Abraham, and Moses, is part of the creative act, which it expresses in rights and duties. The farmer must deal with the land according to the requirements of this Covenant if he wishes to enjoy the fruits of his labor (Job 31:38–40). He must give the fields the seventh day of rest, the seventh year of fallowness, and the jubilee of the forty-ninth year (Lev. 25:1–7; Ex. 23:10; Lev. 20:22). The earth has the right to that rest which comes from divine beatitude, just as do Israel, the farmer, the slave, and the animals. Man must allow the earth its liberty and its generosity by giving it its legitimate rest. He must grant it the first harvest of the fruit trees, and the corners of the fields must never be harvested by the owners, so that the poor may have their part of the inheritance.

The notion of property is affected by the Hebrews' conception of God and earth. Strictly speaking, YHWH is the sole proprietor of all creation. Man has a life-interest in the land. The family, the tribe—more than the individual—may enjoy its possession. Its transmission follows strict laws that limit its use.

"The land also shall not be sold forever: because it is mine, and you are strangers and sojourners with me" (Lev. 25:23). Herein lies the principle of the inalienability of a patrimony. A right of immediate repurchase is granted to the family, and the jubilee dissolves the effects of all real estate transactions (Lev. 25:1–22). Jeremiah's repurchase of the field of Anathoth proves that these laws were applied in the daily life of the Hebrews and that they explain their life style very well (Jer. 32:6–11). The seventh year's release (Deut. 15:1–13) and the restitution of the jubilee, tithing, the prohibition of loans at interest—are all limits on the principle of private property. These measures, which hinder free enterprise and the principles upon which today's "consumer society" are based, characterize Hebraic antiquity, which defines itself as a *sacrificial society*.

A Gift of God

For the Hebrew, the land is important inasmuch as it is a divine creation, an essential factor in the economy of salvation. It is a reality promised to the chosen people: the necessary support of the incarnations of history. It is the indispensable partner of its historic destiny. But in addition the Hebrew believes, and feels fully justified in so doing, that the land of the promise embodies truly exceptional beauty and features. He has numerous synonyms to label this cherished land, whose conquest cost so dearly. It is the Promised Land, the land of the Covenant, the Holy Land, the land of Judah, the land of beauty.

More recently, the Hebrew expresses the essential meaning of the country that has become his in one word, the Land.

A small country—tradition held that in patriarchal times the Holy Land was but the stone upon which Jacob rested his head to sleep. In the times of the trials, the time of Zerubbabel, for instance, it encompassed some 2,000 square kilometers, and what remained of Israel centered around Jerusalem. But even in the period of greatest splendor, under Solomon, or after the heroic campaign of the Maccabees, the country was contained in narrow limits that never exceeded some 26,000 square kilometers. From Nahr el-Kasimiyeh to Beersheba, it is 230 kilometers; in breadth, from the Mediterranean to the edge of the desert, the distance varies between 27 and 150 kilometers.

The Hebrew celebrates the beauty of his country in poems that have kept their meaning, freshness, and depth after many centuries. Love of country always opens onto a vision that transcends it and develops into the love of creation and the creator. The natural configuration of the Holy Land has favored such sublimation.

The Land of Beauty

Paul Claudel's page on the topography of Rio de Janeiro is famous —God decided to outdo himself. He made the purest sky, the most beautiful bay, the most shimmering sea, beaches, mountains, forests, flowers, birds, and insects, which must have stripped the heavens. A swarm of angels intercedes and disturbs the creator, who lets his *chef-d'oeuvre* fall to earth in the chaotic splendor of Rio. It must have been the same for Israel, except that in this case even the angels cooperated, and more carefully. Not only are the components of the countryside extremely beautiful (the Hebrew feels and proclaims this from birth until death), but together they make up a miniature universe, a microcosm.

The expanse is so limited that, from certain vantage points, the naked eye can see forty types of landscapes and climates. The eternal snows of Hermon are a few hours away from the windswept and burning deserts that surround the country. Coming from the east after traveling a few days in the deserts, among mountain crests and dry ravines where scraggy thistles are the only sign of life, one discovers the beautiful banks of Lake Tiberias or the Jordan. The green pastures, which seem to have been transported from Switzerland, Provence, or even Normandy, border either gallery-like forests (which seem imported from the depths of Africa) or lunar landscapes of the Jordan basin or the Dead Sea. The Hebrews express these rugged contrasts by saying that their country is both "the land of milk and honey" and "the land of lead with skies of brass which devours its inhabitants." It is never monotonous. Even the deserts of Judah, the Negev and Sinai, offer variety reminiscent of the Gobi Desert or others of Africa and America. The traveler and pilgrim is constantly in suspense before an ever-changing landscape, as if the earth were giving an inventory of its wonders and presenting itself in human dimensions to human comprehension. Gentle contrasts; magic colors play in the blue skies. Asia, Africa, and Europe (and not only its southern shores) seem to blend into a country that resembles all of them, and yet is original. The conquerors from Mesopotamia, Egypt, Greece, or Rome, as much later the Crusaders and pilgrims from all over the globe, have been able to find some spot in this small country that resembles their native villages.

Nature's Fantasy

Modern geologists and geographers analyze the reasons for nature's variability. They point to the terrestrial accident that caused this kind of natural miracle, which redirected Canaan from its desert vocation to make it a natural museum where every specimen lives and grows. The country lies between the Mediterranean and the Jordan, between 31° and 33° 20′ north latitude and 34° 20′ and 36° east longitude. To the east, the vast Syro-Arabic desert, a rocky steppe almost without water or oases, cuts the country off from Mesopotamia, Persia, and India. By caravan route, 1,250 kilometers separate Jerusalem from Babylonia. Even for the camel, introduced into this region toward the middle of the second millennium, the crossing is a feat. To the west, the Mediterranean coast, rectilinear, almost totally lacking in natural shelters, crossed by strong currents, and not very inviting to moorings except for sparse maritime trade, gives the country rain and climatic conditions that correct its subtropical position. Sinai surrounds the country to the south and protects it from the escapades of its noisy Egyptian neighbors. Only the north is open, the route for the Mesopotamian invasions.

The country, surrounded by sea and desert, is an oasis bounded on one side by the Dead Sea and the Jordan fault, an unequaled geological phenomenon. This depression comes down from the Taurus, across Coelesyria, and reaches its deepest points where the Jordan meets the Red Sea (−394 meters) and at the bottom of this sea (−793 meters). The Jordan is the only important river in the country; 288 kilometers long, it is remarkable (in spite of its size) for the rich vegetation of its banks, which contrast with the surrounding lunar landscape.

The Dead Sea, which the Hebrews call the Sea of Salt, is below sea level and is the most curious part of the depression. The heat of the surrounding mountains evaporates its contents at the rate of eight million cubic meters yearly, which equals the daily flow of the waters of the Jordan and its tributaries (of which the most important is the Yarmuk). This phenomenon explains the exceptional density of its waters (1.225), which makes it possible for one to float effortlessly.[1]

Transjordan, 9,481 square kilometers, extends from Mount Hermon to the torrent of the Yarmuk, in its northern section (Golan); from the Yarmuk to the Wadi Hesban to the north of the Dead Sea, in its central section (Gilead); and from there to the Wadi Hesi, to the south (Moab).

Cisjordan, 15,643 square kilometers, is divided in two by the Esdraelon Valley. North of this valley are Galilee and Carmel, at the crossroads of the principal caravan routes that connect Egypt to Syria and Mesopotamia; hence the strategic military location of Megiddo, so strongly fortified by Solomon.

To the south of the Esdraelon Valley stretch Samaria and Judea, whose hills reach 1,027 meters at Sirat-el-Bella, south of Jerusalem, and lesser heights near Beersheba (where the Negev begins and whose plain eventually fuses with the deserts of the south). This is the heart of the Hebrews' country.

Finally, there is the Mediterranean coast, which is crossed by powerful currents that hinder navigation. With the exception of Tyre (of insular origin) to the north, it offers only mediocre ports: Acre and Haifa, protected by Mount Carmel; and Jaffa and Gaza farther south. The plain of Sharon is rich; the Bible tells of its beauty and gentleness. From Jaffa, toward the southwest, stretches the country of the Philistines, which Shephelah, a region of small hills, and the site of Samson's battles, connects to Judea.

Climatic Whims

Added to the extraordinary variety of landscapes and people is the extremely variable climate, to which man cannot be indifferent. He must always be alert to the dangers facing the life of his country.

The land of Israel, situated on the fringes of Arabia and touching the Mediterranean, is the site of a constant duel between the influences of the sea and the desert on the mountains, the plains, and the depressions. This situation is aggravated by the Jordan depression, which complicates the interplay of the natural topographical factors. There again, man is the prey of marked contrasts. The zone is subtropical; therefore the average temperatures are mild for the two seasons into which the year is divided, dry and wet. The Passover marks the beautiful change from one to the other. But in each place and in each season there is a broad temperature span. Between noon and midnight the difference may be ten, fifteen, or twenty degrees, and sometimes even more—often greater than that between summer and winter in many countries. In the mountains the climate is especially invigorating, favoring the development of the hale and hardy—to resemble the country. It rains only rarely, but when the short rain season comes, it is fierce. For the Hebrew who listens for it and fears it, it represents the worst and the best of things, symbolizing the fullness of God's spirit and the force of his fury.

The farmer knows that the heaviest rains are brought by the west and northwest winds, coming from cold and dark sources. Though the rains are intermittent between the end of November and the end of February, and rather heavy in January, the drought is constant in the summer. The winds of the west and southwest, of tropical or Mediterranean origin, are damp and cause heavy nocturnal mists, which are useful to the trees and to some summer plantings. The desert winds from the Red Sea are feared most. If they blow too long at the time of the formation of the fruits, they can jeopardize their harvest, and sometimes even ruin the principal crops. The breezes have their own language. When they come from the sea, in the summer, they join the dominant wind. Often in midafternoon they blow up columns of sand, whirlwinds. Generally the areas that are open to wind get lots of rain. Jerusalem gets almost as much as Paris' 575 millimeters, while the coast, which has a rainfall of up to 2,000 millimeters, is as favored in this respect as the wettest parts of alpine or maritime Europe. Yet it is only a few kilometers from the world's most arid deserts. The contrasts are sharp in this country, where the poet writes of both heat and cold, fire and frost, dew, rain and wind, the blazing sun and the freezing snow. Snow caps Mount Hermon year round not far from the caravans, which are scorched by the desert winds. And the pilgrim who walks from Jerusalem to Jericho, only 24 kilometers, descends a 1,000-meter precipice and, indeed, makes drastic changes of climate in a few hours.

The constituent elements of the countryside and the climate are so numerous and varied that the light is forever changing. It seems as though men and nature are sculpted in its splendor rather than illuminated by it. It is the earthly proof of the glory of the heavens and their creator, whose first command, on the first dawn, was to give it being. "Let there be light" (Gen. 1:3). Ever since, it has reigned over the beautiful land. No Hebrew can ever doubt this fact.

The Promised Land, where Asia and Africa meet, finding on its shores and mountains a land in proportion to man, to his step and strength, and yet disproportionate in its infinite horizons, its heights and its sky—perhaps more than any other region—justifies the psalmist's chant: "The heavens show forth the glory of God, and the firmament declareth the work of his hands. Day to day uttereth speech, and night to night showeth knowledge" (Ps. 19:2–3).

The Products of the Earth

The flora and fauna reflect the deepest character of the country, which is to present the variety of a universe in the framework of a province.

Both are extraordinarily rich, most generally Mediterranean and sub-tropical—but desert to the south and tropical near the Dead Sea.

In his kingdom the Hebrew finds the entire earth and rejoices in it, to the extent that his country and the universe become one. There are forests of oaks, terebinth trees, sycamores, pines, acacias, fruit trees, plum, apple, pear, mulberry, fig, citron, pomegranate, olive, occasional cypresses and cedars, carob trees, oriental plane trees, walnut and almond trees, nettle trees, holm oaks, holly oaks, palm trees, and vineyards. In Hebrew, the almond tree is called the *sentinel;* its delicate array of blossoms announces spring. How could the returning traveler doubt that his country, too, had not been *chosen?* Add to the wide variety of trees the multiscented plant kingdom—broom plant, myrtle, acanthus, capers and mustard, lentiscus, hyssop, camomile, vervain, cumin, fennel, and the spices of the East—jasmine, lilies, roses, and every garden flower—pistachios, laurel, balsam, jujubes, willows, reeds, rush, papyrus. All of this is more impressive because it all grows near the lunar-like banks of the Dead Sea or the arid deserts.

Flower and sky are ever present. Every page of the Bible sings their praises. The worst punishment for Israel is exile; the greatest blessing is its prosperity, won by its submission to the divine will.

Throughout the year the Hebrew sees the fertility of the fields. The desert leads him to believe that this is a miracle due to God's grace. He knows that plants and trees have an intrinsic value; he has no right to destroy them. The law forbids chopping down a fruit tree, nor can its fruit be eaten before its fourth year (Lev. 19:23–25). (The regulations concerning the fields have been stated above.) Identification of the human with the vegetable is so great that Deuteronomy assimilates man to the tree in the fields.

Tenacity allows Israel a wheat crop for its staple, bread. The barley that Ruth gleaned is not only food for the poor but also for the horses, mules, and donkeys. Wild corn and sorghum add variety. The gardens produce beans, onions, leeks, eggplant, peppers, cucumbers, squash, pumpkins, melons, saffron, garlic, and all kinds of salad greens, lettuce, chicory, watercress, and even endive.

The Hebrews love flowers to the point of eating some, such as the iris and other lilies. The countryside is filled with tulips, crocuses, hyacinths, narcissus, gladiola, lilies. Red anemones are everywhere and, with the olive, are the country's symbol. For the Hebrew, the olive is the personification of beauty, health, fertility, peace, and happiness. Its oil serves for the consecration of its Kings and priests, for ladies' perfumes, and for cooking. Indeed, seven vegetable types symbolize the country: the olive, the palm, the pomegranate, the fig, the vine, wheat, and barley.

The Animals of the Fields

Genesis gives an initial classification of the animal species and their origins from water, air, or earth. In this tiny country the Hebrew can observe almost everything the creator has made and that Noah preserved from the flood. Man, created in God's image, is the master and crowning glory of creation. Master of the animal kingdom, he is limited nonetheless by the Covenant linking him to God and to the earth. The Law strictly defines his relationship to the animals of the earth. Violating the Law in any way invites damnation and death. The first right of animals is that of lawful existence. Even the wild animals must respect the natural order of which they are an integral part.

> Thou shalt not be afraid of the beasts of the earth . . .
> The beasts of the earth shall be at peace with thee.
> —Job 5:22–23

The concern for peace is so great that the Prophets foresaw an era when not only will the wild animals respect man but they will stop devouring each other: the lion and the lamb will coexist peacefully. This philosophy is all the more surprising in a country filled with all kinds of game: lions, bears, wolves, tigers, leopards, panthers, lynxes, hyenas, buffalos, wild oxen, boars, jackals, wild dogs, rhinoceroses, crocodiles, hippopotamuses.

From this wide choice the Bible distinguishes the pure and the impure. More than the vegetable kingdom, the animal is part of man's universe because it has blood, and blood is the "soul," blood is life (Lev. 17:13–15). Man can become impure by eating or even touching animals such as reptiles, moles, rats, and lizards (Lev. 9; Deut. 14). These cause man, and any object they touch, to become impure.

Man's dietary restrictions are clear: Everything is forbidden except ruminants with a cloven hoof, fish with fins or scales, certain birds and grasshoppers. In every case blood is forbidden, and its consumption makes one liable to death (Lev. 17:14, 19:26; Deut. 12:23). Man who would eat "flesh with its blood"—which is its soul—would become part of the animal and so disturb the psychic plenitude of God's people. The laws of purity are categorical, protecting the greater part of the animal kingdom from man's desires, and certain prescriptions must be followed. An acceptable animal cannot be slaughtered; its throat must be slit and it must be bled so that drinking its blood will be avoided. Young birds, but not the mother, may be taken from a nest (Deut. 22:6–7). All cross-breeding is forbidden, as is the harnessing of two different types of animals to the same plough, an ox and an ass, for example (Deut. 22:10).

A Mosaic of Nations

The history of the land of Canaan has been determined by the nations that surround and make inroads into it. Parallel to the natural diversities is a multiplicity of ethnic, religious, and cultural factors, among which the Hebrew must draw his existence.

The two most powerful poles in this area are Egypt and Mesopotamia. One has to refer to these two empires constantly to study the rise of civilization in this part of the world during the second millennium and the first half of the first millennium.[2] Mesopotamia and Egypt are the Hebrews' cradle. Abraham is born and grows up in "Ur," the Chaldean Uru (today's Muqayyar), near the Persian Gulf, center of the lunar god's cult of sin. The temple dedicated to him was a four-sided building 350 by 248 by 400 by 197 meters, flanked by a rectangular tower measuring 65 by 43 meters. Babylonia and Assyria had two separate histories in the third and second millennia, but they merge in the second millennium and first half of the first millennium and become strong enough, ultimately, to rout the Hebrews.

The Hebraic name for Egypt, the "black country" (Kemet), is *Mitsrayim,* and it appears in the biblical stories of the patriarchal period. Jacob's and Joseph's tales in Egypt are unforgettable. (Thomas Mann has succeeded in updating them.) Later, the Hebrews, enslaved in this country, will be delivered by Moses, the inspired leader who is trained at Pharaoh's court.

After having succeeded in freeing their country from the domination of the Hyksos (1800–1580), the Pharaohs of the eighteenth dynasty sent their armies eastward for their empire's security. Amenophis I occupied the land of Canaan and pushed beyond, toward Syria. In 1479 Thutmose III undertook an expedition against the Asian states, which he defeated at Megiddo. Under Amenophis IV, Egypt's possessions of Canaan and Syria were threatened by the revolt of the local princes and the invasion of the Hittites and the Hebrews. Seti I (1314–1292) reconquered Palestine and stopped the Hittite advance. They were defeated by Ramses II at Kadesh on the Orontes in 1288. In 1223 Menephtah led an expedition against Canaan, again in revolt. He immortalized his triumph by the famous stele that boasts of Israel's annihilation: "Israel is destroyed, its seed is no more." This stele marks the first appearance of Israel's name on a profane document. It expresses no excessive confidence in its future.

Mesopotamia and Egypt are the two giants whose culture and science inform the history of the Near East. But alongside them are a multitude of peoples, nations, city-states, and tribes that add distinctive characteristics to the region. The discovery of the el-Amarna documents (1887) and numerous archeological findings in the Near East have shed new light on this period. Better known since the Boghazkeui findings are the Hittites, whose capital stood at Hattushach in northern Cappadocia. These people, whose native territory was eastern Asia Minor and northern Syria, strongly influenced the civilization of this area, where they appear quite early. Abraham bought lands from them south of Canaan.

The Amorites and the Canaanites are the oldest inhabitants of the country (very little is known of their relationship). The former also settled in Transjordan (Num. 21:14). Scholars have felt that Mesopotamian civilization began with the Amorites, whose history goes back to the fourth millennium. Of Semitic stock (unlike the Hittites), they settled for a long period along the coasts of Phoenicia and on the eastern banks of the Jordan. They, too, are in constant conflict with Mesopotamia and Egypt.

The nomadic Arameans wander in the Near East from upper and

lower Mesopotamia as far as the Mediterranean shores. There they succeed in becoming a power in the city-states recorded in the Bible: Aram-Zoba, Aram-Maachah, Aram Beth Rehob, surrounding the political center Aram-Damascus. As will happen later to the kingdom of Samaria and Judea, the Aramean states fall under Tiglath-Pileser in 732, when Syria becomes an Assyrian province. Aramean becomes the diplomatic and commercial language of this part of the world for several centuries after the eighth century. Considered to be closely related to the Arameans, at Passover the Hebrews repeat: "My father was a wandering Aramean who came into Egypt" (Deut. 26:5).

After the Amorites, the Canaanites, the Hittites, and the Arameans, mention is made of the Philistines, Aryans from the north and from the sea, who settled in the maritime plain in the south of the country; of the Phoenicians, well established among the peoples of Canaan, settled on the northern coast as far as Acre and in Lebanon, in Gebal (the Greek Byblos), in Sidon and Tyre; of the Ammonites, who settled in Transjordan, around their capital Rabba, presently Amman; of the Moabites and the Edomites, who settled in the mountains whose names they bear; and finally the tribes of faraway Arabia (Jer. 25:24; Ezek. 27:21, 30:5; Gen. 22:20; II Sam. 8:8; Job 1; Gen. 18, 37:28).

The Land's Influence on the People

The crucial historic factor that precipitated Moses' mission takes place in the land of Canaan, where well before the conquest the Aramean dialect of the patriarchal period was replaced by the "language of Canaan." It is also in Canaan that the Hebrews absorb the cultural influences that mark them: the Ugaritic texts have shown us what poetry, psalmody, and certain biblical legends owe to the Canaanite traditions. It is on their land that the Hebrews adopt some names for God—*elyon, baal, adon*. There they discovered not only the vine and the olive but their mystical significance. Libations and some sacrificial rites come from the cults of Canaan. The conquest of the country only confirms and expands the ties between Israel, its land, and certain aspects of the religious and cultural life of the Canaan it replaces.

The Hebrew invasion of Canaan may be compared to the barbarian invasion of the Roman Empire or the Arab invasion of Byzantium.[3] This close tie between the land and the people of the Bible was initially corrosive. In the time of the Judges an uncontrolled, pervading anarchy encouraged the challenge of Canaan's two conquerors, the Hebrews and the Philistines. For a time the debilitated country found itself outside the mainstream. Egyptian control was relaxed, thereby favoring the establishment of the Hebrew clans and an egalitarian structure in their new country.

Unity and Diversity of the Land

The geographical structures of the country encourage the breakdown of the people into small, distinct groups that become competitive rather easily. Parallel to the constant struggle of desert and sea influences are the deep antagonisms that divide the Hebrews, now contained in small geographical divisions. The changes are far reaching. The basic unit of society is no longer the family or the clan but the city and the region it commands. Everything works toward this revolution, but especially the aforementioned geographical contrasts. They give rise to different types of men in their microcosms, in the universe—whose contradictions they sense. It becomes necessary to combat the tendencies toward disintegration and thus strengthen the institutions of traditional and religious law to compensate for the danger coming from the territorial structures of the Hebrew society established on the land. The new situation also reinforces Jerusalem's centralizing influence.

The conquest of the land assures a more profound revolution, and the people, having become sedentary, reject nomadic or semi-nomadic activities for agriculture. Henceforth the land must be protected not only from the enemy but from drought, the deserts, swamps, and all natural catastrophes. Love for the land is a function of the constant toil that is necessary to win it.

Foreign elements are not lacking on this land even after its conquest, and are all the more dangerous to national unity because their civilization is superior to that of the conqueror, and their stability is greater. This factor aggravates the devisive tendencies of the tribes of Israel, composed of little groups that originated either in Asia or Africa and that settle in Canaan over several hundred years. Eight centuries separate the first Patriarch from the first King of Israel. Thus there were on this conquered land different types of Hebrews, all of whom did not belong to the family of Israel in the same way, in the sense that Moses meant. Some remained even in Egypt— Egyptian sources mention the *Apiru* under Ramses III and Ramses IV long after the exodus. Mosaic law itself distinguishes between the Hebrew slave and the man of Israel who may not be enslaved.

An Unbelievable Complexity

The complexity of the questions that arise from the settlement of the people on the land is not surprising. So many nuances and contrasts differentiate the land and the people that analysis might even be discouraged. But the historian cannot avoid the complexity with which he is faced when he examines how the Hebrews have been able to preserve their originality and their unity when faced with so many internal conflicts. Exposed to the influences of their idolatrous neighbors, and living in the same geographical and social context, they tend naturally to forget their own God and to offer sacrifice to the Canaanite Baal, lord of fertility and fecundity, and to his feminine counterpart Astarte, goddess of love. These deviations appear only after the settlement in Canaan, where the farmers, depending on the fruitfulness of the earth, practice an orgiastic cult of the goddess of strength and joy, Astarte, who is identified as nurse and mother earth.

The geographical parceling of the contrasting regions that make up the country, as well as the complex variety of the peoples, tribes, languages, and religions that constitute the environment, results in the dissolution of the clan and the concomitant weakening of the ancestral traditions and rites that preserve them. The Hebrew is in a situation to accept, in their place, the traditions and religious and cultural forms that the local Canaanites profess. It is especially in the rich agricultural areas that the newly arrived Hebrews adopt ancient Canaanite feasts related, as we shall see, to the seasons of the year. This is the make-up of the popular religion of some of the Hebrews—a religion strongly censured by the Prophets.

They are followed by an active and powerful minority who prevail over local influences and impose, through the centuries, the traditions and teachings of ethical monotheism. The priests, even when within the Canaanite sanctuaries, offer sacrifice in the name of the God of Israel. The inspired ones, the *nebiim,* travel throughout the country, overcome with the mystical enthusiasm of their faith in one God, to pass this faith to the majority of their brothers. On occasion, bloody encounters occur between the followers of the native traditions and those who are faithful to monotheism and a transcendental God. Finally, the message of the desert, received in Sinai, imposes itself on Canaan, which has become the heritage of the children of Israel.

From this conflict, which the Prophets describe as a struggle between good and evil, arises a syncretism that is a product of this coveted and beloved Canaan. The god of the Canaanites, Baal, the master, becomes one of the names of Israel's God, as we have seen. The children of Israel are named according to the local divinities—Bealiah, Yerubbaal, Eshbaal. In Samaria, the inscriptions give proof of the extent of religious syncretism. Men refer indiscriminately to the name of Israel's God and to the local deities, yet consider themselves orthodox worshipers of the God of Abraham, Isaac, and Jacob.

Such is the land and such are the problems it presents to the new conquerors. Herdsmen, artisans, farmers or businessmen, newly arrived or well established on this land, which is both that of Canaan and Israel, let themselves be influenced differently by the major spiritual, religious, and cultural currents that compete with each other. The land encourages unified settlement as well as division. Unity is felt most when there is an external threat: after the conquest, the tribes regroup around a leader, a Judge, to fight foreign oppression. When Israel sees enemy armies approach its borders, it lays aside its differences and recovers its unblemished heroism. The burdens of the mundane are set aside in order to defend ideals. Trials give rise to strengthened national unity, which had been weakened by the contradictions of the land. The tribes of the north tend to organize on an amphictyonic basis; the southern tribes form a confederacy under the aegis of Judah. The twelve tribes gather at Shechem in solemnities through which they thank God for their Covenant. But these meetings are useful only in times of stress, when the richer, better-organized, better-armed Philistines oblige the people to unite. Because of this, and under the impulsion of a seer, Samuel, there is a desire for the establishment of a monarchy, which, essentially, must fight against the forces of anarchy.

In peacetime, too, it is necessary to find that terrestrial but mystical reality which allows the people to overcome their contradictions, their apathy, their refusals and denials. Then the land takes on meaning, an eternal value so important that it makes dissension disappear. David's genius was his understanding of how—and how much— Jerusalem could help in the unification of the land.

Jerusalem: The Choice of a Site

The contrast-filled country we have just described, in which the planet exists as a microcosm, can be found in its entirety in the capital, *Yerushalayim*. Again, the paradox this city incarnates in the history of Israel must be noted.

Our knowledge of the history of Jerusalem for five centuries of the royal period comes from two principal sources. The first, of course, is the Bible, which makes it possible to reconstruct the condition of Jerusalem's urban development with great precision. Descriptive texts are numerous in almost all the books: the conquest and adornment of the city of David (II Sam. 5:4–12); the building of the city by Solomon (I Kings 6, 7, 9); the works of Hezekiah (II Chr. 32; II Kings 20:20) and Manasseh (II Chr. 33); the nightly walk of Nehemiah through the ravaged city (Neh. 2, 3, 12). To these direct witnesses must be added indirect knowledge from the Pentateuch, the Prophets, and the Hagiographers.

The second source of information is archeological discoveries, which have increased so much recently. The site of the royal city becomes more and more definite. The main tendency is to expand it from Ophel, the hill on which the city of David rose, to the southwest hill—to Mount Zion and the Armenian quarter. The city, 800 meters above sea level, develops around its 6-hectare living center, thanks to the efforts that supplied it with water.

Water Supply

Man's work has had to make up for the shortage of water, since natural sources are in shortest supply in this part of the country. As Albright proved, the Hebrews perfected and made wide use of cisterns in all their settlements, thus protecting themselves from long droughts and total dependence on springs. Cisterns made it possible for the Hebrews to survive their long stay in Canaan. On occasion, natural caves are sealed and well cared for, and serve as huge reservoirs for rain water, which is also stored in water-tight tanks. Thirty-six cisterns, carved in rock—one with a capacity of 16,000 cubic meters, one 19 meters deep—have been discovered around the site of the Temple of Jerusalem.

Distant springs also are harnessed to man's service. The Hebrews built a huge and complex system of canals and tunnels for the transportation of water from springs to the population centers. Hezekiah channels the Spring of Gihon, with a flow of 50 cubic meters per hour, and sends it to the pool of Siloam in Jerusalem (II Chr. 32:4, 30). This is a technical wonder: 512.5 meters long with a gradient of 2.18 meters, which is a slope of almost 2.4 millimeters per meter.

These works explain the location of urban settlements near springs in the Canaanite period, around cisterns and pools in the Israelite period, and along aqueducts during the Roman period. Jerusalem owes its supremacy to the unusual abundance of its water supply— fed from the Spring of Gihon, the En-rogel fountain, the private wells of each house, the pools of the valleys, and finally the aqueducts.

The Building of the City

The city is linked to the memory of Abraham, who on Mount Moriah showed his willingness to sacrifice Isaac to YHWH.

The Horites, followed by the Jebusites, fortify and occupy the site until the Israelite conquest in the time of David. The latter chose to found this tiny mountain city, which belonged to neither the northern nor the southern tribes, as the capital of the unified kingdom and the home of the dynasty. There he builds his residence. From one of its windows, Michal sees David dance with the handmaids of his servants while conducting the Ark of the Covenant toward the sacred mountain, Moriah, and reproaches him bitterly. From his terrace David sees Bathsheba bathing in her pool. He wants her, loves her, and marries her, after having caused the death of her husband Uriah. Here the prophet Nathan censures his King and begs him to repent. And it is from this house that David is driven when his son Absalom perpetrates his coup d'état. He flees by way of the Kidron Valley and the Mount of Olives toward the Jordan Valley. Here, too, where he had wept over Bathsheba's son's death, he covers himself with ashes in mourning for Absalom. And here he ends his days, beside an extremely beautiful girl who lies next to him to warm his old body. It is in this house, finally, which his architect Hiram built for him, that he chooses Solomon as his successor, writes his will, and dies pathetically (I Kings 1, 2).

King Solomon builds his capital. He builds the Temple there, his palace, high ramparts, fortresses, the Millo, numerous buildings, the House of the Forest of Lebanon, the building for his Egyptian queen, the Hall of Columns, the throne room where he judges his people, winning a worldwide reputation for his wisdom. The capital, built by the toil of two generations, David's and Solomon's, is of incomparable beauty. Jerusalem's stone has helped make it so.

The city of David is central to the history of the Hebrews. Too many events to mention occurred there. Kings succeed each other and are buried in the Tomb of the Kings, which archeologists have not yet located. There Athaliah reigns, sets up the worship of idols, and is assassinated and then devoured by dogs. Egypt in the time of Shishak, Syria in the time of Hazael, and Assyria and Babylonia covet this city, which is as rich as it is beautiful, and attack and pillage it as soon as they are able. Within its walls the Prophets from Nathan to Ezekiel deliver their message to all Israel. They launch YHWH's attack on the idols who have won his people and who are adored in the very temple of Solomon. Because of them, the city survives its defeats and rises from its ashes to become the symbol of the ideals taught there, from Nathan to Jesus, and the spiritual center of the three great monotheistic religions. In the time of the Kings, the Temple and the royal palace are the head and heart of the nation, the symbol of its unity and quality.

Solomon's Temple

In the heart of the capital Solomon put up two sets of buildings that formed one unified complex: the Temple of YHWH and the royal palace.

The Temple is in three parts: the vestibule (*ulam*), 11 meters wide, 5.5 meters long, and about 16.5 meters high; the *aula* (*hefhal*), 11 meters wide, 22 meters long, and 16.5 meters high; and the *cella* (*devir*) or Holy of Holies, a perfect cube of 11 meters on each side. The total length of the building was 38.5 meters, with a uniform width of 11 meters. On the exterior the Temple was flanked by supplementary constructions to the north, west, and south. Its three-story annex was 10 meters high, divided into ninety small rooms with windows that gave light to the *aula*.

The dimensions of Solomon's Temple were modest when compared to the other great sanctuaries of antiquity—those of Luxor (260 by 55 meters) and Karnak (its hypostyle alone was 133 meters long, 52 meters wide, and 21 meters high) in Egypt, or the temples of Ur and Esagila in Babylonia. Nonetheless, it was striking for its rich decoration and splendid liturgy. The walls, ceiling, and floors were decorated with cedar and gilded angels, palms, and flowers. In the Holy of Holies was the Ark of the Covenant, guarded by gilded olive-wood angels 5.5 meters tall, whose wing span was 2.75 meters. The *aula* was furnished with a golden altar for bouquets, a cedar table covered with gold for the bread offerings, ten solid-gold candelabras and accessories, as well as tongs, snuffers, flower arrangements, censers, and knives. In the atrium was the bronze altar of the holocausts, whose great basin was held by twelve bulls; ten bronze shells, mounted on wheels, were used for carrying water (II Chr. 1:3, 3, 4; I Kings 6, 7; Ezek. 40, 42).

This type of spiritual-temporal complex was not rare in antiquity, but Jerusalem's was the most developed. The Temple is the hub of the nation, focal point of all blessings, all purity, all forgiveness, and all life. If the universe holds together, it is because of God's presence in his sanctuary, where he receives the worship of his faithful. He has chosen to identify his person, his name, his glory, his heart, and his Torah in this chosen place where he reigns as a King in his palace (Ex. 20:24, 25:8; I Kings 8:13, 9:3; Jer. 34:15; II Chr. 7:16). Here the

Hebrews come to commune with YHWH and be inspired by him. The Kings, Judges, Prophets, and faithful come here to receive the spirit and counsel of their God and to relate their hopes and petitions. Isaiah and Micah express Israel's certitude when they say:

> And in the last days the mountain of the house of the Lord shall be prepared on the top of mountains, and it shall be exalted above the hills, and all nations shall flow unto it. And many people shall go and say: "Come, let us go up to the mountain of the Lord, and to the house of the God of Jacob: and he will teach us of his ways, and we will walk in his paths" (Mic. 4:1–3).
>
> For the law shall come forth from Zion, and the word of the Lord from Jerusalem. And he shall judge among the nations, and decide for peoples; and they shall beat their swords into ploughshares, and their spears into pruning-hooks; nation shall not lift up sword against nation, neither shall they learn war any more (Isaiah 2:2–4).

Jerusalem is the center of Israel and of the world, the source of their salvation and their blessings. More and more, the city becomes the center of the life of the people. After the destruction of the kingdom of Samaria, and later upon the return from the exile of Babel, Jerusalem will be the spiritual center of the people of Israel, occupying a transcendental place which the Prophets continue to glorify. It is here that Judah and Israel will again find their unity. The entire earth, recognizing its center, will be transformed, regenerated, renewed, and saved by the powers of the blessing and holiness of YHWH (Joel 4:18; Zech. 14:9).

Conquest, Security, Defense of the Land: War

A society reveals its true character when it is faced with the exigencies of war, which is part of the natural order of things. Life, peace, and happiness are gifts of God, supernatural realities constantly reestablished by meriting them. Winning wars is not unrelated. War reaffirms Israel's right over the Promised Land. Victory proves the reality of the promise made to Abraham and YHWH's superiority over the gods of the seven nations dispossessed of Canaan.

Biblical Israel is too often at war. Even in the desert it was organized for the military action which was to ensure its conquest of the country. The Song of Deborah and the story of Sisera's murder by Joel (Judges 4:17) relate the warrior legend of ancient times (Judges 5). In every case victory depends on YHWH. That is why a military leader's first effort is to foster the spiritual strength of the people and purify the integrity of their soul, a condition for victory. Military law is very strict regarding the purity of the fighters. The soldier must be in a state of perfect ritualistic purity in order to fight. Even an accidental nocturnal emission may defile him and make him ineligible. Israel's camp must be free of all stain. Latrines isolate their excrement. A spade with which to bury it is part of the military gear (Deut. 23:10-15; Num. 5:1-4) of the soldier. If he is impure, for any reason whatever—even simply frightened, or if his marriage is unconsummated, or he has a vine laden with fruit, or his newly built house is not yet dedicated—he must leave the front and join the back lines (Deut. 20:5-8; Judges 7:2-4). The soldier's continence (I Sam. 7:6, 14:29-30, 21:6; II Sam. 11:11; Judges 20:26), sobriety, even his fasting, strengthen his communion with God and so fortify the army by adding the spirit of holiness to it. The warrior, his arms, his camp, and his people must be sanctified by YHWH in order to merit victory (Deut. 23:15; I Sam. 7:9, 13:9, 21:6; Jer. 6:4; Joel 4:9). Ultimately, victory depends neither on arms nor circumstances but on the spirit that inspires the warrior.

The Warrior's Weapons

During the period that interests us, the art of warfare undergoes a change due to the introduction and perfection of new weapons, which cause a revolution in strategy and tactics. Iron replaces bronze, increasing the mobility of wagons, the striking force of spears, javelins, pikes, battle axes, swords and daggers. The bow, considerably improved, compels the strengthening of coats of armor, cuirasses, helmets, gloves, greaves, and shields. Almost all the armies of the Near East are equipped with these improvements. The art of warfare is, after all, international. Archeological discoveries of recent years (the epigraphical materials of Mari, Ugarit, El Amarna, and Anatolia), numerous Bible references, and Mesopotamian and Egyptian documents have shed light on many war-related questions in biblical antiquity. The battering ram and the chariot are the most potent weapons in the military arsenal during the first half of the first millennium B.C. The chariot, harnessed to two horses, comes into general use and solves mobility and striking problems. Two soldiers are positioned in the wooden chariot, the fighter and the driver. According to Egyptian monuments, the Hittite chariots held three fighting men. The chariot is equipped to protect its soldiers from arrows and javelins. Its utility depends on its workmanship, and its manufacture requires dozens of pieces, described in detail in the documents of the time. The states possessed the secrets of production and, as today, the small states depended on the powerful ones for their military equipment. A large army might have several thousand chariots; lesser kings had to be satisfied with a few dozen. Solomon owned 1,400 chariots and 12,000 horses, which he maintained in such specialized cities as Jerusalem and Megiddo (I Kings 10:26).

Organization of the Army

During the nomadic period the army was the entire population, but the establishment of a career army was the work of the first Kings. David is the architect of the new organization, which allows for mercenaries attached to the King and serving as his guard (mishmereth). David conquers Jerusalem and defeats the Philistines with career troops, which he, like his successors, maintains at great expense. In case of war, general mobilization of all eligibles occurs.[4] When the country is threatened, the war cry is sounded: "To your tents, Israel!" Fortresses, built at the most vulnerable strategic points, have their garrisons reinforced. The country folk take shelter in the rampart-protected cities.

Under the monarchy, Israel's army is basically defensive. The period of conquest, initiated by Joshua, is terminated by David. There is not one war during Solomon's reign, after which the schism-weakened country is not able to defend itself against its covetous neighbors, who will carve it up. The notion of a holy war to spread the true faith has always been foreign to the history, the spirit, and the possibilities of the Hebrews.

Espionage, tricks of war, ambushes, surprise attacks, and lightning campaigns are not our style now, but Israeli military history offers a good sample of them. Noise is often the best weapon. To attack the Midianites, Gideon mobilizes three hundred soldiers and equips them with a ram's horn trumpet, an earthenware jar, and a torch, and at night his troops surround the sleeping enemy camp. On the signal, Israel's soldiers break the jars, light the torches, and, without moving an inch, blow into the horns with all their might. This sows panic in the Midianite camp, and they are defeated.

To these very human means the Hebrews add an especially fearsome weapon, YHWH's personal intervention.

YHWH's Intervention

To direct a blessing upon themselves, not only do the soldiers carry their insignias and banners, efficacious symbols, with their equipment, but also sacred objects which assure YHWH's presence. The Ark of the Covenant, when it accompanies the army, is the surest means to victory, for Israel's enemies are also YHWH's enemies. The Ark's appearance assures the enemy's defeat because invisible powers have come into play (Num. 10:35; I Sam. 4:3–8). Celestial legions, angels, and even gods participate in the fray, whose outcome depends on them alone. That is why before any undertaking the oracles, those seers who sometimes hold opinions contrary to the King's, must be consulted. The King's choice prevails, and the war's outcome separates the true from the false prophets.

After the Battle

Victors and vanquished return to their homes when the battle is over. In case of defeat, the evils of war are exacerbated by the price to be paid to the enemy: a tribute in gold or silver, pillaged and conquered cities, enslaved women, deportations and murders.

If victory has ensued, the army is treated to celebrations with music and dancing and acts of thanksgiving, which precede the fulfillment of vows and the sacrificial offerings that prepare the return of the purified soldiers to normal life. Sometimes terrible tragedies occur. The victorious Jephthah, for instance, slew his own daughter to present her as a burnt offering (Judges 11:34).

The country is enriched by the booty taken from the defeated—weapons and equipment, provisions and flocks, jewels and other objects from the pillaged camps and cities, along with the flocks and harvests of the annexed territories. The Law tries to control natural desires and determines that the booty be divided equally among the people, the soldiers, and the Levites (Num. 31:25). The King and the generals take the most valuable things for themselves or for the Temple (Judges 8:24; II Sam. 8:7, 12:30).

The captives, when they are not executed, are subject to enslavement, forced labor, or ransom. The soldier may marry his captive, who then regains her freedom (Deut. 21:10). The joy of booty sharing is described in all its crudeness by the chronicles. It must be superseded, however, by exploitation of the victory in the political arena for the negotiation of a peace treaty (Deut. 20:10; Josh. 9:6).

The End of All War

The Hebrew is very conscious of the sorrows caused by war crimes and so places peace among the highest considerations. It is not by chance that his most ordinary greeting, his hello, is *Shalom,* peace. Peace and blessing are so closely linked to justice that they cannot be dissociated from it without unleashing the horrors of war, so hated by the people. The most prevalent topic among the Prophets is also *peace.* They preach peace even when there is none, the disillusioned Jeremiah and Ezekiel claim (Jer. 6:14, 8:11, 28:9; Ezek. 13:10–16). And Micah more bitterly states: "They preach peace if man give something into their mouth" (Mic. 3:5). Peace is not only the absence of war but a state which excludes all injustice, imperfection, and sin. It is a state in which the soul achieves its fullness and strength. And, above all, since it has settled in its country, Israel's most constant hope has been to develop without fighting and to enjoy its prosperity and safety among its vineyards and fig trees. In some circles this vision, which is common to all, must be accompanied by the annihilation of the seven nations whom the Hebrews have dispossessed of their land for the conquest of Canaan (Deut. 20:17; Josh. 9).

The city people and the peasants are far from sharing this view. They adopt, with reservation, the idealistic image of Israel's future peace. The Prophets all return to this theme, which inspires them more than any other. And, perhaps for the first time in the history of mankind, war is considered evil in itself and destined to disappear:

> I will make thy visitation peace, and thy overseers justice . . .
> Iniquity shall no more be heard in thy land, wasting nor destruction in thy borders, and salvation shall possess thy walls, and praise thy gates. Thou shalt no more have the sun for thy light by day, neither shall the brightness of the moon enlighten thee: but the Lord shall be unto thee for an everlasting light, and thy God for thy glory . . . And thy people shall be all just (Isaiah 60:17–21).

Peace is accompanied by the triumph of its messenger, Israel. The nations will no longer persecute it, nor will they try to enslave it or drive it out, but instead will come to it bearing precious gifts. The tribute will really be addressed to YHWH, the God of Israel, who will have accomplished the miracle of the total pacification of the universe, which will have witnessed the change in man's heart, in his instincts and his thoughts, and pacified all creation, even the animal kingdom, in this amazing new era. The nations will no longer rule the earth. God alone will. Israel will no longer need weapons on the day of the triumph of its King, the Messiah:

> Rejoice greatly, O daughter of Zion, shout for joy, O daughter of Jerusalem: BEHOLD THY KING will come to thee, the just and saviour: he is poor, and riding upon an ass. I will destroy the chariot out of Ephraim, and the horse out of Jerusalem, and the bow for war shall be broken: and he shall speak peace to the Gentiles (Zech. 9:9–10).

The Second Gate The People

The Name of a People

The Hebrews have been sensitive to the power of the word. In their realism they, like their Mesopotamian and Egyptian neighbors, are aware of the relationship between the object named and the word which designates it. The name is a living reality that designates another living reality—the soul that informs it—and acts upon it. The word is in itself a creative reality. Thanks to the word, Elohim creates the heavens and the earth, light and darkness. Thanks to the word, man can relate to creation, watch over it and fulfill it, or, to the contrary, hamper and destroy it. The word controls benediction and malediction, peace and war, life and death.

The Hebrew does not distinguish between the word and the reality it designates. The word *davar* indicates the word and the object at the same time. Changing a name is equivalent to changing a destiny. Body and soul are so tied to their names that it is impossible to separate one from the other. The soul of an individual, of a people, or of any other terrestrial or celestial reality is the manifest form of the body. In turn, their names effectively express their living unity.

This explains the importance of the name by which the Hebrews have identified themselves as a people. Modern historians link the *'ivrim,* the Hebrews of the Bible, to the nomadic communities labeled *Habiru, Hapiru,* or *Apiru,* which appear in the second millennium B.C. in various parts of the Near East, in Canaan, Egypt, Syria, Hittite Anatolia, and Accadian Mesopotamia. These nomads are sometimes responsible for *razzias,* against which the Canaanite princes must defend themselves by asking help of the Egyptian suzerain.[1] Whatever these distant relationships may indicate, the word 'ivri, Hebrew, is at least phonetically related to the root 'avar, to pass. Essentially, the Hebrew sees himself as a man on the move, crossing frontiers. He is not tied to a territory as are those earthly men, the Canaanites, Moabites, Edomites, Egyptians or Mesopotamians, who have life and name only by virtue of the land. He is the man of the great migrations, which led Abraham from Ur to Canaan, Jacob and Joseph to Egypt, and that brought him back from Egypt and from Mesopotamia toward his Promised Land. From the time of the exodus from Egypt, the Hebrews trace the origins of their existence as a people. And the constitutive act of the nation was made not at the moment of Canaan's conquest at the time of Joshua but at the foot of Sinai in an almost uninhabitable desert, when Moses gave his Law to those rescued from Egypt. The unusual, the unforeseen, the paradoxical—often the incredible, sometimes the impossible— that is what the historian of these people on the move discovers.

Hebrew history begins with nomadism, which dominates the entire formative period of the nation, when it had neither country nor state. So the Hebrews appear just as they recognize themselves— men of passage, transition and exodus, of uprootedness, on the only land they have ever considered their own, which is as diverse and paradoxical as themselves. The unifying factor is a historic conscience, a common ancestry in Shem, the son of Noah, great-grandfather of Eber. They are brothers in Abraham, Isaac, and Jacob. This historical statement cements the ties resulting from a community of language, faith, religion, civilization and, ultimately, destiny on the same land.

The human and spiritual potential of the Hebraic people gives rise to the existence of a territory by a procedure that is contrary to the nature of things. It is not the country which feeds the people and inspires its civilization but, in a constant struggle, the people who— to possess a land for themselves—must conquer it by their own powers. The nomadic Hebrews yearn to be settled and covet the only land worthy of their destiny. Formerly slaves in Egypt, they conquer it by attacking the Canaanites as soon as they are able to. Exiled to Babylonia, they have only one concern, one obsession: to return to their country and rebuild it. Crushed by the Romans in what appears to be a definitive defeat, they muster the remnants of their hopes and strength to give the lie to their misfortune—and wait two millennia for the chance to return to rebuild their national home and country in the place of the promise.

In a sense, the nomad lives in contradiction to nature. His home is the desert, the steppe. The poverty of the ground on which he feeds forces him to keep moving, concerned for his chances of survival in a harsh environment. These factors have played a constant role in the life of the Hebrews, who seek a supernature that satisfies all creation in the fullness of its glory.

In addition, the nation takes shape surrounded by peoples who are strong in numbers and of dominant cultures and civilizations. When the Hebraic people were at the first stages of their historic existence, the Egyptian and Mesopotamian civilizations were already more than 2,000 years old. Egypt's united monarchy dates back to about 3200, when the cities of Lagash, Ur, and Uruk were competitors; Susan civilization goes back even further; and Crete has been using metal since the year 3000. The region where the Hebrews wished to found a state already had a richer past than some areas of modern Europe. Historical comparisons do not usually stand up, but the arrival of the Hebrews in Canaan may be compared in our day to the settlement of Bedouin tribes in the great Western cities while still preserving their character. Millar Burrows does not exaggerate when he writes: "In some aspects the Hebrew invasion of Palestine was comparable to the Barbarian invasions of the Roman Empire or, centuries later, that of the Arab invasions of Byzantium." [2]

Historical research has proved that close ties have existed among the various centers of Near Eastern civilization since the last Bronze Age. Certainly the center of Canaan, which the Hebrews chose for their homeland, must have been a crossroads where many races fought and mingled under the dominant influences of the Egyptians, Babylonians, Hittites, Phoenicians, and Canaanites.

"They went from nation to nation, from one kingdom to another people," sang the psalmist, with the precision of a historian (Ps. 105:13). Such was the otherworldly Hebrew. But, in the diversity of its images, this people identified itself by another name, Israel, and again by a man's name, Jacob—a man who was marked with a supernatural sign. The name indicates the reality of the being. After having won his struggle with the angel, Jacob changed his name and became Israel. And it is by this term that the Hebrews prefer to call themselves. They are the *Benei Yisrael*—the children of Israel.

The origin and meaning of the name are still debated. It is almost certain that it is not of Canaanite origin but Amorite or proto-Aramean, and that the Hebrews brought it to their adopted country.[3] What does it mean? Philologists cannot wholly explain it. *El* is God's name, the all-powerful and the source of all power. *Israel* may mean "the one who mastered God," who persevered, who persisted, the one who found his strength anew. God is both the servant and the master in his kingdom, joining the realities of God to those of man before establishing them on the earth to work the final fulfillment of his vocation.

The Hebrews, or Israelites, also call themselves Jews. This term, whose etymology is not known, means exactly the opposite of what it has come to mean in most Moslem and Christian languages. The very sound of the word Yehudi indicates specific meanings to the Hebrew. The concept phonetically contained within the root of the word means to praise, celebrate, exalt. It also indicates a man, Judah, the son of Jacob and Leah (Gen. 29:35), a tribe, the Judeans, and finally a land, Judah. The Jewish word Yehudi is not found only in Maccabees and the New Testament, as has been stated erroneously;[4] it is also found in Kings (16:6), Chronicles (I, 4:18), and in numerous passages in Jeremiah, Zechariah, and the book of Esther. In biblical times (after the schism) reference was made to the kingdom of Israel in the north and the kingdom of Judah in the south, and the latter alone survived the Babylonian exile. Hence the term Jews for the descendants of the Hebrews.

In every case the people label themselves in reference to a concept, a concept of passage, perseverance, or praise. The concept then designates a man who fulfills its message—Eber, Israel, Judah —then all his descendants, Hebrews, Israelites, Jews, and the land they settled on. Semantic analysis masks the complexity of the components of the Hebraic fact, which evidently is characterized by the union of a spiritual message, a people who accept responsibility for it, and a land promised for its fulfillment. With the centuries, Israel's names take on symbolism and an affective content with subtle nuances. When Moses spoke to Pharaoh—with one exception—he used the term Hebrews for his people; he used the term Israel to address them, however. A single people is described under its various forms—their wandering, their divine relationship, or their historical continuity. Poets add to the list of names: *Yeshurun,* the righteous, the people, the holy people, the great people, the smallest of all peoples, the people of God, the nation of YHWH, the eternal people, the chosen race, the unique. The importance of these concepts for Hebrew thought will be explained below.

"My Father Was a Wandering Aramean"

The traumatized and traumatizing awareness of its oneness does not prevent Israel from realizing its relationship to other nations. Every Hebrew who takes his sacrifice to the Temple of the Lord is supposed to remember his distant origins and say "My father was a wandering Aramean, who went into Egypt to live and from a small people became a numerous and powerful one" (Deut. 26:5; Ezek. 18).

It is here that the Semitic and Asian roots of Israel develop. They draw from the realities of the ancient East, from the nomadic and unsettled Arameans, who wandered as far as the Arab-Syrian steppes. Similar to the Hebrews, at the initial stages of their history the Arameans were in search of a land, which took them to the banks of the Euphrates, to the region of Aleppo, then to central Syria. Egypt's decline in the thirteenth century, followed by that of Babylonia and the Hittite Empire, facilitated the development of a powerful kingdom centering on Damascus. Their common origins, rather than allaying the rivalry between Israel and Aram, increased it. For ages the Hebrews had to wage a debilitating struggle against their Aramean cousins, and occasionally they became their vassals.

At the Crossroads of Nations and Religions

Archeological research has evidence of Canaan's settlement thousands of years before the birth of Israel. Indeed, the Canaanites enter their historical period 3,000 years before the Christian era. From that time the country has had a composite population, for it was at the crossroads of various cultures.

From the third millennium on, Semites lived in the fortified cities of Megiddo, Jericho, Lachish, Gezer, and Jerusalem. Their cousins, the Amorites, were settled around Lebanon, assuring contact with the peoples of Mesopotamia via the Euphrates. To the east of the Jordan were the Moabites; to the south the Egyptians, coveting the land of Canaan as early as the middle of the third millennium. Their armies invaded it repeatedly during the Fifth and Sixth Dynasties. From then on, their cultural, political, and military influence is constant.

Around 1900 the Hittites appear to the north and build their powerful state, during the middle of the second millennium. Their culture shows a predominance of Aryan elements. In the fourteenth century they control Syria and extend their influence to Egypt, and of course Canaan.

The West also has been here: pottery from Cyprus and Greece, dating as far back as the eighteenth century, has been found in the country. And the Philistines, having come from the north by sea, settle on the coast. The Hebrews will have endless problems with them.

Semitic people make up the main element of the country's population. The Canaanites and the Hebrews are related to the peoples on the shores of the Red Sea (Zimran, Midian, Dedan, Asshur, Shuah (Gen. 25:1, 2) and in the extreme south of Arabia, in the fertile mountains of Sheba (Nebayot, Kedar, Adbe'el, Dumah, Massa, Tema, Yetur, Naphish, Mibsam, Mishma) (Ezek. 27:21; Prov. 30: 1; Isaiah 60:7, 21:14).

For the people of the East, of which Israel is a part, Jeremiah uses the general term *Benei Qedmah,* the sons of the East (Jer. 49:28).

Superimposed are the Babylonian influences. They appear in Genesis, the codes of the Covenant, sapiential literature, and hymnology.

From the Egyptians the Hebrews learn the meaning of sacred literature, their sense of the technical miracle that authenticates the mission of the one sent from God, and also, perhaps, the teachings of Akhnaton's monotheist reform, a century before the exodus, which brings to light the powerful monistic thought of the Egyptian priests.

Hebrew, a Sacred Language

More than in the Hebrew conscience, its ancestral traditions, its community of interests or geographical borders, the identity of this people is found in its language. The spoken language informs daily life and, in large measure, determines the spiritual universe, social climate, and mental horizons of a nation. In the complexity of peoples who share the ancient East, language is the surest key to understanding their relationships.

The Hebrew is defined, first of all, by his language, which determines his "belonging," his culture, his formation, his spirituality, as well as his mental dynamism and aspirations. Just as the Hebraic people develop from the Aramean and Canaanite world, their language belongs to the Semitic languages, so called because the majority of the peoples who speak them are related, according to the Bible, to Shem, the son of Noah (Gen. 10:21–31, 11:10–26). Modern philology classifies these languages into three groups: eastern, northwestern, and southwestern. They suggest the existence of a primitive language common to the Semites, from which they were derived, as were the Romance languages from Latin. This original Semitic language is unknown to us, but it is possible to reconstruct it because of the idioms that developed from it, and that caused its breakdown and eventual disappearance.

Hebrew belongs to the northwestern group of Semitic languages, which contributed an alphabet to the world. It was invented by the Phoenicians and spread to the Arameans, Canaanites, and Hebrews. The Greeks borrowed it and adapted it to the needs of their language.[5] Hebrew will be the language the Aramean tribes from Haran will adopt in Canaan. We know the primitive form through the commentaries and certain grammatical forms in the letters of El Amarna. The Bible contains the most complete portion of Hebraic literature. The calendar of Gezer of the ninth century B.C., the ostraca of Samaria, the various seals, stamps and coins of the biblical era, the Siloam Inscriptions at the end of the eighth century, the

coins of the time of the Maccabees, the texts on the stones of syna-
gogues, tombs, sarcophagae, and the Dead Sea manuscripts and the
rich rabbinical literature: such are the samples of the Hebrew language before its present-day revival. It has been, and remains, the
strongest factor in the unity of the people of the Bible. It gave them
their identity and homogeneity, and has enabled Israel to triumph
over the contradictions and adverse circumstances of time. Language has been a major element of the unity of the Hebraic people
throughout its history.

Hebrew has always been a language spoken by a small group. At
the end of the royal period in the Near East, the majority spoke
Aramaic, a language the Hebrews themselves will adopt upon their
return from the Babylonian exile. More than three chapters of the
book of Ezra (4:8 to 6:18, 7:12–26), five chapters of the book of
Daniel (2:4 to 7:28), a verse of Jeremiah (10:11), and two words
of Genesis (31:47) are in Aramaic. This language, raised to a sacred
status, will be used by the Hebrews for important translations of the
Bible and Targums and for the composition of the Talmuds of Jerusalem and Babylonia.[6] The voluminous monuments of Jewish literature will give Aramaic an importance which Nabatean or Palmyrene
never had.

One of the clues to the mystery of Israel lies in the characteristics
of Hebrew, a language with internal inflection. The basis of the language is verbal roots that evoke the subject, object, idea, emotion, or
sentiment to be expressed. Each root contains the master idea, which
will be found in the context in all its nuances and forms. The role of
vowels (sometimes long, sometimes short) is precisely to give the
words the desired meaning. It has been said that Hebrew is an "aris-
tocratic" language, revealing itself only to the expert. Its consonantal
framework makes sense only to the initiated.

Hebrew is a language of rhythm and number. Invariably, particles
serve for articulation, and its fundamental syntax is based more on
the coordination than on the subordination of ideas. So it is also a
"visual" language, made for evoking images, movement, and the
concrete gesture rather than the subtle analysis of ideas. A language
of global knowledge and particular revelation rather than abstract
reflection, whose genius takes ideas out of the realm of the abstract
to put them to action.

The Power of the Language

On returning from the exile the Hebrews discard their old alphabet
for the one they bring back from Mesopotamia, but traditionally the
verbs are linked to numbers and the letters to figures. The Hebrews
give each letter of the alphabet a numerical value, so that their
writings are also numerical documents, as was the Mesopotamian
custom. In subsequent periods, the reinforcement of this peculiarity
was to help the research of the cabalists, bent on finding the secret
(*sod*) of biblical revelation. Under the name *gematriah,* they will
later develop the science of the secret numerical equivalents of biblical texts. Be that as it may, the scribes had to study and teach this
peculiarity of the language, which relates to the sense of man's initiation to a greater truth. So the total of the letters in the word *ehad,*
unity, is equal to the total of the letters in the word *ahavah,* love,
and the sum of both words equals the total in "the God of unity and
love," YHWH (13 plus 13 = 26). The very structure of Hebrew,
like most Eastern languages, favors the play of words and the enig-
mas and mysteries with which each text, and most particularly the
holy writings, are filled.

The fundamentally undifferentiated character of the Semitic
tenses gives these languages an unsurpassed power of suggestion.
For the Hebrew, the preterit always partakes of the aorist, the future
never ceases informing the present. The language, and the thought
it transmits, impose themselves as an imperative—a barrage of real
facts, not ideas—and make one aware of the full meaning of the
words. But the language goes beyond analytic awareness; it transmits
the revealed mystery with immediacy to the reader, who becomes
one of its elements. Thought is impressed on the Hebrew by a non-
discursive dialectic which "frees" the things that pass. The darkness
is suddenly filled with a presence that, without formal, logical order,
yields the universality of reality to man's consideration. The rhythms
of the language, which is often sung, operate as if by themselves to
erase the transitory from the mind and offer it the secret realities of
heaven and earth—a mysterious language, which is the instrument
of its own enrichment. "Holy language"—to use the words of the
Hebrew; that is, a language set apart, in a sense cryptographic,

which has distinguished the people under its powers and given them a time and place that maintain their uniqueness. The "word of YHWH"—to use another favorite expression of the Prophets of Israel—infuses a divine spark in man's conscience. Words of "assurance," which do not hypothesize but *reveal,* explain and shape the real order of the world. Because of the attributes of their language, and the Bible's language, the daily life of educated Hebrews refers inevitably to a body of transcendent values that, for better or worse, rule out triviality and take on importance within a separate historic process, a "holy" process. Even the humor of the biblical people is felt to be special.

The destinies of the Semitic languages have been very diverse. Accadian was the most archaic. Its prestige in the Mediterranean East was linked to the conquests of the Babylonian and Assyrian empires. In the middle of the second millennium, it was the diplomatic language for the entire Near East, including Egypt and Cyprus. The fall of Babylon, the transformation of its empire into a Persian satrapy, Alexander's conquest, and the foundation of Seleucia on the Tigris (to erase the very memory of the former queen of the Orient) resulted in the obliteration of Babylonia and the replacement of its language by Aramaic. All the northwestern Semitic languages eventually suffered the same fate: Amorite, Canaanite, Phoenician, Punic, Aramaic, Nabatean and Palmyrene, eastern Aramaic (these last few maintain some semblance of life in the Syriac and Oriental liturgies and theologies and in the dialect of a few villages)—all have been forgotten by the people who used to speak them and have become dead languages. They have been replaced by Arabic, which mushroomed after the appearance of Islam. Ethiopian, which, like Arabic, is a southern Semitic language, survives in different dialects in Abyssinia.

Hebrew is the only language in the eastern and northwestern groups that has survived. It survived the fall of the Israelite nation as a liturgical and theological language, and continues to help the refugees of the exile survive. A strange dialectic assures the survival of the language in the memory of a people whom it is able to save from extinction and whose resurrection it makes possible at the time of the return.[7]

The Monarchy

After having left nomadic life and conquered their country, the Hebrews must tend to organization and security and face what appear to be insurmountable problems: internal tribal rivalry, separation accentuated by the country's character, outside pressures against the security of their institutions, and retaining the purity of their religion. The Canaanites, Philistines, Hittites, and Moabites carry on a continuous policy of harassment toward the newcomers. To cope with the domestic and foreign problems of their society, the Hebrews adopt a form of government that is fundamentally foreign to them, the monarchy. For 445 years, from King Saul to the period of exile, such a regime makes it possible for them to overcome internal contradictions, give form to the Hebrew civilization, and deliver the message of the Prophets.

We will have a king . . . like all nations (I Sam. 8:19–21).

The chapter of the first book of Samuel that describes the inauguration of the monarchy is very significant. The elders ask Samuel to face up to the failure of the government and to name a King so that the Hebrews may be like other nations. That is what everybody who is privileged with being different wants to do: be like everybody else, conform. This request by Samuel's contemporaries will be repeated for thousands of years by their heirs, the Jews. They still say the same thing today, without being totally successful.

Against the Prophet's will and God's plan, the Hebrews dissent. And God himself says that the voice of the people must be heeded. In his name, around 1031 B.C., Samuel crowns Saul the first King of Israel.

The united Hebrew kingdom will be headed by three Kings successively: Saul, David, and Solomon. It will last almost a century, during which time the Hebrews represent an important political factor in western Asia. The Bible relates the legends of the first three Kings in detail, which will have a lasting influence on the sensibility and hopes of Israel. It is all the more remarkable since the monarchy is inaugurated against national tradition and divine right and, after a brief period of glory, will lead the people from one catastrophe to the next, until its ultimate demise.

The jealousy of the leading citizens toward the other nations must be noted. Each Canaanite city was headed by a king, and Joshua had to overthrow thirty-one of them to conquer the Promised Land. The oldest documents, those of El Amarna, for example, attest to parallel situations in Canaan and in Syria. The five Philistine principalities of the bordering plain and the four Gibeonite cities were governed by the same rules. The kings, sometimes of foreign origin, dominated their cities and the tiny territories they sometimes commanded. Royal power depended on a militia, occasionally supplemented by mercenaries. Dynastic principles determined continuity.

The Hebrews also consider the powerful examples of the hereditary monarchies of Egypt and Mesopotamia. Israel's leaders want to become like the others because they are tired of the disorder of the twelve-tribe federation; they are also concerned with the interregnal anarchy of their Judges, seers, and Prophets and with their God-given mission, which they fulfill as inspired leaders rather than political beings. They want the respectability of the monarchical institution. The conflict resulting from this change may be detected in the Bible: there are two currents of thought, one in favor of the monarchy (I Sam. 9:1, 10:16, 11:1–15) and one opposed (I Sam. 8:1–22, 10:18–25, 12, 15). If the former should win, they will owe it to the pressures exerted by the enemy Philistines against the Hebrew settlements throughout the country. The enemy must be met by a state united under royal power. This power alone makes it possible for the Hebrews to survive the chaos and anarchy at the end of the period of the Judges (Judges 17:6, 21:25).

Saul is the founder of a monarchy which remains in embryonic state for the two decades of his reign. His power, like David's and Solomon's, stretches "over all Israel and over Judah" (II Sam. 5:4–5). This expression confirms the dual character of the Hebraic royalty from its inception. Judah has always had a separate history within the confines of its inspired mountains. It takes strong personalities—Samuel, Saul, David, and Solomon—to overcome the conflict of interests and views that always obtained between north and south.

The Second Gate

Saul, the First of the Three Kings

The charismatic personality of the first three Kings of Israel and Judah has an effect on the society. Samuel chooses Saul on God's orders by virtue of his visionary powers. The son of Kish, a *gibbor hayil,* a leader of the tribe of Benjamin, Saul is young and talented. He is out looking for his father's asses when he meets Samuel, who recognizes him immediately and informs him of the royal destiny in store for him by God's command. In the course of a sacrificial meal, he tells him that his father's asses have been found and that he will be King in spite of his humble family origins in the country's smallest tribe. Samuel proceeds to the King's anointing, and to his proclamation that assures the change in his person: "The spirit of YHWH will triumph in you, you will prophesy with them; you will be transformed" (I Sam. 10:6). Filled with the spirit of YHWH, the King can accomplish his work, for Elohim is with him. In effect, this overgrown boy, made King and Prophet by Samuel, is no longer the calm watchman of his father's asses but an ecstatic visionary and fearsome military leader.

The city of Jabesh, in Gilead, threatened by the Ammonites, calls for his help. The spirit of YHWH seizes Saul, who butchers a pair of oxen and sends the pieces to all parts of the country with a message: "Whoever does not follow Saul will have this done to his oxen" (I Sam. 11:6–7). The people rise up as one. Nahash, the Ammonite who wanted to pluck out the right eye of all the inhabitants of Jabesh, is beaten and his troops are routed. In Gilgal the people of Israel proceed anew with their joyful coronation (I Sam. 11:12–15). Like the Judges previously, the first King of Israel confirms the divine choice by his deeds. His victory, as much as his election, establishes him as leader. An alliance is formed between the King and the people, confirmed and sanctified by God. The future proves that the strength of Saul's soul, inspired by God, matches the greatness of destiny. He defeats the Philistines, as he had the Ammonites. Each victory increases his charisma. With God as his deputy, he becomes the real possessor, the heir, the *nagid* of Israel's wealth (I Sam. 9:16, 9:20, 10:1). He is quite naturally the chief who leads his people to victory, thereby proving the reality of his powers and the strength of his benediction. In peacetime he demonstrates his royalty by the wise execution of justice.

Saul, King of Israel, continues to live on his farm, surrounded by his farmhands, whose activity he directs in the same way as any wealthy farmer. He has neither palace nor temple. The Ark of the Covenant, the spiritual center and mystical rallying point of the people, is detached from his person and his residence. Nothing in his life style puts him above his people—he remains what he was before his coronation. He raises his family to the first ranks of the tribe of Benjamin and becomes the savior and King of Israel, supported by his generals and soldiers, without having made an established institution of the monarchy. Indeed, Saul continues the tradition of the Judges. His destiny is reminiscent of Jephthah's from Gilead. They call him *melech,* king, instead of by the traditional titles of heroes, *gibbor hayil, moshia* (savior), *rosh* (leader), or *shophet* (judge) (Judges 6:14, 8:22). In fact, Saul closes the period of the Judges and opens a new era of the monarchy, which has its true founder in David. Sick, and weakened by internal and foreign enemies, King Saul comes to a tragic end and commits suicide after the defeat of Gilboa.

David

Saul's meeting with David, David's and Jonathan's love, the events telling how the blessings of the Lord abandon Saul and how he drags his son Jonathan with him—all this occurred 3,000 years ago. Yet it still has a contemporary quality and incomparable tragic flavor in the Bible text. The confrontation between Saul, the aging and psychologically troubled King, and the successful young David, aspiring to realize Samuel's promise, is a drama in itself, detailed with the objectivity of a historian and the precision of a psychologist. David is poor and unknown; yet he is chosen as the heir of Saul, whose downfall is explained by his numerous infidelities to God's order.

Saul and David fight for the same throne; nonetheless, they are so unlike that they seem to serve two divinities and two different nations. Samuel, the Prophet who has taken them from their ancestral flocks to present them with the inheritance of the house of Israel, is torn between the two. He symbolizes God's conscience in facing the ambitions and crimes of temporal power. In spite of everything, it is he who makes and unmakes Kings. And the biblical writer shows in detail how Saul's greatness originated from the divine power invested in him, and how his downfall begins in the secret flaw of his soul. David's power begins with the holy anointment he receives from Samuel, who braved Saul's anger. He knew that in anointing the son of Jesse he risked being put to death by the tyrant he had formerly called to power.

"Samuel took the horn of oil and anointed David in the midst of his brethren. And the spirit of the Lord came upon David from that day forward" (I Sam. 16:13). In his village of Bethlehem, David, like Saul, is an unknown young man when he becomes the object of the visitation of the man of God. Once again divine election makes a King from a shepherd. Saul had been put to the test and rejected because of his unfaithfulness. Another choice, as free and unexpected as the first, is expressed in the name of God by his oracle, the seer Samuel. Everyone accepts his choice. If Saul and David achieve greatness, if they win decisive victories over their enemies, if they prove the wisdom of their judgment, they owe it to neither genius nor intelligence but to YHWH's spirit in them. When their sins make them unworthy of divine help, they are ruined and they die. And it is YHWH's spirit, in the name of whom David fights, that inspires him when he heaves the fatal rock at Goliath. It is the same spirit that on two occasions allows him to escape the jealous Saul's attacks. That spirit protects him in his flight as he gathers 400 and then 600 adventurers, who become valiant warriors under his orders; it lets him defeat the Philistines and the Amalekites at each new confrontation; it brings about Saul's defeat, suicide, and the death of his three sons.

From then on David is free to mourn the deaths of his King and his beloved son Jonathan. No longer does anything separate him from the throne Samuel had promised. He is proclaimed King of Judah at Hebron in 1013. He holds this position for seven and a half years, while Ish-bosheth (Eshbaal), Saul's fourth son, rules over Israel at Mahanaim, where he had transferred his capital. A civil war opposes the kingdom of the north and that of the south. The Bible recounts the complicated intrigues in the royal entourage, the confrontation of Abner and Joab, Ish-bosheth's assassination at the hands of two officers, who instead of receiving the expected reward from David are punished for their crime.

It is under complex circumstances that, after the entente between the nation and its sovereign, David is made King by the entire country. The new King is not only a shepherd and a musician but a military genius who pursues the Philistines, to break them forever. It is from them that David, fleeing from Saul's anger, learned the art of warfare; it is among them that he recruits his elite guard, the Cherethites and Pelethites. With the Philistine danger disposed of, David can consolidate his power. His most consequential act will be the choosing of Jerusalem, a neutral city, apart from tribal rivalries, for the capital of the united kingdom.

Jerusalem was to be more than just a royal city. "The city where David camped" was to become the city of God. David confirms its ancient, sacred character by taking the Ark of the Covenant there and making preparations for the building of the Temple, a popular decision. With his funds he buys the Jebusite Araunah's field and builds an altar, which was to mark the site of the altar of the future Temple. Jerusalem, the spiritual center of the nation, soon becomes the capital of an empire. The Arameans and the Ammonites are defeated. Moab, like Amnon and Edom, becomes dependent on Israel. The Amalekites are annihilated. David rules from the Red Sea to the Euphrates and commands the most important, strategic, and commercial routes of the East.

The kingdom is not built without serious misfortunes befalling the King, who saves the life of Merib-baal, Jonathan's ailing son; but all the other descendants of Saul are slain by the Gibeonites. David's adultery with Bathsheba and the death of the scorned husband cause scandal and bring him the Prophet Nathan's censure (II Sam. 12). The death of his child of sin casts a bad light on the intimate life of the King, but love triumphs in spite of sin and crime. The son of David and Bathsheba, Solomon, will be the greatest of Israel's Kings.

Critical events multiply around David. Amnon, his elder son, violates and then abandons his half-sister Tamar. Absalom, who avenges the honor of his betrayed sister by trapping and killing Amnon, has to spend two years in exile before the King's anger subsides and he is forgiven and allowed to return to the court.

The aging David has to confront his son Absalom, who plots against him for the succession. In the tribe of Benjamin, in the north and in the south, revolt breaks out. David is once more able to force destiny and overcome the conspiracy. Joab, David's faithful general, defies the King's order and slays Absalom, who is hanged from a tree by his hair. David must again quell Sheba ben Bichri's revolt. Finally, he witnesses the rivalry between his son Adonijah, supported by Joab and the priest Abiathar, and Solomon, supported by Bathsheba, Zadok the priest, and Nathan the Prophet. While Solomon is anointed with the holy oils by Zadok and is acclaimed King by the people gathered at the Spring of Gihon, David dies, ending a glorious reign of forty years. He is remembered as a versatile man of genius—musician, poet, lover, warrior; calculating, generous, and vindictive; savage mystic and meticulous administrator; a visionary who founds the holy city of Jerusalem as the city of God and a dynasty that will last until the exile. Immortalized in the memory of the people, he continues to live as a symbol of the faith of Israel.

Solomon

Solomon, who completes the portrait of the monarchy, marks it with some of his own characteristics. As his successor, he fulfills his famous father's last wish: the elimination of Joab, David's old and faithful lieutenant, and Adonijah, his half-brother. He maintains an expensive war machine, which he has inherited, and chooses Benaiah as its commander, the general whose support had been decisive for his crowning. He has to contain Egypt's incursions, and resolves this problem in his own way, by marrying the daughter of Pharaoh. A pacifist by nature, Solomon does not take power lightly, and without striking a blow he keeps his inheritance almost intact and brings about an unsurpassed level of prosperity.

Under his rule, every individual in Judah and Israel is safe "under his vine and fig tree" in the plush countryside. The King excels in justice. His judgments form his legend and become proverbial. The treasures David accumulated in his wars are used for building the royal palace and the Temple. His subjects provide for his harem, tables, and stables, for Solomon loves all the luxuries of the Orient.

His human inclinations do not diminish his mystical aspiration. The Temple, which he builds to fulfill his father's vow, is one of the most imposing of the ancient Orient, and his nearby palace underscores the union of the God of his fathers, the monarchy, and the holy city.

As was also the case with David and Saul, there is sharp criticism of the shortcomings of Solomon's reign. Instead of strengthening the aspirations of primitive Mosaism, he does not hesitate to make alliances with pagan powers, or fill his harem with Moabites, Edomites, Sidonians, and Hittites, or to make an Egyptian his queen. He imposes a cosmopolitan atmosphere on his capital, where all nations may feel at home. He builds chapels, which are open to diverse cults. To this religious weakness his rule adds another: a cumbersome state machinery. Harsh assessments and taxation ultimately give rise to general discontent and divide the kingdom immediately after his death, in 933.

During the period this study is concerned with, royalty played a dominant role in the life of the people. Yet it must not be forgotten that it was established by the meeting of divine will and national traditions. The books of Samuel and Kings condemn all the Kings of Israel and spare only a few Kings of Judah from their judgments. Those parties that were favorable to the monarchy (II Sam. 7:8–17; Ps. 2, 18, 20, 21, and all the Royal Psalms; Isaiah 7, 9, 11, 62 seqq.) were not successful in quieting the voices of those who condemned the "King's law" (I Sam. 10:27). In fact, Israel from its beginning has been a religious community whose organization has sometimes required the structures of a state—sometimes monarchical structures—but it remains essentially a group of men under their God and his Law. The monarchy and the state are sometimes a necessity to which the Hebrews submit, in order to assure their survival, but basically they are independent of their administrative organizations and are informed by the order of the spirit.

Choosing and Anointing the Kings

From 1031 to 720 for Israel and to 586 for Judah, the Hebraic city was governed by Kings who received their inspiration, and sometimes their legitimacy, from the tradition of Saul, David, and Solomon. As in all the East in the thousand years that preceded the Christian era, accession to the throne was based on divine appointment. In Israel, too, royal power comes by virtue of God's free choice. When the King fails to live up to the royal covenant, he loses his legitimacy and his dignity. God is free to name his successor without restriction; it is not necessary to exercise the principle of dynastic succession. Primogeniture plays only a secondary role because of the competitive factions and the numerous wives of the King. Women are normally excluded from the succession. Only one reigned in Judah, Athaliah, who assumed power on the death of her son Ahaziah. She ruled for seven years, before being assassinated in her palace by the partisans of Joash (II Kings 11). This account reveals to the minutest detail the organization of a palace revolution, so common in the history of Judah and Israel.

Royal power is based on a covenant between God, the monarchy, and the people. The King, the elected one, is anointed with holy oil in the sanctuary in a unique liturgical act and then receives from the priest the *nezer* and the *eduth,* equivalent to the crown and the scepter, ritual signs of royalty in Egypt and Mesopotamia.

The anointing creates a new person, whose vocation is to act under the impulsion of God's spirit. A change occurs in him and gives him the reality of his powers. As God's anointed, he can accomplish sacred acts. He is the savior of Israel and is gifted, if he is faithful to his call, with supernatural powers (II Sam. 19:10; II Kings 6:26, 13:5; Ps. 72 seqq.). If he is not, as in Egypt, a god (the son of Ra), he at least lives in the intimacy of the creator. Through God's wisdom he knows everything, as does an angel of the Lord (I Sam. 29:9). Psalm 2 goes still further: "You are my son; I begot you today." This statement supports the idea that the creator adopts the person of the King.

The continuous exercise of religious powers follows from this. Saul makes sacrifice to God. David erects an altar, plans for the building of the Temple, and organizes the levitical functions. Solomon builds the Temple, dedicates it, and completes the work of religious organization his father had started (II Sam. 24:25; I Chr. 22, 29; I Kings 5, 8). After the schism, Jeroboam establishes the sanctuary of Bethel, recruits and organizes its corps of priests, and fixes the religious calendar. All the Kings of Judah and Israel, in addition to their temporal power, unrelentingly exercise the spiritual authority whose supreme immediacy they represent. Ahaz orders liturgical reform, which the priest Urias carries out in the sanctuary (II Kings 16:10–18). The altar of the God of Israel is replaced by a copy of the altar that was in Damascus at the time of Tiglath-Pileser, King of Assyria. He eliminates the Temple walk reserved for the King of Israel, to give indisputable homage to his suzerain, the King of Assyria. And the priests, without murmur, zealously carry out unprecedented orders from their King.

Joash budgets the proceeds of his collections to the Temple's repairs. His ordinances are respected by the priests, who are public servants appointed (and sometimes dismissed) by him (II Sam. 8:17, 20:25; I Kings 2:26–27, 4:2; II Kings 12:5 seqq.). Josiah oversees the control of Temple finances (II Kings 22:2–8). He is particularly successful with the great reform inspired by the discovery of the book of the Torah in the Temple of Adonai by the high priest Hilkiah (II Kings 22:8–11). The Kings of Israel and Judah bless the people in the exercise of their sacerdotal prerogatives.

Since the anointing of the King is basically a rite of covenant, it is concluded by sacrifices whose blood offering seals the ties that henceforth unite the person of the King to his God and to his people.

The House of the King

With the institution of the monarchy, Israel becomes an international political power. David concludes a pact with a Canaanite prince, Hiram of Tyre. Solomon weaves a network of political, maritime, and commercial relations throughout the ancient world. The monarchies of Israel and Judah attempt, with varying success, and often at the price of their autonomy, to maintain relations with nearby cities, states, and empires.

For matters of administration, defense, and international commitment, the King surrounds himself with a court of ministers, high-ranking public servants, general officers, "servants of the King" (*'avdei hammelech, sarim*), ministerial-level officers, and secretaries. David and Solomon also copy the governmental organization of the cities of Canaan and neighboring countries. The royal chronicles have preserved the names of the most important of David's ministers: Joab ben Zeruiah, minister of the army, commander-in-chief of Israel's armies, and Benaiah ben Jehoiada, chief of the personal guard made up of the Cherethites and the Pelethites (II Sam. 8:17–18, 20:23–26). There were also some administrative and diplomatic functions, which must have been innovative for the Hebrews in the early periods of the monarchy, that are curiously modern: the secretary was probably the spokesman for the royal government and the scribe presided over written communications with neighboring kingdoms. The duties of the minister of war, the chief of the guard, the secretary and the scribe, set up by David, continued during Judah's long monarchical history with only one important change—the ministry in charge of the royal household. After Absalom's revolt, as a result of the ever-increasing burden of taxation, David established a new central post in his government, the minister of taxation, whose duty was to assess the taxes the people owed the King. In addition, the King had advisers and friends who informed him on general policy and the pitfalls of foreign affairs or party intrigues. Ahithophel was qualified to counsel the King; Hushai the Archite was called the friend of the King. The royal courts of Judah and Israel must have had many such officials, so vitally necessary in moving through the web of intrigue surrounding the Kings. Sometimes David chose his counselors among the musicians, who were his friends and brethren.

Chronicles (I Chr. 27:25–34) completes the description of the civil and military organization of the royal house of David, pointing out offices that shed interesting light on the economic history of the ancient world: an officer over the King's treasures, another over the stores in the cities, villages, and castles, one over the farmers, one supervising the tillers, another over the dressers of the vineyards and one over the wine cellars, and others over the herds of Sharon and the valleys, the camels, the asses, and the sheep.

Such was the highly organized division of labor in the government. This inventory is unique in our documentation and shows the wealth and independence of the royal household. It is clear that this administration was reinforced in David's time by an additional structure: the religious organization centered around the Temple. The aging David counted the Levites, who numbered 38,000: 24,000 presiding over the offices of the Temple, 6,000 scribes and judges, 4,000 clerks, and 4,000 musicians. David organized and divided them into classes of Levites, priests, cantors, and clerks. The Temple's administration was headed by the high priest and the officials in charge of its treasuries and holy stores (I Chr. 23, 24, 25, 26).

The royal administration and the ecclesiastical staff were backed by a large and powerful army. The royal chronicles give another impressive count of the military forces in David's time, though the figures are obviously exaggerated: more than 340,000 soldiers, provided by each of the twelve tribes, and contingents varying from 120,000 to 3,700 soldiers. It was this tremendous assembly of officers and soldiers, armed with spear and shield under the waving banners of their tribes, who at Hebron acclaimed the young King David on the day of his coronation (I Chr. 11:10).

The King and His People

The monarchy was not Samuel's creation *ex nihilo,* or Saul's, or even David's; it was an extension of the national realities in the time of the Judges, organized to fit the needs of the new kingdom. Such an alliance links the King and his people and is the basis for the privileges and duties of the citizens and of the sovereign who rules them. A synallagmatic relationship unites them under God's dependence. Each individual engages himself in this solemn act to follow YHWH and obey his Torah.

In order to govern the country, the King appointed a prefect to lead each tribe (I Chr. 27:16–22, 2:1–2). Their frontiers had not changed since the conquest. Abroad, the territories are ruled by governors, *nitzavim,* or left to the rule of local kings who, as vassals, must pay their tribute (II Sam. 8:2, 10:19).

Solomon assures a reorganization of the kingdom, but still on the basis of twelve regions (I Kings 4:7–19): the hills of Ephraim; the country of Dan, with regions added from conquests over the Philistines and Canaanites; the plain of Sharon; the region of Dor; the plain of Esdrelon and Beth-Shean; the territory of the former Manasseh of Transjordan, enlarged by David's Aramean conquests; the region of Mahanaim in Transjordan; the territory of Naphtali to the north of Lake Tiberias; those of Asher, Issachar, Benjamin, and finally Gilead (probably the ancient territory of Gad in Transjordan).[8] The twelve prefectures are under a minister who is responsible for the prefects (I Kings 4:7). He controls the payment of taxes, which are equal to a month's upkeep of the entire royal household and army, including the fodder for Solomon's large cavalry and the cart horses for each of the twelve tribes. In addition to tax supervision, the prefects oversee the general functions of the country's administration and are charged with maintaining law and order.

Taxation and Recruitment

The burdens of the household are augmented with construction plans. Solomon, like Herod a thousand years later, was a great builder. He undertakes the building of the Temple and his palaces at Megiddo, Hazor, and Gezer. He obtains his resources by impositions on the people, which are translated as seasonal civil service for the benefit of the public works: the corvée, or *sevel*. Everybody is liable to the corvée, which is strictly controlled. In Solomon's time the chronicle mentions 70,000 statute laborers, 80,000 quarry men, and 30,000 workers, 10,000 of whom were designated for the transport of timber from Lebanon, which the woodsmen of Tyre chopped (I Kings 5:20–32); 3,300 leaders of the statute laborers administered this huge work army, composed partially of Hebrews and most likely a majority of Canaanites. The citizen thus becomes taxable and recruitable at pleasure, and bitterness grows throughout the tribes.

What is more, the royal army must be maintained in Jerusalem and the fortified areas. The army's equipment is principally chariots, which were introduced in David's time. The captains of the chariots make up an elite, who are admitted to the royal entourage and occupy such strongholds as Gezer, Hazor, and Megiddo (whose excavations reveal ancient splendors).

Heavy taxes are added to the corvée. Royal chronicles are not very informative about the fiscal system, or the state revenue, or that of the Temple, or that of the numerous royal undertakings and holdings, but the King is free to draw from any of these funds.

Very likely the Hebrews were forced into making regular contributions, in addition to the *sevel*. "He will take the tenth of your corn, and of the revenues of your vineyards, to give to his eunuchs and servants" (I Sam. 8:15). This text was more than a threat; it refers to actual practice in neighboring kingdoms whose kings required a tenth of all the citizens' revenue. Although there is no precise documentation on tithing in the royal period, throughout the centuries references are made to this custom, which is definitely in operation after the return from the exile, when the people solemnly vow to give the Temple a third of a shekel per year, the first fruits of their harvests and flocks, and a tenth of their revenue from the earth and woods (Ezek. 45:13 seqq.; Lev. 7:29).

Custom also has it that every eminent person who was received at the royal court presented himself laden with gifts, whose value varied according to his importance—and his hopes. Naaman, the minister of Aram's armies, offers the King 10 talents of silver, 6,000 pieces of gold, and ten changes of raiment—but it is true that he came to be cured of leprosy by the Prophet Elisha (II Kings 5:5). Gifts flow to the palace on the occasion of coronations, as tokens of allegiance. Under David's and Solomon's reigns the vassal states pay a heavy annual tribute. According to the records, Mesha, King of Moab, contributed 100,000 lambs and the wool of 100,000 rams (II Kings 3:4). It is understandable that he revolted at his first chance, at Ahab's death (II Kings 3:4).

If foreign conditions required it, the King levied supplementary taxes. Menahem raised the considerable sum of 1,000 silver talents for the king of Assyria by taxing each notable in Israel 50 shekels (II Kings 15:19–20). Jehoiakim assessed the notables of Judah, according to their wealth, a total of 100 silver and 10 gold talents to appease Pharaoh (II Kings 23:33).

Because of the political and economic crises at the end of Solomon's reign, the labor and tax burdens are augmented. This is a cause of revolt in the north and it provokes the schism that marks the end of Hebrew political expansion. In the East, rampant with turmoil due to dynastic changes in Egypt and the Edomite and Aramean revolutions, the relations between Judah and Israel were conspiring to affect the future of Hebraic civilization.

Relationship between Judah and Israel

Immediately after Absalom's revolt, David opts for the reinforcement of the throne, which henceforth depends on the regional and military structures of the tribe of Judah, at the expense of the old egalitarian nomadism. Upon Solomon's death, the claims of the tribes of the north are essentially on the economic and social planes. "Take off a little of the grievous service of thy father, and of his most heavy yoke, and we will serve thee," say the elders of Israel at Shechem to Rehoboam (I Kings 12:2–6). Solomon's heir goes beyond the advice of his counselors. He adopts the attitude of his childhood companions—young, vainglorious wolves who urge him to test his strength. "My little finger is thicker than the back of my father. And now my father put a heavy yoke upon you, but I will add to your yoke: my father beat you with whips, but I will beat you with scorpions (I Kings 12:10, 11).

"To your tents, Israel!" The battle cry begins the revolt. Rehoboam accepts the fait accompli; is he not reaping what his father has sown? Jeroboam completes the schism and founds his own kingdom, Israel, opposing Judah. Jerusalem, thus divided, has to be mindful of Shechem on both the religious and the political plane.

Thus the Hebrew homeland will be divided for many centuries. But here and there some tribes remain faithful to the regime, and Judah to David's dynasty. The two new kingdoms lose many rich territories and survive by virtue of extremely hard work and new techniques. Under Solomon, iron implements become widespread and make it possible for the Hebrews to build wells, canals, and conduits and so control the water supply, the means of life and prosperity. This revolution makes the mountains inhabitable; they can then be cultivated to make a new era of prosperity possible. A step has been taken to free man from his enslavement to nature. Now

the mountain civilization of Judah and Israel is free to develop in
its eagle nests.

The Schism

The schism was effected without bloodshed. Rehoboam did not send
his armies out against the tribes of the north (as David had done)
to put down the revolt. The action is accepted. The duality that satisfies the instincts and ancestral traditions of the people must be
satisfied, even if it contradicts the interests and hopes for a greater
unity.

In the time of Solomon it was conceivable that Israel had created
a state sufficiently strong—geographically, demographically, politi-
cally, economically, and militarily—to undertake new conquests
and, like the other great nations of the ancient Orient, to aspire to
a vast empire. But a complex mechanism is at play which changes
the course of Israel's destiny and its spiritual calling. Temporal Israel is at its strongest during the unified monarchy. But as soon as
its contradictions become apparent, the possibilities for an empire
are weakened and the Hebrews are prey to powerful neighbors and
to the anxieties of their prophetic vocation.

Hebrew monotheism was close to disappearing when the Philistines were on the verge of conquering the entire country and enslav-
ing the twelve tribes. The monarchy had been established to oppose
this danger, but its very triumph—the great political and economic
power it achieved in three generations—brought monotheism to the
same point. The ethical monotheism of the Hebrews maintained its
primacy—and survived—primarily because of the breakdown of
royal power after Solomon's death. When Rehoboam, Solomon's
son, succeeded him in 933, a revolt broke out and resulted in the
secession of the ten northern tribes, who founded the kingdom of
Israel around Shechem, the capital where Jeroboam ben Nebat will
reign. The two tribes of the south, Judah and Benjamin, remain
grouped around Jerusalem on territory that, with Edom and the
Philistine country, forms scarcely a quarter of Solomon's kingdom
and has a third of its population.

The long period from the schism (in 931) to the fall of Samaria (in 721) does not destroy the common destiny of the two rival kingdoms, despite their political and sometimes military encounters. What unites them is always stronger than what divides them. Their literature, language, faith, and origins remain the same and their hopes are informed by the love of the same God. The political frontiers cannot sever this spiritual communion, or the close economic ties which are interwoven over this tiny and endangered land. Every economic, spiritual, political, and military crisis in one kingdom is felt by the other.

In Jerusalem the people remain faithful to David's dynasty, but in Israel (as elsewhere in the vicinity) dynasties scarcely outlive their founders. They are born and die amid bloodshed, crime, and conspiracy. The dynasty of Jehu, the most enduring, has only four Kings. The others are even more ephemeral, and their fall initiates the massacre of the royal families and their followers. The revolution affects all echelons of central and provincial power. The country is small, ambitions are strong, the armies are powerful; and from the outset there is alienation from the house of David and the dynastic principle it mystically symbolizes.

The Kingdom of Israel

The kingdom of Israel, from the secession of 931 to the fall in 721, is characterized by frenetic events. During the 210 years of its autonomy it counts nineteen sovereigns, in contrast to the twenty Kings of Judah between 931 and 586, over 345 years.

Jeroboam ben Nebat, founder and first King of Israel, intends to put the kingdom on a solid basis, protected by autonomous institutions. (The chronicles tell us nothing about his military and administrative actions, which must have been considerable.) He must create a new political center and defend it against its numerous internal and foreign enemies. On the other hand, we are told a great deal about his extensive religious reform. He understands that his kingdom has a future only to the extent that there is a religious center to counterbalance Jerusalem's mystical attraction in the minds of the people. "The king deliberated; he made two golden calves and said: 'Go ye up no more to Jerusalem: Behold thy gods,

O Israel, who brought thee out of the land of Egypt' " (I Kings 12: 28–33). He places one of these golden calves in Beth El, the other in Dan, in new temples served by the priests he employs (without considering the exclusive privileges of the tribe of Levi), and he also reforms the calendar. These changes are more effective in solidifying the schism than all the administrative reforms and military precautions taken together.

The installation of the golden calves resembled nearby practices —the bull was a sacred mount of the Syro-Phoenician, Mesopotamian, and Egyptian gods. But Jeroboam knows his limits: in contrast to the foreign practice, his calves are not mounted by a human figure. His is a bold stand against the severe Mosaism of the Judeans and an obvious reference to the past, when Israel wandered over Sinai. That is all it is. He does not go as far as the sacrilege of idolatry but remains faithful to the God of Israel.

In the logic of his choice, he spurns the principle of centralization, which was favored in David's dynasty. His kingdom does not have a single, mystical capital. He moves from one city to another, to Shechem, Penuel, Tirzah, as if to maintain some ancient custom.

He carries out his reforms under pressure from Egypt. In 923 King Shishak invaded Judah and Israel, and the list of cities he conquered is preserved on the walls of the temple at Karnak—150 of them, mostly in Israel. Remains of an arch of triumph which Shishak built after having pillaged the Temple of Jerusalem (he spared the city, on payment of a very high ransom) (I Kings 14:25; II Chr. 12:2 seqq.) have recently been discovered in Megiddo.

Hence Rehoboam's wish to defend the country with a strong chain of fortresses which would extend and consolidate the fortifications built by David and Solomon. Taking advantage of Israel's weakness after the Shishak campaign, Rehoboam, and even more so his son after him, Abijam, attacks the northern kingdom. The defeat of the north is fatal for Jeroboam's dynasty. His son, King Nadab, is assassinated, and the minister of the armies, Baasa ben Ahijah, seizes Israel's throne (909–886). The new King excels at political and military reorganization, but his recourse to Ben-hadad I, king of Aram, puts an end to his dynasty. Baasa's son Ela (886–885), while drunk, is killed by a colonel of the chariots, Zimri, who succeeds him (885) but reigns for only seven days. Omri, the commanding general of the army, cuts off the city of Tirzah and Zimri takes refuge in the tower of the royal palace, in which he is burned alive. Omri has to quell another rebellion, Tibni's, before being crowned (885–874). He founds Samaria, and his son Ahab reigns over Israel for twenty-two years (874–853).

Samaria, Capital of Israel

In 880 Omri, King of Israel, chooses the site for his capital 10 kilometers northwest of Shechem. (Today the place is known as Sebastia, after the city Herod rebuilt on this hill, at an altitude of 430 meters.) The region is fertile, rich in water, and strategically commands the northern routes. With notable building talent, Ahab continues his father's work, but under Jehoram the city declines. Attacked by Ben-hadad the Aramean, it suffers severe famine. Later, under Jeroboam II, the city achieves its greatest prosperity, which is displayed with such splendor that it draws the censure of Amos (Amos 3, 4). And then poverty again, preceding the fall of Israel (II Kings 17:5–6, 18:9–10).

The site was excavated in 1908. The royal palace, its connecting buildings, and its fortress and ramparts were unearthed, as were numerous objects, coins, ostraca, and carved ivories that date back to Omri's time. Between 1931 and 1935 a sanctuary and some tombs were found. What emerges is a rather precise picture of his city with an enclosed area of about 7.5 hectares. The fortress and the palace and its additions are the upper city, while the populace was grouped in the lower city and, during peaceful intervals, in the surrounding countryside. The houses were solidly built, flush with the rock or on a stone foundation, a method no doubt taken from the Phoenicians.

Sixty-three of the ostraca on the site are legible and pinpoint several facts regarding the method of writing (with black ink), the names of people, and the King's system for making assignments. The carved ivories make up the richest collection of art objects thus far discovered in Israel. They are Phoenician-made, and most of them date back to the reign of Ahab, who built a house with them and whose palace contained delicately carved ivory beds.

The Cordial Alliance

Under the rule of Jehoshaphat ben Asa, King of Judah, and Omri (885–874) and his son Ahab (874–853), Kings of Israel, there is a rapprochement between the two Hebraic kingdoms and a reappraisal of their foreign policy, as well as an administrative and cultural evolution. Once the difficulties of the schism are overcome, the political and economic advantages of an alliance are realized, and then are strengthened by the marriage of Jehoram ben Jehoshaphat and Athaliah.[9] This union symbolizes the end of the difficulties between the two states, which regain most of their former wealth.

Peace favors reforms. Jehoshaphat builds on his father's work; he sets up judges in the border fortresses and a supreme court in Jerusalem. He destroys the places of idolatrous worship and spreads the teaching of the Torah. It is likely that he also divided the kingdom of Judah into twelve administrative regions, strengthened his army, and completed the centralization of the Judean monarchy around Jerusalem.

In Israel, Omri (like Solomon before him) allies himself with Sidon and Tyre. He consolidates his kingdom by military victories against Moab, and probably Aram. More important is his founding of the city of Samaria and giving it capital rank. In this way he displays his sovereignty, refusing to rule from the ancient, conflict-torn cities of his kingdom. Omri's choice of Samaria is not unlike David's choice of Jerusalem: not being able to find a "neutral" city, the Kings found a new one. Both capitals will ultimately confront each other in a struggle for prestige, whose memory is still kept alive by the Samaritans.

Ahab follows his father's footsteps and reaps the rewards. Israel becomes one of the most important kingdoms of the Near East. Recent excavations reveal the wealth of its economy, its arts, its commerce, and its impressive urban development. Thus Israel builds itself a political and economic center that controls the important trade routes of the region, and upon which Judah, Egypt, Tyre, and Edom converge.

Ben-hadad, King of Aram, covets Israel's wealth. But twice beaten, in Samaria and in Aphek (I Kings 20), he accepts the alliance offered by Ahab. Today it is conceded that Assyria's military rise, beginning in the ninth century, was dangerous both to Aram and to Israel and ultimately induced the rapprochement of these enemy countries.

The Assyrian Challenge and a Time of Trial

From the ninth to the seventh century the Assyrian army was the most fearsome military instrument ever at the disposal of any state in the ancient Near East. Only the Babylonians and the Medes would eventually break this terrible war machine, which dominated the Near East for three centuries and caused the fall and destruction of the kingdom of Israel, weakened by the internal strife that reoccurred after Ahab's death.

Bloody images illustrate this period. Ahab, disguised as a trooper, dies in the battle of Ramoth-gilead and, pierced by an arrow, remains fixed to his chariot until nightfall, while his army flees. His body is washed in the pool of Samaria. Dogs lick his blood and prostitutes bathe in it (I Kings 22:36). Later, another tragedy: Mesha, King of Moab, beaten by the coalition of the Kings of Israel, Judah, and Edom and driven to despair, sacrifices his son by his own hand to the god Chemosh.

Death roams everywhere. Joram is killed by Jehu, who also murders Ahaziah. Jezebel, dressed in royal raiment and Eastern headdress, dies with a challenge on her lips. In Samaria the leaders kill seventy sons of Ahab and send their heads in baskets to Jehu, who had ordered this massacre. The new King, en route to his capital, Samaria, kills forty-two Judean princes who had come to inquire about the royal family. Revolutionaries surround the Temple of Baal and murder its priest and congregation, before razing the building and its annexes.

Jehu, cut off from Judah, which is governed by Jezebel's daughter Athaliah and then by her son Jehoash, thinks it wise (in the second year of his reign) to ally himself with Shalmaneser (842). The Assyrian monarch records on a black obelisk the moment when Israel's ambassadors brought him their tribute of gold and silver ingots, gold vases, and precious gifts.

This incident foreshadows the advance of the Arameans, who invade a large section of the country. They pillage fortified cities and murder thousands, sparing neither women, nor old people, nor children, and kill the men with unsurpassed cruelty. They invent new instruments of torture, such as iron-edge blades that are used by the military to facilitate massacres and increase terror.

The small nations take advantage of the confusion in Israel: the Ammonites, Moabites, Edomites, Philistines, and Tyrians join in the pillage and subdue the weaker villages. The reign of Joachaz (814–798), son and successor of Jehu, plunges the country into the worst poverty. Damascus forces Israel to reduce its army to 50 horses, 10 chariots, and 10,000 foot soldiers. Then Hazael's successor, Benhadad, besieges Samaria and causes a famine so severe that some of its women are forced to devour their own children (II Kings 6: 24–30).

The Prophets and the people see the apocalyptic meaning in these horrors. Moments of respite or even notable victories, such as Aphek's, only foreshadow deadlier dangers. For almost half a century two Kings, Azariah of Judah (768–739) and Jeroboam II of Israel (785–745), take advantage of the decline of Damascus and the Assyrian withdrawals under Assurbanipal III (772–755) and Assurninari IV (755–746) to act together and give the Hebrews a prosperity unexperienced since Solomon's time. Kings and people dream of a lasting peace while prophets of doom raise foreboding voices.

The Fall of the Kingdom of Israel

It was then that new men appeared in Judah and Israel, whose energetic competition undermined the state and gave the nation and its ideals a chance for survival. The books of Kings and Chronicles relate the history of this era, and not only describe but explain the events and the people, based on the oldest sources: the *Archives of the Kings of Judah and Israel* and the archives of the Temple. The biography, programs, wars, and constructions of each King, as well as his virtues and vices, are presented in a critical spirit. The general tendency, however, is to criticize all the Kings of Israel, who are accused of "hurting YHWH's eyes" because they perpetuate the schism. Moreover, their economic and political relations with the Phoenician cities and "the kings of Syria and the coast" opened the way to Canaanite religious and cultural influences over Israel. After Ahab's marriage to Jezebel, daughter of the king of Tyre, the baal of Tyre is adored at the Samaritan court.

Jehu's rebellion removes, along with Ahab, the pagan influences, but it cuts the ties between Israel and Tyre, an ultimately destructive course for the kingdom. Israel's decay begins with Jehu, and except for a few periods of respite will continue until its fall in 721.

Jeroboam II ben Jehoash, crowned in 782, succeeds during one of the weak periods of the kingdom of Damascus in establishing an entente with Judah, thus stabilizing the economy of Israel and promoting its cultural influence. Prophethood has renewed importance with the advent of Amos and Hosea. But after Jeroboam II dies in 753, the process of decomposition accelerates. The four last Kings of Israel are powerless to forestall the fall of their kingdom, which is threatened by the Assyrian armies.

Tiglath-Pileser, master of Damascus, Israel, and Judah, conquers Babylonia once more in 729. His successor, Shalmaneser V, is crowned in 727 and rules for five years. King Hoshea of Israel, supported by Sua, an Egyptian dynast, stops paying his annual tribute to Assyria. Shalmaneser captures the rebel King, who is soon abandoned by Egypt. Samaria, besieged, makes a desperate stand against the Assyrian army for three years, and falls in 721. A Babylonian chronicle, written in the fifth century and based on the oldest sources, states that Shalmaneser V besieged Shamrayn, the Aramaic name for Samaria, which Sargon I finally conquered. Apparently Shalmaneser V died immediately after the surrender of the city, perhaps following an army revolt. He is replaced by Sargon II, who quells a vassals' revolt in 720, before completing the destruction of Samaria and Israel. Sargon II deports 27,000 inhabitants of Samaria and populates it with subjects from other parts of his empire; he deports Arabs, Babylonians, Cuthans, and people from Avah, Emath, and Sepharvaim. These massive deportations are customary for the conquering Assyrians—and the Babylonians are quick to adopt them. The Samaritan and Israelite exiles are soldiers, priests, leaders, and civil servants, who are relocated in Mesopotamia and Media. The great masses, who are left alone, are supplemented with foreign elements who will institute a new ethnic and religious unity, that of the Samaritans (II Kings 17).

Sargon II's deportations give rise to the myth of the ten lost tribes. In fact, the deportees made up a minority among the people, but there is little documentation of their fate. Settled in Gozan, Assyria, they apparently served in the Assyrian army as entire units, as was customary. What became of them? Some, no doubt, were assimilated by the population among whom they lived. The stronger ones must have waited for favorable circumstances to return to their homes or to Judah.

The Kingdom of Judah Survives Alone

The misfortune which had ravaged Israel now lurks at Judah's borders, at the gates of Jerusalem. At Moresheth the Prophet Micah foresees the worst: "Zion shall be ploughed as a field, and Jerusalem shall be as a heap of stones, and the mountain of the temple as the high places of the forest" (Mic. 3:12). He calls his people together and urges them to greater justice, virtue, purity, and love in order to merit, possibly, divine pardon and to escape ruin.

Hezekiah (717–687), in whom Isaiah doubtless saw the Prince of Peace, the wondrous Child on David's throne (Isaiah 50), continues Ahaz's policy and pays tribute to Assyria, but is ready to break with his fearsome sovereign at the first opportunity. When he does so, under the influence of the Egyptian faction and against Isaiah's call for neutrality, he is defeated by Sennacherib's armies, which conquer Judah's fortresses one after the other and besiege Jerusalem. The capital is temporarily saved, but only by a miracle. The Assyrians, disturbed by rumors from Egypt, or learning of new troubles to the east, or ravaged by a plague in the army, have to lift their siege rather suddenly. Jerusalem is delivered. The Temple is safe. Isaiah's prophecy is fulfilled before everyone's eyes.

Nonetheless, Judah remains under Assyria's yoke. The long reign of the son of Hezekiah, Manasseh (687–642), initiates a period of political and religious reaction. The extensive reforms of Hezekiah's rule are nullified and their proponents are executed. The old Prophet Isaiah—according to a late tradition—pays for the courage of his predictions with his life. Idolatry reappears. The provincial sanctuaries are opened to pagan cults, ritualistic orgies, and in the Valley of Gehenna, in Jerusalem, children are offered as a holocaust to the idols. Manasseh sacrifices his son, as Ahaz had done. The priests take up the ancient practices of divination and augury. A statue of the Assyrian divinity Ishtar, queen of heaven, is erected in the Temple. Sacred prostitution is reinaugurated: women offer themselves to the faithful in honor of the queen of heaven. The offerings go to the Temple and the children born of these rites are raised to its service. The Assyrian worship of constellations and idols, as well as imitation of the foreigner, become widespread.

The son of Manasseh, Amon, is assassinated in the second year of his reign, 639. His eight-year-old son Josiah is brought to the throne by the group who snuffs out the revolt. This is the period when the Scythian hordes overrun western Asia and threaten Assyria and Egypt. New Prophets, Nahum and Zephaniah, forecast ultimate catastrophe, a last judgment from which Judah will emerge purified.

Josiah and the priests indulge in the purificatory reform. The finding of a copy of the Torah in the Temple serves as a solemn occasion for the proclamation of the Law of God as the law of the land. Josiah orders the total destruction of the idolatrous altars and symbols and the suppression of pagan liturgies throughout the kingdom —and even in Samaria, where the high places are abolished and the Temple of Bethel is destroyed. With great pomp Jerusalem celebrates the restoration of monotheism at the feast of Tabernacles in the purified Temple. For a time the country enjoys relative prosperity and security.

Only Jeremiah condemns the superficial reform, which does not get to the heart of spiritual transformation, the condition for salvation. A new judgment of God, he announces, will make the nation repent and will save it from the evils which lurk over it. In fact, Nineveh falls in 612, under the combined attacks of the Babylonians, the Medes, and the Scythians.

The Egyptian armies spread over the coast once more and the Hebrews meet them at Megiddo, where they are beaten. Josiah dies in 609. His son Jehoachaz, who is named King by the people, reigns for three months—before being bound in chains and deported to

Egypt. His brother Jehoiakim replaces him. His reign marks a rapprochement with Egypt, religious regression and return to idolatry, and worship of the queen of heaven. Meanwhile, Egypt is beaten by Babylonia in 605. Nebuchadnezzar, the victor, directs his armies toward Syria, Israel, and Judah, and Judah falls in 604.

The End of the Kingdom of Judah

The history of the twenty-year Babylonian domination of Judah is related by the royal chronicles and the book of Jeremiah (II Kings 24, 25) and is complemented by the *Neo-Babylonian Chronicles*. It is known that in 604 Nebuchadnezzar conquered Syria and Israel and destroyed Ashkelon, whose inhabitants he deported. Jeremiah, braving the ire of the nationalist party, preaches repentance and unconditional surrender to Babylon, believing that the revolution is doomed to failure (Jer. 26:12, 27:6). In 601 Nebuchadnezzar tried to invade Egypt—at the same time that Jehoiakim chose to rebel (II Kings 24), miscalculating Babylonia's power, which only Jeremiah and his partisans appraised objectively. The pro-Egyptian party supports the revolt. Three years later, in 598, Nebuchadnezzar appears at the head of his army to punish Judah. Jehoiakim dies and is replaced by Jehoiachin (597), who defers to Babylon and pays the heavy tribute that is imposed. He turns over all the treasures of the Temple and the palace to the occupier. Nebuchadnezzar deports 10,000 people, the King and his household, ministers, officers, and leaders. Only Jehoiachin's surrender to Nebuchadnezzar, as he passes through Jerusalem's gates with his mother and his entourage, spares the city from total destruction. Jehoiachin, Nebuchadnezzar's prisoner, is treated as a King in exile. In his captivity he is supported by the Babylonian government. The *Babylonian Chronicle* records this in the state accounts.

Zedekiah (597–586), son of Josiah, is the last King of David's dynasty. Once again the country is divided into partisans of Mesopotamia and friends of Egypt. Jeremiah, however, is not deluded; he goes into the streets of Jerusalem with a yoke on his shoulders to symbolize the Hebrews' servitude toward Babylon. Hananiah ben Azzur predicts the end of the oppression and removes the yoke from him publicly. Jeremiah writes to Babylon to exhort the exiles to be patient and to advise them to prepare for a lengthy exile.

Zedekiah finally yields to the pressures of the pro-Egyptian faction of the revolt against Babylon. In 590 he takes up arms on the side of Egypt, whose armies have set off to conquer the five Phoenician cities. Then Nebuchadnezzar decides to end Egypt's aggression once and for all and to crush Judah. In the heart of winter, 588, he attacks Jerusalem and builds a wall around the ramparts of the capital to starve it into submission.

The Egyptians come to Jerusalem's assistance and the siege is temporarily lifted. Jeremiah, leaving the city to go home to Anathot, is accused of going over to the enemy's side and is thrown into a dungeon by the pro-Egyptian faction. The Prophet continues to advise Zedekiah to surrender at the opportune moment. Nebuchadnezzar, having driven the Egyptians away, attacks the city again; on the ninth of Tammuz, 586, a break is made in the ramparts and Zedekiah tries to flee. He is overtaken at Jericho and brought to the Riblah camp, Nebuchadnezzar's headquarters. Forcing him to watch, they slay his sons and Judah's nobility; then they put out his eyes, chain him, and take him to Babylon.

A month later, the seventh of Ab, in the heart of summer, the chief Babylonian general, Nebuzaradan, returns to destroy Jerusalem. What remains of the treasure and the bronzes from the columns and pools are taken. Jerusalem, its Temple, and its palace are sacked, its ramparts are leveled, and the populations of Jerusalem and Judah are deported to Babylon (II Kings 25:8 seqq.). In 582, five years after the massive deportations, Nebuchadnezzar returns to finish the task and to direct a third wave of deportations, 745 men from Judah. Judah and Jerusalem will never really rise from their ruins, in spite of the heroic attempts a half century later, in 538, after the return from the exile. The Davidian monarchy is destroyed forever. Six of its rulers—Ahaziah (841), Athaliah (841–835), Joash (835–797), Amon (642–639), Josiah (639–609), and Jehoiakim (608–597)—have died a violent death, as had the founder of the Hebraic monarchy, Saul, and nine of the eighteen Kings of Israel.

The Biblical City

The Relics of the Tribal Organization

During the entire monarchical period the historical conscience of the Hebrews is keenly aware of the origins of their people, whom the Nazarites and the Rechabites continue to idealize. As nomads, the Hebrews led their flocks of sheep and goats and, restricted by weakness to sparse hillside pastures, lived a frugal existence in tents and caves, depending on alliances or engaging in conflicts with other tribes. They preserve the accounts of the journeys of Abraham and Lot, of Isaac and Jacob. They recount their alliances with Gibeon and Shechem and boast of their conquests: Jericho, which surrenders at the sound of their trumpets, Ai, and Deborah's victory, and Jael's killing of Sisera. Even when they are settled in Canaan, their literature still mentions the tents.

Leaving their nomadic or semi-nomadic lives after the conquest of Canaan, they undergo a total change in life style. Bit by bit they discard their tents for houses in the cities. The erstwhile shepherds become farmers. They must learn, frequently from the Canaanites, the crafts and techniques of their new jobs. This change, and its concomitant conflicts, is a main factor of Israel's history.

The tribe, like the family and the nation, is set up as an independent body, claiming eponymic descent from one of the sons of the Patriarch Jacob. The biblical city is born from the twelve tribes of Israel, united under one faith and one Law.

The Hebraic Family

Hebrew society is based on the couple and the family: in the beginning God created Adam and Eve. Anthropologists have defined the Hebrew family as endogamous, patrilineal, patriarchal, patrilocal, extended, and polygamous. These six characteristics are found among the other Near Eastern peoples, but only among the Hebrews are they combined.

Endogamous, the Hebrews prefer marriage within the tribe. Filiation was perhaps originally matrilinear, but in the historical period it is the father who determines the family relationship of the new-born child: Isaac is foremost the son of Abraham, *ben Abraham.* The father in the patriarchal family is lord and master. When a man marries, he takes his wife into his father's family and home, where he remains a member. The extended family, the *mishpahah,* is com-posed of the head of the family, his wife or wives, his sons and their wives and children, and his unmarried daughters. All the property of the *mishpahah* is held and managed by the head of the family. The members of this economic entity devote themselves to animal husbandry, farming, the crafts and arts, and business. The biblical family also contains slaves and hired hands, whose number depends on its finances. Their tasks vary from domestic chores to war and administration. A family may be made up of dozens, even hundreds, of individuals and, though living in one or several villages, always observes the Law and the strictest solidarity, a constant in ancestral nomadism.

The tribe is made up of a group of families with blood ties. Each descending from the same ancestor, the members of the tribe are *brothers* of the same flesh, blood, and bones. Hence the importance of genealogies, so carefully recorded in the Bible. Each child of Israel knows that he belongs to a house, *bayith,* that he is a member of a family, *mishpahah,* which belongs to a tribe, *shevet.* But he also knows that all the tribes of Israel have the same Patriarch, Jacob, the son of Isaac, the son of Abraham. In this way the tribe is able to absorb foreign groups. The tribe of Judah took in the remains of the tribe of Simon, as well as the descendants of Caleb and Yerah-miel. He also knows that all humanity descends from Adam and Eve or from Noah, permitting exogamous unions: Moses, Boaz, David, and Solomon (among many others) marry foreigners.

After its conquest, the country was divided among the tribes. With legalistic precision, the book of Joshua records the list of tribes and their boundaries, which will be reviewed at the time of the schism (931).

From south to north the country is occupied by the tribes of Sim-eon and Judah, Benjamin, Dan, Ephraim, western Manasseh, Asher, Issachar, Zebulun, and Naphtali. To the east of the Jordan are the second half of the tribe of Manasseh and the tribes of Reuben and

Gad. The tribal pattern evolves in time and reflects the life of the people. Uncertainties and textual contradictions feed the historical debate about the groupings of the tribes and their borders. The question is complicated by the problem of identifying place names, but contemporary research has made notable progress in resolving this problem.

The tribe contains an internal government that also is based on blood ties: the *z'kenim,* or elders, who form a council composed of the heads of the principal families. It directs all tribal matters concerning domestic and foreign relations. In times of crisis a chief takes responsibility for the tribe's fate. The tribe provides the army with a contingent whose function varies according to its size. The tribe's territory is determined by tradition. The lands are controlled as family property, and springs, wells, and cisterns are objects of endless quarrels between neighboring tribes.

Permanent settlement tends to break down tribal organization and geography accentuates the process of fragmentation. Territorial seats will be changed considerably by the establishment and then by the division of the monarchy. Geographic localization tends to have primacy over blood ties. Prophetic teaching tends to idealize the past by contrasting the nomadic and tribal ideal with the burdens of owning the land. As a reaction against sedentariness, the Rechabites (founded by Jonadab ben Rechab under Jehu in the ninth century) expressed their opposition to the new customs throughout biblical history until the period of Jeremiah (Jer. 35:14).

The Cities of Refuge

In addition to the territories allocated to the tribes, including the Levites, the country has cities of refuge (Deut. 19:1–13), an institution that seems to antedate the centralization projects of the monarchy. Its goal is to provide refuge to an accidental killer. If the elders of the city where the killing took place determine that it was criminal, they may ask for the extradition of the guilty party for trial. In the royal period, the Kings tend to exercise the right to give refuge (II Sam. 14:4–12). Qadesh, in the tribe of Naphtali, Shechem and Hebron in Cisjordan, and Golan, Betzer, and Ramath in Transjordan were the six cities of refuge apportioned to the whole territory of Israel to ensure the operation of this biblical institution, which checks automatic vengeance by kin.

The Rich and the Poor

By necessity the nomadic society is essentially egalitarian. The tribe is composed of families that are based on a strongly homogeneous society. Class divisions do not appear before the sedentary period, when the new stability calls attention to differences stemming from the variety of talents and possibilities.

During periods of prosperity the rich and powerful use every opportunity to amass land, houses, gold, silver, and other goods. When economic decline occurs, economic differentiation accelerates. The rich use the pre-capitalistic exploitative practices that are found among the Hebrews and their neighbors. Any catastrophe, whether national or international, hurts the poor most. Foreign invasions, epidemics, floods, and drought ravage the crops and flocks, and the fearsome appearance of locusts furthers the social divisions by destroying the fruits of many years' labor for some while strengthening the power of others. Dynastic crises, so numerous in the north, are often followed by a settling of accounts between the victors and the vanquished. The Prophets are relentless in their denunciation of such exploitation: "Woe to you that join house to house and lay field to field, even to the end of the place: shall you alone dwell in the midst of the earth?" (Isaiah 5:8).

These imprecations become more vehement as the social dangers represented by the loss of real estate become more serious. Navoth stands up to Ahab when he wants to confiscate his vineyard. And the prophetic voices denounce plundering (I Kings 21:1 seqq.). The social and political consequences of the loss of real estate, which the laws try to limit, are very serious (Lev. 25:23–35, 39–40), tantamount to a death sentence for the victims.

In the period of the conquest, the country had been allotted to the tribes and families in equal parcels. From this rose the strong reaction against the land seizures in Mesopotamia and Egypt in the dark periods of their history, and which Israel saw again at the time of its greatest maturity. The national conscience was alerted to the drastic human and moral consequences of such a process. The land, source of all good, is more than an object for the Hebrew, as has been noted; it is a creature of God, belonging to God, and to be disposed of only by God. The conquest of Canaan was executed on his order, as was the division of the land among the tribes and families. The concentration of property wealth went against not only the general welfare but against the divine will. Hence the guarantees of property rights. Separation from the land can occur only when an insolvent debtor sells his property to pay his debts, or when a thief must pay for his transgressions. Even in these cases the family has preemptory rights; it may "liberate" such property that is up for sale to preserve the social balance of the tribe and to prevent the property's falling into the hands of "strangers."

Along with land, uncoined silver was a dominant factor of wealth under the monarchy. Country-wide social crises and wars, which are rampant in the endemic state, and regular or extraordinary payments to suzerains cause a shortage of silver, which affects the economy. There is no record of a loan during the royal period, but it is known that in the provincial Aramean capital of Guzana in the twelfth century, interest on silver loans reached 50 percent, and 100 percent on grain loans. In Assyria the average rate of interest went above 25 percent. One may easily conclude what sort of situation prevailed in Canaan, poor and torn by so many conflicts. This is no doubt why Mosaic law forbids loans at interest and attempts to end the abuse of usury by very strict measures.[10]

Mosaic law, which is similar to the law of many ancient civilizations, allows a debtor to free himself from his debts in the form of units of labor, which for large debts may last for months or even years, so that a Hebrew may become the slave of his creditors, at least temporarily.

The country never had flourishing businesses or industry. Craftsmen made chains, veils, headbands and bonnets, little ankle chains, belts, perfume containers, medals, rings (even nose rings), fine clothes and cloaks and capes, shawls, mirrors, fine linen, turbans, and mantillas (Isaiah 3:16–25) for their female clientele. But industry and business were in the hands of the more important neighbors of Israel. The country was flooded with products from Damascus, Mesopotamia, and Egypt.

Hebraic society was composed primarily of farmers. Even when dispossessed of his land, the Hebrew hires out as an agricultural worker. Isaiah mentions annual work contracts (Isaiah 21:16), but generally the worker was paid on a daily basis, as guaranteed by law, in silver or goods. The salaried classes must have been numerous, in spite of the lack of biblical texts referring to them, but farmers and workers made up the great majority of the population (Deut. 24:14–15; Lev. 19:13).

Among the salaried class were artisans, masons, carpenters, blacksmiths, smelters, engravers, weavers, tailors, embroiderers, millers, bakers, fullers, potters, locksmiths, jewelers, perfume makers, well sinkers, and engineers. These occupations are kept in the family and passed from father to son. The craftsman is assisted by his children, hired hands, and slaves. As is still the custom in Eastern cities today, the various occupations are located in certain streets, neighborhoods, or villages, according to their specialty. Obvious reasons of economic geography determine this division. In Jerusalem there was a bakers' street (Jer. 37:21), a goldsmiths' quarter (Neh. 3:31–32), a valley of cheese makers, a field of launderers (Isaiah 7:3), a weavers' and a potters' gate (Jer. 19:1). In the south of Judea, in Beth-Ashbea (I Chr. 4:21), as in Debir (a city of a thousand grouped in 250 houses), fabrics were manufactured and dyed; in Lod and Ono, in the plain, people worked with metal and wood. Probably following Mesopotamia's example, these corps of occupations soon organized into corporations. It is possible that in the time of the monarchy certain marks on pottery represented the trademark of a corporation and not just that of an individual. The King managed the large state industries, such as the foundry of Ezion-geber and the pottery works of Gederah and Netayim (I Chr. 4:23).

These activities were second only to agriculture in the national economy. Since important commerce was in the hands of the neighboring nations—the Phoenicians, Assyrians, and Tyrians—the Hebrews had to be satisfied with the everyday trade: the farmers, the breeders, the artisans sold their products directly to the consumer in the city markets. There do not seem to have been classes of Hebrew businessmen: the businessman of the country was the "Canaanite." The royal household, for both political and economic reasons, had developed a sort of commercial monopoly. Solomon joins with Hiram of Tyre to arm a flotilla on the Red Sea (I Kings 9:26–28, 10:11, 22): his ships carried the copper of Ezion-geber to Arabia and Ethiopia, in exchange for which he imported gold, ivory, and the products of those countries. Solomon carried on a trade in chariots with Egypt and horses with Cilicia. Ahab owned bazaars in Damascus, as the Syrian King Ben-hadad had previously in Samaria (I Kings 20:34). The commercial ties of the royal palace stretched to Tyre, to Ethiopia, and probably to the entire ancient Near East. Thanks to the colonial enterprise of the Phoenicians, they were, in time, to reach all the countries of the Mediterranean. In periods of crisis, the ancient egalitarian ideal made social conflicts all the more serious, especially as the great majority of the population, farmers included, was concentrated in tiny urban establishments.[11] Demographic concentration made the crystallization of distinct social classes unbearable among the people of the Covenant. The social cleavage between rich and poor aggravated the struggle between local power and the state centralization desired by the first three Kings of Israel, and favored the movement toward regional separation.

"Israel Has Gotten Fat"

During the royal period, as has been mentioned, society is no longer based on the tribe but on the family clan. Social life is concentrated in the cities, the largest of which have 20,000 inhabitants and the smallest only a few hundred. It has been rightly noted that the *huqqim* of the Bible essentially constitute a municipal law. The legislators' concern is at the city level more than at the national level.[12] The principal laws of Deuteronomy reflect this attitude regarding the cities of refuge (Deut. 19), the unknown murderer (Deut. 21:1–9), the rebel child (Deut. 21:18–21), the adulterer (Deut. 22:22–29), or the levirate (Deut. 25:5–10). Hence the importance of notaries in the council of elders, *z'kenim*, to manage the city. In Samaria and in Jerusalem the *zeqenim* on the local level and the *sarim*, ministers and high officials of the King, are a force which may, on occasion, check the royal will. It is the "VIPs" (*gedolim*) or heroes (*gibborei hayil*) who easily become the targets for the invective of the Prophets. The psalmist equates wealth, importance, authority, and power with evil. He who "gets fat" walks in the ways of iniquity. The prophetic ideal strengthens the tendencies inherited from the nomadic life and condemns the abuse of power by the rich. The land is the most important source of wealth, and families take good care of their inheritance, rarely making property transactions. We have the inventory of Nabal's fortune in the time of David: 3,000 sheep and 1,000 goats. His wife Abigail, eager to be in David's good graces, gives him a present: 200 loaves of bread, 2 containers of wine, 5 sheep, 5 measures of grain, and 100 bunches of grapes. Nabal's wealth was several hundred dollars, and his offering, readily accepted by David, must have been relatively modest (I Sam. 25:2–35). An inventory of Job's goods gives an idea of a huge fortune: 7,000 sheep, 3,000 camels, 500 pair of oxen, and 500 asses (Job 1:3). Job's fortune, very likely mythical, was more than two hundred thousand dollars. These comparisons are difficult to make, however, and the Bible relates them in more modest proportions. Abraham is described as a nomad who has a large tent; Saul works his own lands and goes to look for his father's stray asses. David, too, is a shepherd; when he appears before King Saul, he brings him an offering of five loaves of bread, a container of wine, and a kid (I Sam. 16:20).

By today's standards this wealth is modest, and excavations reveal a relative equality of standard of living. In David's time all the houses seem to have been of the same type and dimensions. In the time of Amos, sharper differences between rich and poor (who live in different neighborhoods) are revealed. This is when the Prophets make themselves heard. From Amos to Jesus, they condemn the accumulation of land and capital, exaggerated consumption, injustice, speculation, fraud, luxury, corruption, and the selfishness of the rich. The poor, the weak, children, widows, and orphans are pitiful victims of social injustice. Tirelessly, the Prophets and biblical legislation take up their cause and try to work for their welfare. Loans must be without interest; the pawned blanket must be returned to its owner each night (Ex. 22:24–26); strict justice must be followed (Ex. 23:6). Deuteronomy expands these laws:

If one of thy brethren that dwelleth within the gates of thy city in the land which the Lord thy God will give thee, come to poverty: thou shalt not harden thy heart, nor close thy hand, but shalt open it to the poor man, thou shalt lend him that which thou perceivest he hath need of. Beware lest perhaps a wicked thought steal in upon thee, and thou say in the heart: The seventh year of remission draweth nigh; and thou turn away thy eyes from thy poor brother, denying to lend him that which he asketh: lest he cry against thee to the Lord, and it become a sin unto thee. But thou shalt give to him: neither shalt thou do any thing craftily in relieving his necessities: that the Lord thy God may bless thee at all times, and in all things to which thou shalt put thy hand (Deut. 15:7–10).

This shows a strong desire to correct the inequalities that emerged with the end of nomadism. The lender's hesitation to lend to the poor immediately before the year of remission is understandable when one knows that during that year debts are canceled (Deut. 15:1) and the products of the earth are left to the poor (Ex. 23:11). This occurs every seven years. Every forty-ninth year, for the jubilee, the people benefit from a general emancipation and every individual regains unimpaired rights over his patrimony. YHWH is the true protector of the poor against the harshness of the rich. And if abundance is a divine gift, experience proves that the rich may be bad and that the just man may be poor. The book of Job strongly protests against this injustice, which Job attributes to God himself. Also, Isaiah and the Psalms take up this idea of the spirituality of the poor, which becomes more important in the later Prophets, at the period of the second Temple, and in the nascent Christian Church. Even if the poor never knew how to organize themselves into a political party in biblical times, they became an inspiration for the ideals of Hebraic spirituality and turned the entire people toward their supranational destiny and their universality.

"The Same Law Will Rule Citizen and Foreigner"

The country of the Hebrews contains many foreigners, the *gerim,* or more precisely the "aliens," the numerous inhabitants who are not of Hebraic ancestry. The law tries to assimilate them to the citizens, *ezrahim,* in every way possible. In fact, they are well integrated into the social, economic, and even the political structures of the nation. It is common to compare the *gerim* to the *perioikoi,* the ancient inhabitants of the Peloponnesus. The *gerim,* like them, are the descendants of the ancient masters of the country. One annoying condition deprives them of the right to own property: the land is completely in the hands of the twelve tribes. In this they are similar to the Levites, who also are deprived of land, God being their domain. The laws of social protection cover the *gerim* and the Levites (Deut. 14:29, 26:12), as well as the poor, widows, and orphans. The law tries to avoid extremes by commanding that they be given the triennial tithe (Deut. 14:28) and the products of the seventh year (Lev. 25:6) and that the cities of refuge be open to them (Num. 35:15). They are free to harvest the corners of the fields, to glean the fallen grapes in the vineyards, and to gather up the grain that remains at harvest time (Lev. 19:10, 23:22; Deut. 24:19–21; Jer. 7:6). The law stipulates the duties of the people toward the *gerim,* who must be loved like brothers—not forgetting that the Hebrews, too, have been *gerim* in Egypt (Ex. 22:20, 23:9; Deut. 10:9, 24:18–22; Lev. 19:34). In the vision where he establishes the country's boundaries after the exile, Ezekiel allocates a share to the *gerim* "who live and have had children among you." They must be treated as citizens and receive their territorial heritage in the tribe in which they live (Ezek. 47:23).

The cultural laws confirm the gradual integration of the *gerim* into the Hebrew society. Like the Hebrews, they must obey the laws for the purification of sins (Lev. 17:15). They owe equal fidelity to God (Lev. 20:2; Ezek. 14:7) They are held, often in a very explicit way, to the same obligations as the Hebrews (Lev. 16:29, 17:8–16, 22:18; Num. 15:29, 19:20): fasting, sacrifices, dietary laws, etc. Apparently assimilation was pushed so far that numerous *gerim* were totally integrated through circumcision (Num. 9:14). Otherwise the differences were only of a social order, such as existed between rich and poor, patrician and plebeian. Legislation that sought to mitigate the problems arising from this situation for the *gerim* and the poor increased the risks to social equilibrium, which already was endangered because of the slave class. And the disillusioned sages know that, in spite of their efforts, there will always be the poor in the world.

"They Will Be Your Slaves"

The status of the slaves depends not only on social, economic, and historic factors but also on the theological aspirations of the Law. It is a truism to recall the cruel fate of slaves in antiquity. In Mesopotamia, Egypt, Greece, and Rome a slave is property like any other piece of property. The "head of a slave" is counted as one counts head of cattle. He is marked as cattle and branded with a sign of possession. Aiding a fugitive slave is severely punished. The sale of a slave is no different from the sale of ordinary merchandise. A female slave owed not only her work but her body to her master, and remained a slave to him even if she bore his children. Except in Hammurabi's Code, a master had the right over the death of his slaves, who had no protection against whatever their master desired.

It is certain that slavery existed in biblical society. The word *'eved,* which some translations understate as "servant," precisely indicates a slave. An eloquent passage of Ecclesiasticus describes the Hebrew slave as an animal. The donkey has a right to fodder, a whip, and a burden; the slave has a right to bread, correction, and work. The master is warned that any good he does for a slave will turn against him: "He works only under the whip: leave his hands free and he will flee . . . watch over his work, or bind his feet" (Eccl. 33:25–28). This cruel picture of a slave's lot is corrected by an ambiguous piece of advice: "If you have a slave, treat him as your brother" (Eccl. 33:32).

Once again the egalitarian bent of the Hebraic society works to correct inequalities. Job cries out: "Did not he that made me make the slave, in his mother's womb the same as me?" (Job 31:15). To this personal identification biblical texts add a collective one which is more to the point: Israel has been a slave in Egypt for generations. The Hebrew, who knows what slavery is, must keep that in mind when he deals with his own slaves. As best it can, biblical Law works to protect the slave. It punishes the master who would kill his slave; if the slave has been blinded, wounded, or poorly treated by his master, he must be freed; he has the right to one day's rest a week; women slaves who have been used as concubines may no longer be sold as merchandise (Deut. 21:10–14). The mistreated slave may always run away. Contrary to most ancient legislation, Deuteronomy formally forbids returning a fugitive slave to his master (Deut. 23:16).

In antiquity, war was the principal source of slavery, as corroborated by the books of Judges (9) and II Chronicles (8–15). The book of Numbers describes the sharing of the Midianite virgins among the victors.[13]

The state controls the slaves attached to its service and those of the sanctuaries. Biblical law never mentions public slaves, but their existence seems certain. King Solomon uses them in his mines, ships, and state industries (I Kings 9:27; II Chr. 8:18). Some of them, the *nethinim*, are in the service of the Temple. After the collapse of the monarchy, only they will survive in post-exilic Israelite society.

Trade in foreign slaves, centered in Gaza and Tyre, is in the hands of the Phoenicians. Slaves originating in Asia Minor are traded there, while in Asia Minor Hebrew slaves are sold. The price of a slave is 30 shekels of silver, according to the Code of the Covenant. That is high, considering the general level of poverty (Ex. 21:32).

Slavery is not necessarily of foreign origin. In certain cases the Hebrew may fall into slavery in the midst of his brethren. Prophetic teaching (II Chr. 28:8–15), the law (Lev. 25:46), and the most innate tendencies of Hebraic society seem to condemn these practices, which nonetheless exist under many forms. Leviticus tells of the Hebrew who sold himself as a slave and commands that he not be put to forced labor (Lev. 25:39–43). When a Hebrew is sold abroad, it is the duty of his people to do all they can to bring him back (Lev. 25:47–53). The slavery of a Hebrew is considered essentially temporary in every way: his servitude is limited to six years, at the end of which he must be freed. The legislator kindly commands: "The seventh year you shall set him free: And when thou sendest him out free, thou shalt not let him go away empty: But shalt give him for his way out of thy flocks, and out of thy barn floor, and thy winepress, wherewith the Lord thy God shall bless thee. Remember that thou also wast a bondservant in the land of

Egypt, and the Lord thy God made thee free, and therefore I now command thee this" (Deut. 15:12–15).

If the Hebrew slave refuses his liberation, he becomes a slave in perpetuity. His ear must be pierced against the door of the house, no doubt to indicate his integration into his master's house (Deut. 15:17). Before the jubilee year, the Hebrew slave can always be re-purchased by paying his master a sum equivalent to the salary for his remaining years of servitude.

The slave's condition depends on the character of the master; and in many cases he must have been better off than the sub-proletariat of modern societies. The slave participates in the life of the family he serves, and legislation promotes this integration whenever possible. The slave must be circumcised (Gen. 17:12–13); he takes part in family worship, observes the Sabbath, and celebrates all the religious holidays, including Passover (Ex. 12:44, 20:10, 23:12); he may marry the daughter of his master and inherit his goods (Prov. 17:2; Gen. 15:3; I Chr. 2:34–35). In these cases he automatically becomes a free man, *hofshi* (Deut. 21:10–14).

The number of slaves was never very great. At the height of its power the monarchy never had a sufficient number for the construction of the Temple or the palace; it had recourse to thousands of hired men. After the schism, military power declines and the Hebrews have to worry about their security rather than increasing the number of slaves. Few can afford to invest in the purchase of slaves, so carefully protected by law. It is more useful and convenient to hire someone. Free workers are always ready to hire out on a clearly defined contractual basis. Thus it may be seen that economic conditions reinforce Hebraic national traditions and egalitarian hopes.

The Limits of Power

The people whose history we have just reviewed knows the limits of power. Henceforth, it makes a connection between its election and the reality of its weakness. How many men does it have? In the lack of statistical documentation, the answer to this question can only establish a scale. Biblical tabulations have been challenged, but Exodus puts the number of Hebrew men who went out of Egypt with Moses and wandered in the desert for forty years at 600,000 (12:37–38). Today these figures are altered to more modest proportions, due to a different interpretation of the terminology. The second book of Samuel records the results of a census taken in David's time: 800,000 eligible men in Israel and 50,000 in Judah, from a total population of some 6 million (24:1–9). This people, who calls itself chosen because of its smallness, can also, in happier hours, consider itself "as numerous as the stars in the sky and the sands of the sea." Israel and Judah had a total of some 500 cities and villages in an area not exceeding 26,000 square kilometers.

It is difficult for the historian to establish the truth. Scant statistics in the Bible,[14] extra-biblical sources,[15] and especially the archeological excavations allow a more precise estimate. Each city of Israel was contained in an area of a few hectares at most. As has been shown, Jerusalem in its most prosperous period could not have exceeded 20,000 hectares, in a country whose Hebraic population probably varied between 600,000 and 1 million. These facts add to the mystery of the political, military, and especially the spiritual resistance with which this tiny people, with such great energy and perseverance, faced the great empires that opposed it.

The Third Gate The Days

The Unity of Daily Life

"And there was night and there was morning, one day," says Genesis of the first morning of creation (Gen. 1:5). As commentators explain, this is not just the first day, it is the only day. And history reflects it forever, throughout man's existence from generation to generation. For everyone it is identical, and extraordinary, diverse, and unpredictable. There is no better way than by the study of daily life through history to evaluate the unity of the human race expressed in the Bible, which tells us that we are all children of Adam, the son of the creator of heaven and earth, forever and ever.

Let us refer to the series for which this book has been written (Librairie Hachette, La Vie Quotidienne series)—what Mireaux and Flacelière write for the Greeks, Montet for Egypt, Contenau for Mesopotamia, Carcopino for Rome, Charles-Picard for Carthage or Auboyer for India, on habitat, dress, occupations, arts, cooking, and urban or rural life, more or less resembles each other. The similarities are inevitable because, since the Neolithic Age, man's diet has not undergone any essential change and the basic needs for shelter, clothing, and tools have remained essentially the same. There is a very narrow margin of originality, and the scarcity of ancient sources makes it all the more difficult to determine. Often the historian must interpolate: to describe the bread the Mesopotamian ate in the ninth century B.C., one is obliged to refer to the work of today's Iraqian baker. What is more, in most cases the reader is surprised to what degree man's basic actions and reactions retain permanence in even the most advanced civilizations.

The hairdresser, make-up man, and tailor of Nephritite or Athaliah, of Pharaoh, Solomon, or Caesar, have more or less the same gestures, techniques, and ambitions as the hairdresser, make-up man, and tailor of a modern celebrity. Even those elements which seem the most barbaric, strange, and inconceivable to our modern sensibility may be found as blatant and shameless in modern society as in ancient times. The horrors of war such as the Assyrians and the Babylonians were responsible for, the massacre of entire populations, mass deportations, and physical dismemberment—everything which shocks our sensibility in our contacts with the ancient world—are still with us today, on a much greater scale. This is not limited to human sacrifice, which is still practiced in the modern world under various forms: the murder of hostages or patriotic hara-kiri are the most current. As for sexual and erotic outrages, phallic cults, and Dionysian or Dagonian orgies, there is little doubt that our contemporaries could not rate as masters in the most "refined" sanctuaries of antiquity.

Developing this chapter is more difficult than the others because the Hebrews do not seem to have produced anything new in science, art, or technology. Whatever they had in this area they borrowed from the Mesopotamians, Syrians, or Egyptians, and later from the Persians, Greeks, or Romans. One must go as far back as the second half of the fourth millennium to find the very first founders of our civilization. The originality of the Hebrews, if there ever was any in this domain, can be measured only by how they sifted and used foreign influences. Their possibilities of fulfillment in everyday life were limited by the fact that they were a tiny people, very uncomfortably settled on a poor and ungrateful land. And it was there that they had to define their faith, and bear witness to it, in a form of challenge to all nations, to mankind, and to a great degree to creation itself, whose natural order they deny. Their ambition is not only to give life a new content but to transform Israel and mankind, so that they may have a vision of a new heaven and a new earth where nations will no longer wage war and where the lion and the lamb will live in peace.

Now we must get down to the business of telling what we know of the principal characteristics of the daily life of the Hebrews. Recent archeological findings make this a less frustrating endeavor than it would have been twenty or thirty years ago.

"You Will Go to the Land I Show You"

At the time of the Patriarchs and the Judges the land of Canaan receives an uninterrupted flow of new populations whose industry keeps adding to its wealth. Recent excavations prove that agricultural and industrial techniques achieved an unprecedented level of refinement. Cappadocian tablets from about 1800 B.C., the documents of Larsa, of Babylon, and the texts of Mari seem to indicate that the country was open to its neighbors and was a hub for the Middle East, without any linguistic barrier. Western Semitic was widely understood and Babylonian Accadian was the commercial and diplomatic language. Close by, Egypt played an important role in the life of Canaan. There were no insurmountable linguistic obstacles in the south either: educated Egyptians knew western Semitic and Egyptian was spoken by the leaders and businessmen of Canaan. The archeological discoveries of Bert-shean, among several other sites, show the high degree of Egyptian influence on Canaanite culture.

Only at the end of the period of the Judges does the camel appear, primarily as a domestic animal for daily work on the land or in caravans. Formerly the donkey, the proud and strong animal of the period, was the most important and most prevalent in the cities and villages, in the fields, and especially on the caravan routes. The horse is rare, and the wagons he pulls are rustic and move slowly. The population experiences a period of transition between nomadism and sedentary life. The local kings live in what resemble fortresses, while the people live under their tents or in rustic huts in the summer. In times of danger they move into the fortresses. In the winter, the more industrious build stone houses measuring 5 by 15 meters, with roofs made of boughs, to protect themselves from the heavy subtropical rains. Historians see the ancestral semi-nomadic customs as one of the principal elements of the feast of Tabernacles (Succoth).

The principal activity is farming and livestock breeding. Nomadism centers around the southern part of the country, and rarely as far as the vast Negev. Copper, iron, and weaving are developed. Brilliant woolen tunics, expertly dyed, are worn over the left shoulder, leaving the right shoulder free and bare. The style is the same for men and women—but the latter were dressed with more care, no doubt.[1] Later, influences from the north and the east were to transform the mode of dress noticeably.

A New Era

The conquest of Canaan initiates a period of anarchy. The Hebrews must adapt to the new country and be assimilated into a new social and economic context which itself is in flux. The Bronze Age has been replaced by the Iron Age. The camel changes the means of communication, and suddenly shrinks and complicates the ancient world—a change as drastic as that which the railroad caused in a more modern period. Suddenly, southern Arabia, Iran, India, and Ethiopia have access to the Fertile Crescent and the Mediterranean, with their vast markets, thus accelerating technical change and progress. The horse becomes more useful because of the improved construction of wagons. New arts and a wide range of specialized occupations diversify societies that have become more open to foreign influences.

Huge galleys, invented by the Phoenicians, not only reach the coastal islands off Canaan (Crete and Cyprus) but faraway shores of the Mediterranean and the Red Sea. Voyages to Spain or Ethiopia become possible.

Besides the technological progress arising from improved water transportation, agriculture and hygiene are revolutionized. From the ninth century B.C. on, each wealthy house has a cistern that stores a year's supply of rainwater. These private cisterns are supplemented by public pools, which makes the situation even better. The boldness of their conception may still be admired by the visitor today: the aqueducts of Megiddo and Siloam, the Pools of Solomon, and the cistern of Gibeon (12 meters deep and 11 meters in diameter, connected to an aqueduct at its base and hollowed out of rock, probably dating to the beginning of the royal period) (II Sam. 2:13).

The City in Biblical Times

Recent excavations give a relatively precise view of the biblical city, not only of its temples and palaces but of its hovels and more humble aspects, from which its daily life may be reconstructed. However, we must approach the notion of city without reference to the current situation. In biblical times each city constituted a kind of state that aspired to sovereignty and independence in whatever concerned its alimentation, security, civil and religious administration, and its economic, industrial, commercial, and social life. This characteristic, common to all antiquity, was accentuated by the geographical conditions in Canaan, which gave the biblical city original qualities very different from those characterizing Nineveh, Babylon, Ephesus, Athens, Corinth, Carthage, or Rome.

The city's primary function was to protect its population from the enemy, which explains its crowded, dense population and its method of constructing solid but inexpensive ramparts from the time of Solomon to that of Herod. The latter's remains have defied time in Jerusalem, Megiddo, Tell Beit-Mirsim, Beth Shemesh, Hazor, Gezer in Mizpah, and other places along the crests that surround the country from north to south, opposite the Asian desert. The Hebrews built two types of ramparts, one with vaults or casemates, the other crenellated, and both were intended to increase their resistance to attack. The ramparts were 15 to 20 meters high and the gates were specially fortified: pincer-type entrances, inherited from the Canaanites, or with up to four pairs of arches, as in Megiddo, Hazor, or Gezer. The people liked to sit on benches along the walls of these gates to chat or even carry on business and decide legal questions. The actual gate, often directly accessible, was sometimes constructed with a more complex approach, as was the last gate built at Tell Beit-Mirsim.

In royal cities such as Jerusalem and Samaria the surrounding wall was complemented by another series of ramparts that encircled and protected the palace. In periods of expansion the cities extended beyond the walls. To ensure the safety of the new sections it was necessary to extend the fortifications and defense towers, the *migdalim,* which are prominent in both the landscape and the military history of the nation. A village is called the "daughter" of the city that ensures its protection and its houses have a different juridical status. The city is also the cultural, economic, and religious center; it is also an industrial and agricultural market; and a royal palace, a sanctuary, or a military garrison increases its importance. Generally the establishment of a fortified place initiates the development of an urban center.

Canaan developed from the numerous caves of the country, used since prehistoric times and still used today in some places; then tents and houses of stone and brick were added. In the royal period a tent is still considered a house and continues to be used for tribal meetings. The site of a city depends first on its ability to ensure security and provide a water and food supply. The case of Jericho, built in a valley, is exceptional. This city was an oasis and water was the determining factor in its becoming a city. Strong ramparts were necessary to ensure its protection, and traces of them, dating back to the ninth millennium B.C., have been found. The sites of dozens of biblical cities which archeological research reveals are commonly distinguished by the existence or traces of the ramparts and towers. The people were forced into small agglomerations. The ramparts blocked the expansion of a city and obliged the local inhabitants to spread into hundreds of smaller urban centers. The archeologist-historian Aharoni has counted 363 identifiable cities in the royal period out of 475 named in the Bible. Obviously, hundreds of other towns and agricultural centers, which have left no archeological or literary traces, must be added to the total.

Geographical conditions determine whether a city is to be a commercial, industrial, or maritime center. Their growth was related to the needs of the population, without a comprehensive plan, but excavations indicate the inherent suitability of the various sites and a general respect for the terrain in antiquity. The buildings have only one or two stories (very rarely three) and thus form a skyline that parallels a site's natural contours. Today the methods of construction in the different periods are known to us, from their origins to the fabulous buildings of Herod's time.

Solomon in All His Glory

Solomon's reputation as a builder is legendary. As soon as an important new find is unearthed, it is attributed to him; so in 1867 an archeological genius, Charles Warren, discovered Jerusalem's Herodian wall and immediately—and erroneously—ascribed it to Solomon. He was mistaken by a thousand years,[2] but Solomon—after all —built so many things: cities, ramparts, fortresses, aqueducts (I Kings 9:10–24). Thanks to his works, the country was transformed. But his unforgettable masterpiece is the Temple he erected to the glory of God. It took thirteen years to build and included the "House of the Forest of Lebanon," which served as an arsenal and royal treasury (I Kings 10:16–21). The lack of documentation makes it impossible to determine the function of the Hall of Columns, but the audience hall served for court ceremonies and as a justice chamber. There Solomon handed down his legendary, wise judgments as he sat on a gilded ivory throne decorated with bulls' heads on the back and either side. Two of the bulls support the arms of the chair and six lions stand at either side of the six steps which lead to the throne. On the seventh step was the King himself, whose human face completes the symbolism of the bull, the lion, and the figures 7 and 12. The narrator concludes his description in admiration: "Never was anything like it made in any kingdom" (I Kings 10:18–20). We know now that Tutankhamen and the Syrian or Palestinian kings who are represented on the coffin of Ahiram of Byblos were made in gold and ivory by the same techniques. The gallery of the "Forest of Lebanon" was lined with 300 large shields of hammered gold, on each of which were 600 gold coins and 300 small shields of hammered gold, each bearing 3 golden coins. The plates, flasks, and goblets for Solomon's table were made of this same gold, which his fleet brought back from Tharsis every three years, along with silver, precious stones, fragrant spices, ivory, and monkeys—or, if from Ophir, with rare woods for the production of lyres and harps.

His guests and family daily help themselves to the food brought to him for his table: 30 measures of pure wheaten flour, 60 measures of regular flour, and the flesh of 30 steers, 100 sheep, and a number of deer, gazelle, antelope, and fattened ducks. People come from everywhere to admire the wisdom and glory of the King of the Hebrews (I Kings 5:14 seqq.).

The three-story palace is 100 cubits long, 50 cubits wide, and 30 cubits high. In the center is a large courtyard. To the north of the palace and harem is the Temple and the altar of sacrifices, inhabited by the presence of the Elohim of Israel, who from heaven watches over his people.

Royal records show Solomon's annual revenue was 666 gold talents, or 29 tons, no doubt an exaggeration, but nonetheless it gives one an idea of the progress that had been made over a few generations and the changes that took place after the anarchy of the period of the Judges, Saul's initial steps, and David's wars.

Modern archeology shows multiple influences for the architectural and artistic splendors of Solomon's reign: Sargon's palace at Khorsabad, Sennacherib's palace with its Syrian facade, and that of Tell Halaf have many characteristics in common with the palace of the greatest King of Israel. The building techniques of his architects are better known because of the excavations at Megiddo and other sites. All of this proves the close relationship and influences of the neighboring countries, Egypt, Mesopotamia, Syria, Canaan, and especially of the Phoenician architects and engineers who directed the construction. The discovery in 1936 of the Temple of Tel Tainat in the plains of Amuq (to the north of Syria) confirms these influences; it is of the same period and type of construction. The Temple of Shiloh no doubt also followed this model, which must have been the classic form in the Fertile Crescent at the beginning of the first millennium B.C. The decoration of the Temple, minutely described in the royal chronicles, shows the same influences: the use of wood (as was widespread in Syria), cherubim, palm trees, flowers, bronze objects, lions, and bulls has also been found among the various civilizations of western Asia and in some regions of the Mediterranean, notably Cyprus, that were in contact with the Syro-Phoenicians in this important period. Amathonte's fountain in the Louvre probably gives an accurate impression of the "Sea of Bronze" in Jerusalem's Temple.[3]

The Hebrews present an original synthesis of the building and decorative elements of their period. The queen of Sheba's amazement at the splendors of the court was not a pretense. Jerusalem was without doubt one of the most brilliant capitals of the ancient world and Solomon one of its greatest and most cultivated monarchs (I Kings 10:1 seqq.).

"The Houses of Your People"

The streets of the city are narrow, roughly paved, and protected from the sun by canopies and crude roofing. The principal streets, which lead to the city's center or skirt its ramparts, are filled with the main bodies of artisans, who have their bustling shops and bazaars there. Jeremiah, for instance, Zedekiah's prisoner, gets his daily bread from the Street of the Bakers in Jerusalem (Jer. 37:21). The gates are privileged places; public meetings, markets, and sometimes court hearings are held beneath their vaults. The houses are built of clay (Job 4:19), rough bricks (Isaiah 9:9), or stone (Lev. 14:40). As the country grows and prospers, a differentiation and regrouping of social classes may be observed.

Stone is the preferred building material, for the country has excellent and easily exploitable quarries. The methods of work in Canaan do not differ from those in Egypt, and the spread of iron tools facilitates the work of the quarrymen. The poorer houses are built of baked or unbaked brick, generally around a court that will be filled with playing children, animals, and older people doing their chores. The cistern is for general use. When there is none, the women go to a spring or public reservoir to draw their water.

Palaces are built of huge hewn stones (I Kings 7:9) and sometimes of marble (I Chr. 29:2). Asphalt, or more usually lime and plaster, serve as cement and wall covering (Gen. 11:3; Isaiah 27:9; Deut. 27:4). The walls are painted in natural colors, with brown dominating. Sycamore, or better still cypress, acacia, olive, cedar, or imported woods such as sandalwood, are used for building and decorating the houses of the rich.

The layout of the homes, as we have recently learned, is generally square. In the center is a courtyard with a well or cistern and a small pool which may serve as a bath or for ablutions. The sturdier houses have a few stories: three levels for Solomon's palace, at least two for the prostitute Rahab's house and for David's before he became King (I Sam. 19:12). In the royal period, the most humble families lived on the upper level, not (as was formerly the case) on the ground floor. The roofs are flat, but slanted to direct rain water to the cisterns, and are made of brick or mud, with occasional clumps of grass growing upon them. A terraced arrangement permits them to be used as storage spaces (a prostitute may even hide fugitive men there). Roofless balconies are used for sleeping during the hot nights and on the stifling days when the south wind blows (I Sam. 9:26). The terraces are places for plotting, for secret meetings (I Sam. 9:25) and, as legend would have it, for love trysts.

"To live in the corner of a roof" is a proverbial expression to designate a sad and lonely life, but it is preferable to living with a cantankerous wife (Prov. 21:9, 25:24). The terraced rooftops also are good places for brooding under Asian skies. The faithful Hebrews build their ritualistic huts there in the autumn, as do the idolaters, whose altars are consecrated to the worship of the stars (II Kings 23:12). The use of terraces is so widespread and common that there are regulations requiring railings. Frequently a guest room is built on them (Judges 3:20; I Kings 17:19: II Kings 4:10). The rich, in addition to their bedrooms, dining rooms and living rooms, have a second residence for the summer (Jer. 22:14; II Sam. 4:7; Amos 3:15). In the mountains in the winter, houses are heated by braziers placed in the center of the rooms (Jer. 36:22).

Room decoration sometimes reaches an elaborate level of refinement, with wooden floors and paneling and beautiful paintings, sculptures, and other ornaments of gold and ivory. The doors swing on hinges at the top and bottom, and the hole into which the axis of the door fits has the name of the female sex organ, *poth*. The locks and bolts are initially of wood and then (notably in the cities) of metal, after the spread of the use of iron. Parchments with important verses from Scripture hang from the doors (Deut. 6:9, 11: 20). Windows are small and symmetrically placed. They open onto the street even in the women's quarters. Trellises or blinds protect the rooms from the sun, as well as from indiscreet glances (I Sam.

19:12; II Sam. 6:16; II Kings 9:30; Prov. 7:6; Song 2:9). The absence of windowpanes is not a problem except in the three coldest months or in the mountains.

Furnishings consist of tables, chairs, benches, cabinets, and beds. The beds are low, in the form of a divan or sofa, and covered with fabric, blankets, and cushions. Sometimes they are upholstered in fine purple linen. Some of the furniture is rather luxurious, made of cedar and decorated with gold and ivory. Metal or pottery chandeliers serve for lighting. The poorest home has at least one oil lamp while the rich have ornate chandeliers which imitate those of the Temple. Meals are prepared on the *kirayim,* stoves with two grates. For holidays and feasts, special chefs are employed to help the women prepare perfect meals (Lev. 11:35; I Sam. 9:23). The Bible enumerates the utensils: kettles, basins for washing the bled meat, pans, platters, pots, mortars, knives, three-prong and other types of forks, tongs, scoops, cruets, jugs, and cups. These utensils are of terra cotta, or preferably copper.

Grain is ground in hand mills in every home. The servants, women slaves, or—lacking these—the lady of the house, with the children's help, turn the heavy millstones that crush the grain. This animates the house, and a home is considered dead if the mill is not working (Jer. 25:10; Eccl. 11:4). A kneading trough is used to prepare the dough, which is allowed to rise before baking. At the Passover, unleavened bread is eaten to commemorate the sorrows of the flight from Egypt. The clay ovens that the Bible describes are the same as the Jews use today in villages of Asia and Africa or that they brought back with them when they returned to Zion, the ancient *tannur,* a pyramid-shaped vault of baked clay about 75 centimeters high. The wood, placed on the ground, heats its sides; the dough is put on the hot surfaces, either inside or outside the oven; and the bread is cooked on two sides (Isaiah 44:15). Public bakers have large ovens and supply the cities (Hos. 7:4; Jer. 37:12).

Bread is the staple—a bread oven is near each home. Different kinds of flour are used to prepare pastries, which the women experiment with to produce new delights. The refinement of cooking is, in certain respects, a result of the status of women. Hebraic cooking is varied. At the beginning of the period with which we are concerned, the soldier's ration consisted of bread, wheat and barley, flour, roasted cereals, fava beans, lentils, beef, lamb, poultry, eggs, game, fish, cheese and dairy products, oil, spices and condiments, honey, fresh and dried fruit, and wine or milk for a beverage. Various cakes complemented the menu, *'ugoth, halloth, reqiqim,* made with a base of flour, oil and honey, and a variety of doughnuts cooked in oil or honey (I Sam. 25:18; II Sam. 16:1, 17:28; I Chr. 12:40).

There are two meals a day, one at noon and a more copious one at night, after the day's work (Gen. 43:16, 43:25; I Kings 20:16; Ruth 2:14–17). Isaiah censures the revelers who start partying at dawn and continue into the night. Hell will delight in swallowing them up (Isaiah 5:8–14).

Meals are taken on low chairs around a table (Gen. 27:19, 37: 25; I Sam. 20:24). Later, it becomes the custom to eat reclining on divans. Amos chastises those who, indifferent to the nation's sorrows, eat lamb as they recline on their ivory beds or soft divans, drinking and shouting songs to the sound of harps and other musical instruments which they invented for their debauchery (Amos 6: 4 seqq.).

Bread also serves as a plate, or is dipped in the sauces placed in the center of the table. Fingers are used instead of forks, and spoons apparently are reserved for kitchen use. Before one leaves the table, grace is said to thank God for the food he has given (this, however, is a later custom) (Deut. 8:10). In the minds of the Prophets and priests faithful to Mosaism, a meal retains a suggestion of its sacrificial origin, which permits the communion of those gathered together with God. This is the source of all life. Hence its important place in biblical narrations, where everything begins or ends with a meal.

Wine

The country is famous for the quantity and quality of its wines—from the vineyards of the plain, the valleys, and the mountain terraces. The Hebrews make other alcoholic beverages with pomegranates, figs, dates, and honey. They also know the process for making beer and spirits.

Although wine may be of Caucasian origin, it enjoys a special place in Hebrew life. They drink it often and speak of it in lyrical terms. The usual beverage for meals and banquets or drinking parties is called *mishte,* and is the favored gift for a King or superior—the custom of giving gifts with strings attached is apparently of noble origin. Wine is also used for medicinal purposes. Liturgically, it is used daily for sacrifices and libations. In literature it is the symbol of joy, of love, and of a mystical life in God. Prophets warn against immoderate consumption, but it is the drunkard whom they condemn rather than the wine (Song 8:2; Isaiah 5:22).

The Hebrew Diet

The religious character of the meal is reinforced by the strict diet of the faithful. To be in a pure state, one must abstain from all unprescribed food. Pure animals are four legged, cud chewing, and of cloven hoof. Animals that fulfill only one of these conditions—the camel, the hare, and the pig, symbol of all impurity—are forbidden. Except for fish with scales and fins, everything that lives in the water is impure. There is no general rule in Mosaic law for birds, but the eagle, hawk, crow, and ostrich are cited as impure. Shellfood, as well as all insects, are impure. The only insects which may be eaten are certain kinds of grasshoppers with four claws and wings. Specific laws forbid the practice of pagan rites—for example, "cooking the kid in his mother's milk." [4] Offering wine as a libation to idols also is forbidden.

Similar rites may be found among the Egyptians, in the books of Zoroaster, and in the laws of Manu. Most peoples have dietary restrictions, but the Hebrews attribute the origin of theirs to their God, revealed on Sinai. The observance of these laws is limited to pious circles. It is impossible to determine precisely to what extent they are followed, but clearly they have no value among those Hebrews who sacrifice to idols. The Bible does not hesitate to describe Elijah feeding on meats which ravens bring to him. These meats were hardly properly killed, but the writer of the Elijah cycle does not seem offended (I Kings 17:6).

Clothing

In the beginning, the Bible teaches, man and woman were without clothes. Cast out of Paradise, they cover themselves with fig leaves and then animal skins to cover their shame (Gen. 3:7, 21). In the royal period the country is rich in textiles. Linen and wool are widespread. Cotton appears only at the end of this period, while hemp remains undiscovered for a long time. Carders, spinners, and weavers are numerous and skilled, and the dyeing trade is strong. White clothing, in harmony with dominant religious symbolism, is preferred. The wealthy choose rich fabrics dyed in shades of purple, crimson, and brown. Lace and embroidery are used for decoration. Assyrian bas-reliefs give a precise picture of Hebrew dress at the time. Shalmaneser III's black obelisk, sculpted in 850, shows a Hebrew delegation sent by King Jehu with the tribute for the Assyrian sovereign. The delegates are dressed in a particular way, completely different from the Assyrians and reminiscent of the styles in northern Syria and southern Armenia.

The Hebrews dress in long-fringed tunics, *ketoneth,* covered with fringed cloaks, *simlah.* They wear their clothes with or without an undershirt, *sadin,* and probably, as the priests do, undershorts, *michnasayim.* These articles are made of linen or wool and are quite full, so that they may be slept in comfortably. Mosaic Law requires that fringes decorated with blue thread be attached to each of the four corners of the cloak to remind the Hebrew of the presence and commandments of YHWH at every moment of his life (Num. 15: 37; Deut. 22:12). To this plain outfit may be added an over-tunic, *me'il,* which is larger than the *ketoneth,* is closed on the sides, and has slits for the head and arms. At the bottom of the priests' *me'il* are a border of pomegranates of different colors and small golden bells whose deftly composed melody has a mystical value.

The priests' *ephod* is sometimes worn by the meticulous Hebrew. It is a short article of clothing, consisting of two pieces joined by precious shoulder straps and made of twisted linen interwoven with gold and dyed purple, violet, and crimson threads. Joseph compares it to the Greek *epomide.* Kings wear yet another large cloak, the *addereth* (Jonah 3:6).

Men wear their hair full, and baldness is already a subject for jokes (II Kings 2:23). The edges of the hairline cannot be shaved (Lev. 19:27), or at least the law forbids this foreign style. A beard is a man's decoration and identity. Everyone grows one. If the Hebrews are the disputatious people, it must be admitted that they have faces to match this reputation. Their headdress consists of a bonnet, *migbah,* around which priests wear a kind of turban, *mitsnepheth* (Ex. 29:9; Ezek. 21:31; Isaiah 62:3), whose color and type vary according to time, place, and style. Evidently it is inconceivable to go about bareheaded. Footwear consists of sandals with straps tied at the calf or, in winter, high leather boots with turned-up ends, Hittite style.

The Pentateuch describes the vestments of the priests in detail (Ex. 39:1–33), yet it is difficult to reconstruct them. Their inspiration must once again have come from Egypt, in a succession of changing styles. The pectoral, *hoshen,* which is hung on the *ephod* by gold rings, is inset, in rows of threes, with twelve different precious stones. The name of the tribe to which each stone corresponds is engraved on them. The high priest's turban is decorated with a golden plaque on which are engraved the words *"QADOSH* for *YHWH"*—"Holy for Adonai." In prosperous times the priests' vestments are splendid and enhance the Temple ceremonies, so beautiful and impressive as to attract great crowds from far-off places.

With the exception of the *ephod* and the *addereth,* women wear similar clothing. Nonetheless, the difference between masculine and feminine styles is visible since the law forbids one sex to wear the clothing of the other (Deut. 22:5). What is different is the quality and color of the fabrics, their length, ornaments, and cut. A woman wears a woolen, linen, or silk belt, *qishurim,* wrapped around the waist several times. It is one of her main decorations. Her cloak, *mitpahath* (Ruth 3:15), is very wide and may cover the head. She also wears a hooded cape with sleeves, *maataphah,* which may be very stylish and luxurious (Isaiah 3:22).

Women's shoes, *tahash* (Ezek. 16:10), are made of fine leather. The *ashasim* are sandals or clogs, probably decorated with little bells that tinkle with each step. Headgear consists of turbans, net bonnets, and linen or silk headbands. The veil is an important piece of feminine finery. The women develop an art of the veil, according to their age and milieu, to express shyness, fear, or love. Apparently nothing requires the woman to cover her face. She seems to be quite free in both her ways and her dress in the high periods (Isaiah 3:16). Her hair is well taken care of, often arranged in braids, and always veiled. She may remove the veil only in the presence of her husband.

We have mentioned the great contrasts in temperature within the same day and between seasons, which necessitates frequent changes of dress, called *halifah,* changing. The rich own an extensive wardrobe (II Kings 5:5); and since clothes are loose and not strictly adapted to the body, they may be given as gifts. (Samson set the price for the solution of a riddle by the Philistines at 30 outfits and 30 pieces of fine linen; then, having lost the wager, he obtained the clothing by killing thirty men of Ashkelon. Naaman, cured of leprosy by Elisha, gave him 10 outfits.) A wardrobe includes winter and summer clothing, work and dress clothes, and, in each case, changes for different times of day and night.

It is probable that the dignitaries of the court and the officials of the army, like the priests, wore a special costume. In times of mourning or on days of fasting and austerity, a kind of hairshirt, the *sac,* made of a rough fabric or hide, was worn to humble and punish the flesh (II Sam. 14:2).

"You Will Earn Your Bread by the Sweat of Your Brow"

The occupations mentioned in the Bible are exercised in the same way as in the neighboring countries. The Hebrews learn them from the Canaanites, Hittites, Philistines, Mesopotamians, and Egyptians, and at the same time influence them. In the royal period, the tiller and the artisan use the tools of the past in an improved form. Sickles with flint blades mounted on wooden handles are replaced by sharp iron sickles, which are more productive. The farmer has to hold wheat in his fist to cut it since the long scythe will not be invented until much later. Hatchets, hammers, scissors, chisels, and iron saws revolutionize daily life and the quality of manufactured products.

Prosperity makes it possible to improve the mass production of everyday objects. The progress represented by the new methods is comparable to that effected in modern industry by the introduction of the chain or cable. Archeological sites reveal these changes. Early in the first millennium B.C., more numerous, varied, and better-made objects appear than in the second millennium. Table service, decorated with regular geometric motifs, is improved and more widely used. Well-made bone carvings are common and demonstrate the same progress.

Spinning and weaving are generally considered women's work (Prov. 31:13). The products are for home use, but also to sell in the marketplace. In Egypt this is men's work, and the Hebrew men participate in it. The technical biblical vocabulary for this skill is very diversified: three-ply thread, shuttle, peg, fastener, roller, warp and woof, spindle, distaff, strand—all these terms of the modern textile industry are current in Hebrew after the first part of the first millennium B.C. (Judges 16:14; Job 7:6; I Sam. 17:7; Prov. 31:19; Ex. 26:31; Lev. 13:48). Remarkably beautiful things are manufactured, such as *tashbetz* (a material dotted with tiny squares), fabrics decorated with geometric designs, gold and silver thread, and embroidery and tapestry work. The fullers and dyers reinforce fabrics by using several strong substances—boric acid, for instance. In Jerusalem the fuller's field was used for the drying of fabrics treated in the capital.

Tanners probably use the Egyptian method of tanning with oil. The leather industry furnishes numerous objects not only for everyday life (shoes, sandals, bags, straps) but also for agricultural and military needs—helmets, quivers, and shields.

An abundant supply of stone furnishes good material for buildings, which are constructed to resist the weather and the attacks of the conquerors, Assyrian, Babylonian, or Roman. David finds his quarrymen and carpenters in Tyre (II Sam. 5:11) and they teach their techniques to the Hebrews, who cut the stone and make bricks according to the classical process (Nahum 3:14; Ex. 5:7; II Sam. 12:31).

The potter has an important status both in life and in literature. His techniques are those of the times. His wheel, *ovnaim,* is made of two round stones and two wooden wheels of unequal diameter, placed one over the other. The artisan squats on the ground. In the eyes of the Prophets his act symbolizes that of the creator, and such is his name in Hebrew, *yotser*.

Here, the glass maker is in the product's country of origin, for its inventor is the Phoenician. This material is no doubt an expensive luxury (Job 28:17).

Architects, engineers, masons, carpenters, cabinet makers, sculptors, blacksmiths, tinsmiths, and decorators are often in the service of the Kings, the principal construction entrepreneurs.

The mines of Ezion-geber prove the existence of advanced techniques (although the processes used are unknown to us) for the treatment of copper. A strange and astonishingly precise text by Job describes the genius of man mastering matter:

> Silver hath beginnings of its veins, and gold hath a place wherein it is melted. Iron is taken out of the earth, and stone melted with heat is turned into brass. He hath set a time for darkness, and the end of all things he considereth, the stone also that is in the dark and the shadow of death (Job 28:1–3).

At this time the Hebrews normally use gold, silver, copper, brass, iron, tin, and lead. These metals are often imported from Ophir, Ethiopia, southern Arabia, Spain, Egypt, and the Caucasus. The steel cited by Nahum (2:4) and Jeremiah (15:12) probably came from the shores of the Black Sea. It is the "iron of the north," *peladoth*. The Hebrews know the techniques for the smelting, refining, and oxidation of metals (Isaiah 1:22; Jer. 6:29; Ezek. 22:18), which are first used in the second half of the fourth millennium, as Jean Perrot's excavations at Beersheba have shown.

The most widely used metal is copper. Since it is easy to work with, it is used for making utensils, armaments, helmets, shields, breast plates, amulets, and art objects. Iron is used for more important items—chariots, swords, spears, and tools. Prisoners' chains and locks are of copper, bronze, or iron (Judges 16:21; Ps. 105:18, 107:16; I Kings 4:13; Job 19:24). Lead is used in making weights, in the mason's plumbline, and for writing tablets (Zech. 4:10, 5:8; Amos 7:7).

Jewelers and goldsmiths are busy with a prosperous luxury industry thanks to the needs of the Temple, the court, and rich ladies.

The master techniques for working metals are known at the beginning of the monarchy. Precious stones, either domestic or imported, are used most commonly for the high priest's pectoral: sardonyx, topaz, emerald, carbuncle, sapphire, diamond, agate, jacinth, amethyst, chrysolite, cornelian, and jasper. These stones are sought after both for their value and their symbolism. They adorn royal crowns, rings, and seals. Pearl and coral are also known. Ivory is used for decorative purposes and is sculpted by specially chosen artists.

Here is another domain of the ladies, who had a great choice of jewels at their disposal. Earrings in many shapes, *nezem, 'aghil, netiphoth;* and jeweled nose rings with an ivory or metal ring, which are suspended over the lips, and some of the rings are quite heavy (Gen. 24:22). The women also have double- and triple-strand necklaces. And they wear various other ornaments: small sunbursts, crescents, gold amulets, various talismans, perfume vials hanging between their breasts, golden chains encircling the face, arm and/or wrist bracelets, rings, worked belts, ankle bracelets, bags and pouches worn on the belt, make-up boxes; *puch* and *kohl* for the eyes and *kofer* or henna for the nails, hair, and hands. Make-up and perfume are kept in vases or special boxes. Hebrew beauties may admire themselves before small portable, oval or round bronze mirrors. Sometimes they even carry them to the grave. Men have only their staff and a seal ring, which notables wear either on a finger or hanging from their neck (Gen. 41:42; Jer. 22:24; Song 8:6).

The perfume maker, *roqeah,* concocts perfumed oils, unguents, and perfumes for Temple use (holy oils, fumigations of the sanctuary) and secular needs, no doubt according to Asian custom. Holy oil is made of olive oil and aromatic compounds mixed with myrrh, cinnamon, aromatic reeds, and cassia. The perfume for holy fumigations is made of storax resin, the aromatic horny plate of shells, a gum resin, *galbanum,* and pure incense, with salt added. These perfumes are reserved for sacred use, but their components, in various combinations (with balm predominating), are commercially available.

In normal times, life in the large cities is rich and varied, as in Jerusalem and Samaria. The important people of this society own homes and summer villas which rival the luxury of the King's. They have several wives and many children. They eat the best foods, drink good wine, and love dancing and music. The young people play in the forests and the vineyards or in games where love and song hold the place of honor. Suicide is so rare that there is no Hebrew word for it. In two millennia of history there are only two desperate acts: Saul's and Ahithophel's.

The bazaars overflow with clothing and decorative luxuries. The passage of a caravan from Egypt or Mesopotamia is an event that interests everyone and changes the balance of local business.

The elegant ladies of Jerusalem and Samaria rival their sisters of Tyre, Damascus, Nineveh, and Memphis. With their wavy hair artfully set, their eyes enlarged by make-up, and in their loose-flowing and sumptuous dresses, they affect a brisk step that draws attention to their beauty by the clicking of their ankle bracelets.

Commerce: Weights and Measures

Since Solomon, the Kings favor foreign commerce and sometimes retain a monopoly for certain products: wheat, olive oil, honey, balm, and horses, for instance. In any case, wholesale and retail merchants pay a tax on their transactions (I Kings 10:15, 5:25, 10:28). It is not possible to draw up a report on Israel's foreign commerce in the period with which we are concerned, because there is no specific information for it. In addition, the Prophets tend not to complain of the state's poor economic condition but, rather, to condemn what today is labeled the "consumer society," or more specifically its screaming inequalities and injustice.

Retail business is a daily reality, and moralists know how to deal with this. "Terrible, terrible!" says the buyer. Yet he congratulates himself when he makes a good purchase (I Kings 10:29). Deceit and fraud are denounced, especially when they concern weights and measures. In Solomon's time a chariot cost about 6.5 kilograms of silver, a horse about 1.7 kilograms. Prices go down as silver becomes rarer.

The units of measure correspond to no official scale, in contrast to Mesopotamia, Egypt, Greece, or Rome. The Hebrews adopt the various metrological systems in use in Canaan, but it is difficult to arrive at an indisputable systemization of the biblical data, which seem to place measures in the realm of traditional evaluation rather than strict determination. Thus, we must wait for archeological research to provide more precise information.

Length measurements include the cubit, *ammah,* based on the length of the forearm—as everywhere on the shores of the Mediterranean; the span, *zeret,* the distance from the tip of the thumb to the tip of the little finger when the hand is spread open; the palm, *tephah,* based on the breadth of the hand; and the finger, *etsbah,* a finger's breadth. The rod, *kaneh,* and the cord, *hevel middah,* seem to have been instruments rather than units of measure. The *gomed* appears only once in the Bible, to determine the length of Ehud's sword (Judges 3:16). Although the metric value of these lengths gives rise to disagreement, the Egyptian cubit suggests the following measures:

Large cubit	0.525 m.	Small cubit	0.450 m.
Span	0.262 m.	Small cubit	0.225 m.
Palm	0.0875 m.	Small cubit	0.075 m.
Finger	0.0218 m.	Small cubit	0.0187 m.

The rod equals 6 cubits.

Distances are established empirically: there is no distinction between the step, *tsa'ad,* and a day's march, whose value is very approximate.

Measures for solids and liquids include the *kor,* the *letech,* the *ephah,* the *bath,* the *seah,* the *hin,* the *omer,* the *qav,* and the *log.* Here again there is disagreement on exact equivalents. The discovery of eighth-century jars with their capacity engraved on them only adds to the controversy as the ensuing systems have significant differences. The equivalents proposed by A. Barrois may be used as a guide:[5]

Kor	229.913 liters	*Hin*	3.831 liters
Letech	114.956 liters	*Omer*	2.299 liters
Ephah-bath	22.991 liters	*Qav*	1.277 liters
Seah	7.663 liters	*Log*	0.319 liter

Other systems put the *kor* at values ranging from 405 to 209 liters.

Area measures also are empirical. The *tsemed,* roughly an acre, is the portion of land two oxen can plow in one day. An area may also be determined by the amount of grain necessary to sow it, or more simply by giving its dimensions.

Weights consist of the talent (*kikkar*), the mina (*maneh*), the *shekel,* the *beqa',* and the *gerah,* which is the lightest Hebrew measure of weight. Debate does not end here either, but again we cite Barrois for the following equivalents:

Talent   34.272 kg.   Mina   571.200 g.   *Shekel* 11.424 g.
Beqa'   5.712 g.   *Gerah*   0.571 g.

According to another system in which the mina equals 60 shekels, the talent weighs 41.1264 kilograms.[6]

Money

The Bible measures wealth not only in property (animals or land) but also—from the earliest times—in silver or gold (Gen. 13:2, 24:35). A dowry is evaluated in shekels, in pendant earrings, and in bracelets. For any transaction, silver or gold is weighed on scales according to the weight system of the country. Ingots are cast, evaluated, and spent by their owners (II Kings 12:10–13). Weight fraud is an ever-present theme among the Prophets.

Money engraved with a seal which authenticates its value appears in Asia Minor in the seventh century and is circulated by the Persians. Only very late biblical texts make mention of it (Neh. 7:69). The oldest coins found in Israel are from the fifth century; the oldest known Jewish coin, which probably goes back to the period of Nehemiah, is silver and weighs 3.88 grams.

The Hebrews did not coin money during the entire royal period. In December 1970 a treasure was found which weighed 25 silver kilograms and dated from the ninth century. It was hidden in pots in the basement of the synagogue of Eshtamoah, near Hebron, and probably belonged to someone called Hamesh. This discovery, the most important one in the Hebron area, broadens our knowledge on the topic.

The Economy of the Country

Agriculture is clearly the principal resource in antiquity. Village folk and even many city dwellers earn their living from the soil. The Hebrews are primarily a people of Asian mountaineers and farmers.

Except for the Jordan Valley, which exploitation soon turned into a desert, agriculture in Canaan depends on the sky—rain water and dew. A single year of drought puts the country in danger of famine and the Hebrews begin to seek food, which they must buy from the Egyptians and Mesopotamians, on the banks of dependable rivers (Deut. 11:10–12). The products of the earth complete the revenues from the animals: meat, milk, wool, and leather. The Hebrews and the Egyptians constantly refer to "the land flowing with milk and honey," an allusion to tilling and animal husbandry.[7]

The country is heavily cultivated. On the high elevations, the fig tree, the olive, and vegetables grow on terraces. On the plains, indefatigable laborers plow, harrow, sow, and harvest their fruits, their wheat, barley and corn. They sing as they convey their loads of grain in wagons to an open threshing floor to be threshed and winnowed. The grain is milled for bread and the straw is kept for feeding the livestock, whose meat is a luxury. Oxen and donkeys pull the rustic carts and wagons. They stomp on the sheaves of wheat on the threshing floor, where the grain mounts up. If pasture land and water are available, the farmer raises sheep and goats. Livestock are plentiful, but the horse is reserved for the rich. A network of irrigation canals and lush orchards, vegetable patches, and gardens abound.

The country is at one of the crossroads of eastern Asia, Egypt, and Mesopotamia. Camel and donkey caravans, and later horse caravans, tap a share of international business, which adds a large revenue to the coffers. Small business is handled by semi-nomadic salesmen; big business is the monopoly of Kings and tribal chiefs.[8] Eilat's control of the coastal and northern plain route is necessary for the security of the great land and maritime trade routes. The journey of the queen of Sheba and her adventures with King Solomon have as their backdrop the economic expansion of the early royal era. These exchanges add appreciably to the stores of gold, silver, precious stones, ivories, perfumes, spices, metals, and other rare products.

After the schism the Hebrews make an effort to control at least a portion of the country's coastline and, in various periods, the strategic points of the "royal way" in Transjordan. In the time of Jehoshaphat and Ahaziah, the kingdom of Judah controls the country of Moab and the Jordan depression as far as Eilat. The excavations of Ezion-geber and Bether indicate a lively trade with southern Arabia. There is also solid evidence of trade with other neighboring countries. Export trade depended on agricultural products: cereals, gum tragacanth, balm, laudanum, wine, oil, honey, and perfumes (I Kings 5:25; Ezek. 27:17; Gen. 37:25, 43:11; Jer. 8:22). Imports were clothing, luxury objects, armaments, horses from Egypt, wood from Phoenicia, and perfumes from Arabia. In El Amarna a letter from Pharaoh to the king of Gezer was found that announced the shipment of silver, gold, clothing, and ivory seats in exchange for some pretty servants.[9]

Fishing and navigation are not important in the economy. The coasts are not easily navigable and the period is not "up to" the enormous projects necessary for their use, as in Tyre, Sidon, Gebal, and Arvad in Phoenicia. Less important ports function in Acre, Dor, Jaffa, and Ashkelon. The mouths of the Kishon, the Yarkon, and the Lachish offer protection to the ships in the small ports that archeological research has discovered at Tel Abn Urvam, Tel Kassila, and Tel Mor. Of the four most important ports, only Dor is in Hebrew hands for any length of time. Supposedly, it was their main port during the royal period (I Kings 4:11). Acre, coveted in the time of David, is brought into Tyre's sphere under Solomon. The Philistines control Ashkelon, Ashdod, and Jaffa without competition from the Hebrews, who did not seem to have maritime pretensions at the time.

Solomon uses the ports freely to import the raw materials for his buildings. Without any problem, Jonah embarks in Jaffa on a ship from Tarsis, which tends to be identified with a Spanish port that exported silver, copper, and other metals. Solomon develops a merchant fleet in Eilat with the help of his Phoenician associates. Their only competitors in the Red Sea are the Egyptians. Possibly one of the goals of Shishak's campaign against Jerusalem in 924 B.C.

(after Solomon's death) was to settle the problem of maritime rivalry.

Israel is poor in raw materials. Yet the Bible speaks of its copper and iron resources, probably referring to the mines that have been uncovered to the east in Transjordan, in Lebanon, or between the Dead Sea and Eilat. There is no proof that the saline waters of the Dead Sea were exploited except for therapeutic purposes.

The crafts were transmitted from father to son; and certain cities were famous for their specialties: Debir, a city of 1,000 inhabitants, for its dyes; the coastal cities for their purple dye; the mountain cities for their pottery and fabrics.

The country is rich, but the wealth is unevenly distributed. The prosperous trade and the accumulation of capital cause the gradual elimination of small holdings and the concentration of rural property in the hands of the affluent. The small, impoverished farmer is trapped by his rich creditors. When he can no longer pay his debts, his land is sold—or he has to sell his children and himself into slavery. A series of laws tends to minimize the consequences of this condition, but without very good results. Nonetheless, slavery in Israel is not the monstrous machine it is in the great empires of antiquity. The very dimensions of the country preserve it both from the extremes of excessive power and the worst hazards of the human condition.

Calendars

"Elohim said: Let there be lights made in the firmament of heaven, to divide the day and the night, and let them be for signs, and for seasons, and for days and years," says Genesis (1:14). The day, of course, measures the rotation of the earth on its axis; the month, the revolution of the moon around the earth; and the year, the revolution of the earth around the sun. The Hebrews take all this into account to measure time.

This history of the calendar is difficult to pin down for a people at the crossroads of several civilizations. The Hebrews adopt diverse and changing methods of time calculation. Their calendar evolved as a progressive synthesis of their knowledge; so they adopted a lunar-solar calendar, as the Egyptians had. In the beginning, the day was counted from dawn to dawn rather than from evening to evening, a modification that was made during the period of the first exile and that has persisted in Israel's tradition. The night was divided into three watches, according to Mesopotamian usage. Later, the Romans' division into four watches will be imposed. The clepsydra and the gnomon are used, as well as the solar dials of the type found in Gezer (dating from the thirteenth century B.C.), for telling the hour.

Months are 29 or 30 days, depending on the phases of the moon. Their names, borrowed first from the Canaanites, relate to agricultural life: the months of grain, flowers, streams, rains, sowing, harvest, pruning, summer fruits, the picking of flax, late sowing, etc. In the official calendar, numbers replace names. The biblical year is counted from the first to the twelfth month. But this is apparently a late change. After the exile, the Babylonian names are definitively adopted.

The twelve-month, 364–365-day year was known to the biblical Hebrews (how they learned this is not known) and appears during the last quarter of the tenth century in the oldest Hebraic document we have, the farm calendar of Gezer. It cannot be accurately determined when they introduced a thirteenth lunar month to synchronize with the solar year, but this custom was known in the royal period (II Chr. 30:2; Num. 9:11; I Kings 12:32). After the exile, the year is "institutionalized." The Babylonian cycle of nineteen years, with a fixed number of embolismic years, is adopted. The numerous reforms that the calendar undergoes through the centuries led the rabbis to establish four beginnings of the year: *Tishri,* the New Year for the commemoration of the creation of the world and for marking the beginning of the seventh and jubilee years; the fifteenth of *Shevat,* at sap-flowing time, the New Year for the trees' tithing; *Nisan,* at Passover, the New Year for Kings and feasts; and *Elul,* the New Year for tithing livestock.

The custom of counting the years from the creation of the world, as the Jews continue to do, is not mentioned in the Bible. The dates are established in relation to outstanding events or to the Judges and Kings. Understandably, this creates considerable difficulty in establishing a sure chronology for the ancient history of Israel. In addition to the official calendar of Judah, the kingdom of Israel had a dissident calendar. Ezekiel envisages a calendar reform. The *Book of Jubilees,* of the sect of Qumran, defined its own way of calculating time. The Hebraic calendar is keyed to the recurring succession of religious and national holidays and the seasons of the year, revealing its double character, historic and agricultural.[10]

The Sabbath and Holidays

The seventh day of the week, the Sabbath, sets the rhythm of the Hebraic year. This original institution of the ancient world goes back to the people's most remote past, which connects creation's divine completion and the creator's rest at the end of the six days' work to that of his people (Gen. 2:1; Ex. 20:8, 31:12, 34:21; Deut. 5:12). Observance of the sabbatical rest is insisted upon in the Torah and by the Prophets. It is the major subject in the preaching of the priests and Levites, who consider it the very symbol of fidelity to the supernatural order established by God for his people. Its importance became even greater in the post-exilic period, when the rules governing it were made more stringent.

Along with the Bible, which commands it, the Sabbath was to become the true "home" of the people who had been driven out of their land. The Sabbath took on the aspect of the religious holiday of Israel very early. It is the sign of the alliance between an obedient people and God and his Torah. It is based on the duty to imitate God, who rested after creating the world. The human, social, and cosmic meaning relates to the memory of the enslavement in Egypt and the providential liberation that ends it. With the Sabbath, leisure is for the first time considered a metaphysical category leading to the last days of humanity, whose ultimate fulfillment it foreshadows.

The day of rest is consecrated to joy in God, sacrificial offerings, education, and the sermons of the priests and scholars. It is a public holiday. Work and business are completely suspended, as if they were the week's tithe (Isaiah 1:13; Hos. 2:13; II Kings 4:23). The Hebrew and the foreigner, the citizen and the alien, animals and things, nature itself, must observe it.

Each new moon is celebrated by special sacrifices, offerings, and libations (Num. 10:10, 28:1–5; Ex. 40:2)—again, a matter of public holiday according to ancient traditions. At the new moon Saul offers a meal which is sacrificial in character, since purity is required for participation. In some periods, rejoicing accompanies the full moon, a custom no doubt taken from the Canaanites (Ps. 81:4, 104:19).

The Hebrew liturgical year is marked by three important pilgrimages, which take place at Passover (*Pesah*), Pentecost (*Shavuoth*), and Tabernacles (*Succoth*). Passover commemorates the departure from Egypt and the events relating to the liberation of the people (Ex. 12; Josh. 5:10–12; II Kings 23:21–23). King Solomon personally officiates at the Temple for the feast of unleavened bread, centering around the sacrifice of the paschal lamb (I Kings 9:25). For seven days, unleavened bread reminds the nation of its misery and enslavement in Egypt.

After the Temple's founding, the tendency to make this holiday into a great pilgrimage is confirmed. Crowds gather from every point for the journey to the capital to offer sacrifices and homage to the King and to the liberating God. This practice becomes more prevalent as the centralization of the monarchy increases. It completes the family tradition of the *Pesah*. As in the time of the Judges, each head of a family is enthroned in his home, or under his tent, recalling YHWH's act as he triumphs over his enemies and frees his people. This springtime holiday, which maintains its country-like character, symbolizes the deepest meaning of the history and faith of Israel.

Shavuoth, celebrated seven weeks after Passover, is the feast of the first fruits of the harvest. It is marked by ablutions, libations, and special sacrifices. Again, a solemnity of agricultural origins is reinterpreted in the sense of the history of Israel's salvation. In the people's mind it becomes the feast of the gift of the Torah on Sinai and the renewal of the Covenant.

Succoth, the feast of Tabernacles, is celebrated at the beginning of autumn (Ex. 23:16, 34:22; Deut. 31:10), at harvest time, "the fifteenth day of the seventh month." It lasts for a week, and adds an eighth, terminal day, *Shemini 'atsereth. Succoth,* too, is linked to the joy of the earth's richness. Its huts, built in the gardens or on the terraces, recall those which the farmers build in the fields at fruit-picking time, when it is necessary to be close to one's work. But this earth-related holiday also takes on a historical significance related to salvation. It recaptures the nomadic past of the people wandering in the desert. A logical sequence of the three pilgrimages of the year is established—the flight from Egypt, the gift of the Torah, and the wandering in the desert—as a prelude to settling in the Holy Land. The people, encouraged by the Kings and priests, reenact the distant memories in large assemblies in Jerusalem.

Two other important solemnities are added to these three (Num. 29:1–12). *Rosh Hashanah,* New Year's Day, is celebrated as the most solemn of the new moons with reference to the creation of the world; it is the Sabbath of the new moons, the seventh of the year. *Yom Hakippurim,* the Day of Atonement, which follows ten days later, is the great Sabbath of the year—a strict fast that foreshadows God's judgment (Lev. 23:26–32; Num. 29:7; Lev. 16).

The origins of these holidays are disputed. In the post-exilic period they grow in importance. They complete the liturgical year, which celebrates the Sabbath, the new moons, the three high holidays of national, historical, and agricultural inspiration (Passover, Pentecost, and Tabernacles), and two holidays that are specifically religious, universal, and trans-historic: New Year's Day and the Day of Atonement. Only one day of fast is required each year, but the men of God willingly add others.

Games and Recreation

The Bible gives succinct information about games and recreation. This was not among the Prophets' interests, yet excavations have indicated that social games were played in Mizpah, Kiriath-Sepher, Beth Shemesh, Gezer, Megiddo, and Debir. Game-playing items have been found there, but how they were used by children and adults is not known. The games mentioned in the Bible are riddle contests, music, and dance, which are enjoyed at banquets (Judges 14:12; Zech. 8:5, Job 21:11). Sacred or profane dancing plays an important role in the feasts of antiquity, including those of the Hebrews. A diversified vocabulary describes the different ways to dance. The crossing of the Red Sea is celebrated with song and dance. Passover, the annual assembly at Shiloh, the processions with the Ark of the Covenant, and probably the liturgies of the Temple also included sacred dances (Ex. 15:20; Isaiah 30:29; Judges 21: 16; I Sam. 18:6; II Sam. 6).

Hebrew literature makes no reference to the games that held such an important place in antiquity, however. There are no direct references to hunting, which so amused the Egyptians and Mesopotamians, or to gladiatorial combats, pantomime shows, and plays. Those authors who see a type of drama or opera in the Song of Songs have little evidence to support their thesis, which projects into the past what is true only of succeeding periods or other civilizations.

It is certain that in the royal period contests of skill and strength had no place in society—much less the horrible spectacle of throwing men among wild animals. The Hebrew is absorbed in other thoughts. We can be sure that the Prophets would have condemned such bloody games.

A favorite pastime was public readings of the Prophets and other writers. These events were held in the squares around the sanctuaries, where, once learned, they were frequently repeated from generation to generation, acquiring an authoritative status.

Leisure plays an important role in the ancient city. For the Hebrews, about a third of the year is holiday. Liturgies, processions, sacrifices, public and private prayers, pilgrimages to the Temple or sanctuaries, and steeping themselves in profound traditions are part of the normal activities of the faithful, obliged by law to refrain from work. Leisure, sanctified by study, is an essential aspect of Hebrew thought and manners, informed by the sublime intimacy of God.

Israel's Liturgies

To adore YHWH is to serve him, be his slave, bow down before him, and seek his countenance. Holidays are the meetings of the faithful, joyful with their Lord. The Prophets use the symbol of marriage to define Israel's relationship to YHWH.

Contemporary criticism no longer defines the patriarchal cult as essentially animistic. The Patriarchs are the object of their God's visitation. They build sanctuaries where he has shown himself. There they offer sacrifices according to the rituals, which include purifications, libations, oil offerings, and benedictions (Gen. 4, 8, 14, 22).

In the period of Moses the liturgies become fixed. The confession ritual accompanies the sacrifice and the eating of the sacred meal (Ex. 18:10–12). The theophanies antedate the various communion rituals (Ex. 19, 24). The ancient patriarchal customs, essentially personal or familial in character, are codified to serve the new faith. The Tabernacle of the Covenant shelters the real presence of YHWH. While Moses communes with his God, a column of clouds rises at the entrance of the Tabernacle and the people rise and bow down in adoration (Ex. 33:8–12).

At the time of the conquest, the tendency toward syncretism becomes stronger. The Canaanite sanctuaries of Bethel, Beersheba, Shechem, and Shiloh are used for Hebrew worship. Altars multiply. Each city and village wants its own place of worship. The liturgical calendar is fixed and the three annual pilgrimages are observed. Pagan customs mix with monotheistic practices, and seers reproach the confusion of Baal and YHWH in the liturgies.

Monarchical power reinforces the influence of Mosaism, for which Jerusalem becomes the most important center. Israel's liturgies become established—in contrast to the wandering of the Tabernacle of the Covenant and the Ark of the Covenant in nomadic times. This is an important change, which must be emphasized. Henceforth the symbolism of the Temple is the soul of the liturgies. The five great feasts are celebrated there with great pomp. The Psalms' influence increases as a book of prayer. Sacrifices, offerings, processions, vocal and orchestral music, and sacred dances attract large crowds to Jerusalem, the source of both the Torah and the word of God. In addition, the priests present the oracles, who enlighten the crowds. They speak in the name of YHWH, whose will they interpret and whose miraculous action they relate to the people assembled in divine joy, which the Prophets and poets of Israel praise. The ceremonies take place in Jerusalem as well as in the ancient sanctuaries where Israel's God is still adored. Late in the post-exilic period a liturgical and sacrificial monopoly affirms itself in Jerusalem. Meanwhile the Prophets, who prefer to be heard in the enclosures of the sanctuaries, denounce deviations from the cult. They condemn violations of the Law, the sacred prostitute, and the hypocrisy of a religion that is practiced without heartfelt repentance. Sacrifices without repentance are hateful to YHWH, who prefers justice and mercy to the external show of the Sabbath, the feasts of the new moon, and the pilgrimages. When the heart is not worthy, it is futile to bow down before YHWH. Amos, Hosea, and Isaiah carry the argument to the point that they condemn not only the worship of false gods, the flesh, power, silver, or nature but the false adoration of the true God.

Sense of Tragedy and Sense of Humor

Considering the various elements that must be touched upon to reconstruct the daily life of the Hebrews, one is struck by the harshness of their conditions: a country on the edge of the desert, where every acre of sand or mountain rock has to be conquered; a hostile and implacable political environment; a people divided by a thousand internal contradictions; a strict God and a stricter Law (we will return to this—a historic destiny marked by an exceptional series of misfortunes: wars, revolutions, famines, epidemics); and the double catastrophe of the fall of Samaria and Jerusalem, which puts an end to the kingdom of Israel and then Judah.

In spite of this gloomy background, their daily life seems to have been dominated by joy, jubilation, cheerfulness, and hope. Few civilizations have sung the joys of man more fervently—one of the greatest paradoxes of the nation's existence. Let us look more closely at this people.

Hospitality is practiced with the generosity of the Orient, as a duty and not as a favor. There are no hotels in the cities; at most, one finds a guest room on the outskirts. The traveler or pilgrim has the right to be welcomed where he intends to spend the night, with the understanding that he is under a reciprocal obligation. Prophetic teaching stresses this duty, whose exercise is a cardinal virtue: love of neighbor. The Law gives many guidelines for loving one's neighbor or the foreigner. The duty derives from the Hebrew's obligation to his God. Hence the continual effort to make manners more civil by religious instruction and respect for the liturgies: to greet a person, one "blesses" him and says "Peace be with you."

Daily language is naturally impregnated with the prophetical ter-minology passed on by traditions which, in the royal era, are taught to all levels of society by the priests, Levites, and scholars. Ordinary people transmit them to their children and the rich hire preceptors to do it. Well-lettered individuals know a large segment of tradi-tional writings by heart. The high standards of prophetic preaching require a broad base of men trained in the disciplines of a highly developed culture that makes the message preachable.

The greeting mentioned above is often accompanied by the "kiss of peace," widespread in the East. At least in select circles, one bows down before a superior and addresses him in the third person. Re-spect for parents and elders and the protection of widows, orphans, and the poor are duties the law holds important (Lev. 19:32; Prov. 20:29). Formulas of politeness, blessings and priorities, kindness in every social situation, and the exchange of gifts and visits are established traditions due to the efforts of the priests and Prophets.

As we have seen, the Hebrews love feasts, the pleasures of the table, and music and dancing (Judges 21:21; II Sam. 6:19); and they gather together for all this in their fields, vineyards, and homes (Lam. 5:14). It is good taste to speak little and wisely (Prov. 10:19, 17:27); braggers, teasers, and the violent are not accepted (Prov. 21 seqq.). Artful speech and subtlety of mind are demonstrated in inventive riddles, allegories, and parables. Delicacy of language is valued, whereas crudity in matters pertaining to sex, the fertility or sterility of women, their confinements, or their illnesses is to be avoided. This is accepted as normal—neither caused by nor leading to "complexes." In fact, Hebrew society strives for a high purity of life style. The Nazarite takes a vow of continence and refrains from alcoholic beverages during his retreat. When disaster threatens, the entire population takes to fasting, penance, and prayer. In this re-spect the prophetic appeals have reached the highest level of excel-lence.

In contrast to this austerity, joy shines from almost every page of the Bible, echoing the lives of its heroes. All suffering ends in happi-ness because of God's salvation, and sorrow is sure to give way to laughter.[11] In spite of the pitfalls of the human condition, laughter and the divine smile are part of the eternity of the creator. This laughter and smile has nothing to do with the raillery of reprobates

123

or the broad joke, for "the laughter of fools is like the crackling of thorns burning under a pot" (Eccl. 7:6). Mockery is condemned, and those who practice it will be dust.

YHWH's laughter resounds in the heavens (Ps. 2:4), as does that of his friends on earth. The most severe of the Patriarchs, the unexpected son of Abraham and Sarah, is called Isaac, "the one who laughs." The announcement of his birth provoked an incredulous laugh from his parents, and this laughing Isaac is portrayed under his tent imprudently dallying with his wife Rebecca (Gen. 26:8). The familiar laugh of God recurs frequently in the Bible. He projects unto heaven the laughter of the people in the joy of their fate and the assurance of their triumphs.[12]

Love

The notion of love in the biblical era suggests its central importance in the life of the people; indeed, it was the very peak of Hebrew aspiration. Just as the family is the fundamental cell of society, all humanity is one huge family—sprung from God's genius and the side of one man, Adam, the father of mankind. Everything that touches upon love—sex, procreation, marital relations, and acceptable and unacceptable unions—has metaphysical importance and is fundamental in Hebrew life.

The androgynous myth appears in an allusive manner in Genesis: Adam is both "man and woman," and humanity develops in an incestuous chain: the sons of Adam and Eve marry their own sisters, and Lot "knows" his daughters (Gen. 5, 10, 19:30). This type of marriage, which was sometimes allowed in neighboring civilizations, was strictly prohibited in the royal era (Lev. 18:9, 20:17). Yet marriage between brothers and half-sisters apparently was not forbidden in either the patriarchal period or the early monarchy. Amnon loves Tamar, his half-sister, and has illicit relations with her. His only crime, it would seem, was abandoning her after the seduction (II Sam. 13:1–23). There were severe sanctions in very ancient law against this type of union, but it was practiced so openly that the Prophets continually censure it (Ezek. 22:11). In contrast, custom encourages endogamous marriage and the law does not forbid it.

The patriarchal family is based on the marriage between uncle and niece, nephew and aunt, and especially between cousins, so as to keep the patrimony intact.

Although marriage to foreigners is disapproved of, the Bible furnishes many such examples, some of them illustrious: Esau (it is true he did not have a good reputation) marries two Hittite women against his parents' will (Gen. 26:34); Moses marries a Kushite and is criticized by his sister Miriam for it; Samson's partnership with the Philistine Timnah was not a happy one, for this hero was destined to be the victim of the women he loved (Judges 14, 16).

After the settlement in Canaan, law forbids marriage with the foreigners of the seven Canaanite nations: Hittites, Girgashites, Amorites, Canaanites, Perizzites, Hivites, and Jebusites. The struggle against idolatry is the main reason (Deut. 7:2–4). Yet, in actual fact, mixed marriages increase in the time of the Judges and in the royal period and are common until the exile (Judges 3:5–6). To put an end to them, Ezra and Nehemiah order the foreign women sent away.

David's line includes foreigners, Ruth the Moabite and Rahab the prostitute. Apparently, during the royal period the interdiction against mixed marriages was less severe than during the patriarchal period or after the exile. It is clear that the settling of the people diminished the dangers of exogamy and allowed a more liberal attitude. Solomon's penchant for foreign women (who filled his harem) is no secret. After the exile, the weakened nation seeks to defend itself and reinstitutes the prohibition of exogamy. Endogamy becomes the fundamental rule.

Marriage

Hebraic marriage has always been polygamous. Ecclesiastes, if it had broached the subject, would have stated in its cynical way that official monogamy encourages clandestine polygamy while official polygamy pushes man—as a reaction or defense, perhaps—to practice monogamy. In either case, things balance out. Instinct tends to justify or correct the direction that the law takes. The problems and sometimes the hypocrisy of monogamy are ignored by the Hebrews;

on the other hand, they tend to dwell on the situation of households made up of one man and several wives. This may have been quite common. Kings prove their power by the number of their wives: Saul has "several"; in Hebron, David has six, and will have more in Jerusalem; Rehoboam has eighteen wives and sixty concubines; and the Song of Songs attributes sixty wives and eighty concubines to its idyllic King.

King Solomon breaks all records with 700 wives and 300 concubines, according to the chronicles (I Kings 11:3). It is understandable that the legislator felt it appropriate to suggest that Kings not multiply their number of wives, who served to cement foreign relations (Deut. 17:17). They belonged to the throne as well as to the King, and at the outset of the monarchy the harem was included in the succession.

The rich and the powerful imitated the Kings and established their social position by increasing the number of their wives and children, who could number several dozen. Rivalry and jealousy came into play between the child-bearing wives and the sterile ones, between Sarah and Hagar, Rachel and Leah, Hannah and Peninnah (Gen. 16, 30; I Sam. 1:6). Quarrels are not rare. Sometimes one wife bargains off a coveted object with another wife for a night with their husband. In this way Rachel received some mandrakes from Leah (Gen. 30:15).

From the dawn of their history the Hebrews knew romantic love. One is still moved by the passions of Abraham and Sarah, Jacob and Rachel, Potiphar's wife and Joseph, Shechem and Dinah, Samson and Timnah, Rehoboam and Maacah, David and Bathsheba, Adonijah and Abishag, and Amnon and Tamar.

Generally, the choice of a wife is the affair of the young man's father (Gen. 24:51)—the agreement of the future spouses is not indispensable. A normal marriage is of family as much as individual interest. The dowry the young man's father must present to the bride's family is determined by social importance and wealth. It is a business transaction. The price of the fiancée establishes her social value and esteem and her rank in the harem. Even her trousseau is part of the long negotiations which usually precede a marriage. The value of a "virgin fiancée" is 50 pieces of silver, a very high price (Ex. 22:15). When the fiancé has no money, he may commit himself to his future father-in-law's service to pay for his bride. Jacob had to work for Laban for fourteen years before having his darling Rachel.

The marriage celebration includes a nuptial cortege, a banquet, and benedictions. It is important, after the consummation of the marriage, to establish the bride's virginity, and a blood-stained sheet is the required proof in case of dispute (Deut. 22:13–18). The fertility of a marriage is the criterion for its success, and God is the master of this; it is God who makes women fertile by "visiting" them —Sarah, Rebecca, Rachel (Gen. 18, 21, 25, 30)—or "remembering" them, as he did the sterile Hannah (I Sam. 1:1–19). The acceptable average progeny of one wife is five or six children, preferably sons (Ps. 128). Heroes often have a miraculous birth: Isaac, Jacob, Esau, Benjamin, Samuel, Samson. A dream, a religious vow, or the visit of an angel sometimes precedes and announces the event (Judges 13; Isaiah 8; Hos. 1; Ps. 127).

Adultery, prostitution, sodomy, homosexuality, incest, and relations with a woman during her menstrual period are prohibited. If one is guilty of any of these, he or she is punished with sterility. The guilty, says Leviticus, "will be destroyed out of the midst of their people" (Lev. 20:18) or "will die childless" (Lev. 20:20), a punishment as serious as the death sentence that usually accompanies sexual infractions. For a man, adultery has only one sense: intercourse with a married woman. Job cries: "If I have committed adultery, may other men lie with my wife" (Job 31:10). The pathos of this cry, in which Job states his innocence, leads one to believe that such sins were anything but rare.

Fornication and adultery cause the sterility not only of women but also of nature. The normal consequence is famine: the country has been made impure and vomits its people (Lev. 18, 20:10–22; Deut. 11:17). Women's adultery and prostitution are the symbols of Israel's collective infidelity by deceiving God and prostituting itself to idols. The crimes are related and their consequences are identical (Ex. 34:15; Num. 15:39; Deut. 31:16). Adultery is such a serious crime, and so severely punished, that a woman who is suspected of it always has recourse to God's judgment, the ordeal, to prove her innocence. This procedure is minutely described in the Bible. The woman who has recourse to it must drink bitter water; if she is guilty, "the waters she drinks will be bitter; her belly will swell, her thigh shall rot and she will be an example to her people" (Num. 5:12–31). Virtue, on the other hand, determines not only her fertility but her physical beauty and that of her children.

The Man Whose Sandal Is Removed

A man who dies without children must nonetheless have progeny. By law, his brother must marry his widow, because polygamy aims at increasing the patrilocal, patrilineal, and patriarchal family. To avoid levirate (an old and forceful institution), Onan, who refused to give a child to his sister-in-law, introduced *coitus interruptus* into universal society and literature—a practice unknown to the animal world. But, like many others, he died a victim of his innovation: "Therefore, the Lord slew him, because he did a detestable thing." [13]

In the royal period, legislation weakens levirate and allows a solution other than Onan's: the *levir* who refuses to do his duty may submit to a public humiliation. The widow removes her brother-in-law's sandal and spits in his face, saying: "So shall it be done to the man that will not build up his brother's house" (Deut. 25:7–10). Obviously, a reform intervenes in periods when family ties are weakened. The story of Boaz and Ruth illustrates these biblical customs (Ruth 4 seqq.).

The levirate gives a woman the right to family status, which includes its wealth and, in principle, the right to succession. Another example of this is the ancient custom by which a son inherits his father's harem. He marries his father's wives, with the exception of his mother. In their eagerness to inherit, Reuben and Absalom prematurely take possession of their father's concubines (Gen. 35:22; II Sam. 3:6; 12:8; 16:20–22; I Kings 2:22). These practices are severely condemned by law and by the Prophets (Lev. 18; 20; Ezek. 22:10).

Virginity is both valued and protected. The violator of a virgin is forced to marry her and to pay the legitimate dowry to her family. If the girl is betrothed to another man, the penalty is death. If the man swears that the woman, married or not, was fully willing—did not shout, if the rape took place in the city—she too will be put to death (Deut. 22:15–29). Rape is an attack on a family's honor and wealth and may cause implacable vengeance (Gen. 34:31) that may lead to the massacre of an entire tribe, as when a man is sexually attacked by homosexuals. In the case to which we refer, a Levite escaped the attack of the men of Gibeah, near Jerusalem, but his wife died from their sexual assault, which also proved fatal to the aggressors. Benjamin's tribe was almost totally destroyed in the war provoked by the incident (Judges 19–21).

The marriage law's two components of polygamy and repudiation allow the repudiated woman to exercise successive polyandry. The husband, sole possessor of all property, has the right to repudiate his wife, who may always rejoin her parents' family after negotiations and the consequent divorce. Sometimes a marriage may be dissolved by the initiative and pressure of influential individuals (Gen. 21; Judges 14). Divorce is confirmed by an official letter in which the husband says that the wife is no longer consecrated, hence is untouchable (Deut. 24:1–4), and that she is free to remarry. The issuance of such a letter may be attended by various forms of blackmail in cases of disagreement. Like marriage, divorce symbolizes an aspect of God's relationship to his people (Hos. 2:4–5; Isaiah 50:1; Jer. 3:8). God always takes back his adulterous people, whereas the law forbids a man to remarry his wife if in the meantime she has given herself to someone else (Deut. 24; cf. II Sam. 3).

The causes for repudiation are broadly defined, such as deception about virginity—which results not only in the divorce of the guilty woman but in her stoning (Deut. 22:13–21). Or, more generally, a man may repudiate his wife "if she find not favor in his eyes for some uncleanness" (Deut. 24); this is primarily infidelity (Lev. 20:8–21), which theoretically is punishable by death, or sterility. In the latter case, provision is made for taking a second wife, whom the sterile wife is foremost in wishing her lord and master to have. The Prophets encourage men to be faithful to "the woman of their alliance," but this admonition is made within the framework of a polygamous system.

Sexual Activity

Normal sexual activity is legitimate and good. God's first command to man when he created the world was "Grow and multiply and people the earth" (Gen. 1:28). Sexual love is not separated from a couple's spiritual love, and there is no Hebrew word that distinguishes the two aspects. There are no complexes regarding sex either. Sexual life is practiced openly but is strictly and fully legislated. This proves less the virtue of the biblical people than the importance of the problem. The documents and various facts and laws that the Bible passes down on this theme have no parallel in any other culture of antiquity.

The married woman is consecrated, sanctified, and set aside for her husband, but copulation causes impurity, as does any other contact with the sacred. After coitus the couple must make their ablutions and purify themselves, although they will remain impure until evening. The law is the same for man, after copulation or any seminal loss. Sexual activity, of whatever nature, introduces man into the universe of the sacred. He must be purified to reacquire the fullness of his secular functions. In addition, custom tends to separate the sexes.

All sexual activity is forbidden with a woman who is menstruating; any direct or indirect contact with her is equally forbidden. The loss of blood results in impurity, as does anything which borders on the mystery of life and death. "If any man lie with a woman in her flowers, and uncover her nakedness, and she open the fountain of her blood, both shall be destroyed out of the midst of their people" (Lev. 20:18). For blood is life, and the loss of menstrual blood, as well as that following childbirth, places the woman in the dangerous and mysterious zone between life and death, between the poles of purity and impurity that are the major terms of biblical dialectics. In fact, the sexual act is allowed only during fertile periods.

Legislation is full of sexual interdictions and severe penalties: death by stoning or "separation from the people." Opposed to the licentiousness that prevailed throughout antiquity—and not only during antiquity—is the effort to discipline and orient couples' sexual activity.

Homosexuality—so esteemed by the Greeks and many others—is

an abomination (Lev. 18:22); and the inhabitants of Sodom and Gomorrah pay dearly for this vice (Gen. 19; Judges 19). The Hebrew Prophets and lawmakers are the first to prohibit it so absolutely.

Bestiality (Lev. 18:23, 20:23), current among the nomads, who satisfied their instincts with their animals, is also punishable by death. Hittite law is a precedent. The interdiction applies to women as well as men and points to country practices. Mention also should be made of the tradition of sacred prostitution and sexual hospitality among nations. The gap between the common prostitute, *zonah,* and the sacred prostitute, *qedeshah,* who works for a sanctuary, is considerable. Both are dedicated to the satisfaction of pilgrims and travelers, but the first is serving man's drives while the second is the priestess of an idol. In spite of condemnation by the lawmaker (Deut. 23:18–19), these practices never totally disappeared. Judah sees Tamar as a *qedeshah* but does not hesitate to avail himself of her (Gen. 38:15; I Kings 22:47). The narrator seems to regard it as a normal incident. Some Hebrews are chastised for having prostituted themselves with the daughters of Moab in Baal Peor (Num. 25:1–3). The royal chronicles relate an impressive series of sacred prostitution in Israel and Judah in the periods of Rehoboam, Asa, and Jehoshaphat (I Kings 14:14–24, 15:12). Under Asa's long rule (911–870), the sacred prostitutes are driven from the Temple, the idols are destroyed, the title Great Lady, *Gevira,* is taken away from Maachah, and the idol she served, Asherah, is burned in the valley of Kidron (I Kings 15:9 seqq.).

The Kings try unsuccessfully to stamp out these activities. Hosea condemns the same crimes (Hos. 2 seqq.). At the end of the royal period, Josiah, in the course of his religious reforms, "destroyed the places of the sacred prostitute which were in the Temple of the Lord where women wove veils for Asherah." More than a thousand years of prophetic sermons and legal repression separate the story of Judah and Tamar and the story of the houses of prostitution that operated in the Temple on the eve of its destruction.

Prostitution has legal rights in the Hebrew culture. In cities, prostitutes receive their clients at home. Rahab blissfully sells her charms in Jericho in the time of Joshua (Josh. 2:1) and is esteemed by the authorities. Jephthah, son of Galaad, and Samson in Gaza have no qualms about visiting such women, and the chronicles relate their act without censuring it (Judges 14). Two prostitutes, confronting each other in a lawsuit, have free access to Solomon's courts. Throughout the royal period the *zonah* and the *qedeshah* are part of city life. They stroll around the streets, court, public baths, and crossroads and stand by the doorways of their homes. They call out to passersby, trying to interest them with a gesture or, more delicately, by playing the harp and singing. Though prostitution is condemned by law, it persists in fact. The lawmaker, having decided there should be no prostitutes or prostituted individuals in Israel, forbade the priests from marrying prostitutes and threatened to burn a priest's daughter who prostituted herself (Lev. 21:7–9). The moralists resign themselves and tend to preach prudence while describing the hypocrisy, arrogance, brutality, and cynicism of these women (Prov. 2:16, 5:3, 6:24, 7:5; Jer. 3:3; Eccl. 9:3).

The care with which illicit sexual activity is defined points up the original character of Hebraic love and sexual life. A constant concern has been to favor demythification and demystification—a liberation and sanctification of sexual activity.

Circumcision

It was not by chance that circumcision, practiced by numerous peoples of antiquity, became a Hebrew rite of alliance with God. The blood of the alliance that unites God and every eight-day-old Hebrew boy is that of the circumcised prepuce. It is in this act that a son of Abraham is known: circumcision is the initiation rite that consecrates man's entrance into the assembly of the children of Israel. It is both a religious and a national rite. A flint blade was used, even in the Iron Age, to recall the Abrahamic origins of this tradition. From life's outset, circumcision consecrates man's sexual organs to God in a bloody sacrifice, resulting in constant concern for a liberation, sanctification, and sacralization of sexual life. Sexual life is a sacred duty and a divine joy that restores man to the fullness of his original state. For although God created Adam man and woman, he proceeded to extract Eve from his body: "She is bone of his bone, flesh of his flesh" (Gen. 2:20–24). This is the origin of the ontological character of love and the desire for the restoration of original perfection, reflected in the Song of Songs: "I belong to my lover, and my lover belongs to me" (Song 2:16). In contrast to the ancient world's mythologies, this verse marks a revolution which assures the liberation of the couple that is sanctified by love. Woman is man's equal in offering love, and together they face heaven, finally freed from the fallen idols.

The Women of the Bible

The Bible offers a fascinating study of woman since Eve, the mother of every living being, up to Shulamite, the exemplary lover of the Song of Songs. Mother, wife, queen, soldier, sorceress, prophetess; young girl, fiancée, sister; prostitute, spy, thief, seductress; head of a clan; hater, coquette; the one who is fragile, fiery, passionate, amorous, clever, teasing, jealous, subtle; mistress of the household; heroine, Lilith, the anti-Eve, destructress; mortal, demon, virago, lover, virgin—these are the roles that appear in the extraordinary gallery that covers two millennia. No equivalent documentation exists in literature.

Essentially, the biblical woman is lover, wife, and mother. She plays a role in the family and society and in economic, religious, and political life, while remaining fundamentally a dependent of her husband or her father. Her economic role is treated in the famous chapter of Proverbs (31), which, with the Song of Songs, is the most eloquent and probably the earliest feminist manifesto. Women are not rare in political life—the prophetesses Miriam, Deborah, Huldah, for example, and the queens Bathsheba, Jezebel, and Athaliah. More often their talents are devoted to the arts, song, dance, music, embroidery, and weaving. They participate fully in the sacred liturgies and play an active role in the community. They may consummate sacrifices but they do not have the power to perform priestly functions. Occasionally they practice divination and necromancy.

Routinely, they keep busy in the home: milling grain, baking bread, preparing meals, drawing water or bringing it from springs in jars they balance on their head; and raising and educating children. Being a wife in a polygamous household, which always includes several dozen persons, or even several hundred, is difficult.

She must oversee the purity and sanctity of this extended family.

She is faithful, strong, discreet, silent; she is both at peace and a peacemaker. She is fervent in the adoration and service of her God, her parents, her husband and children. If she must fight for her country, she is implacable: Jael assassinating Sisera, Judith decapitating Holophernes, Jephthah's daughter offering her life to her father in sacrifice.

The woman, in principle subordinate to the man, is his equal before the law in certain circumstances. Father and mother are due the same respect from their children. Men and women are subject to the same punishment in adultery and incest, and generally to the same penal and criminal legislation. The woman is idealized—to the point of symbolizing the honor of man, wisdom, the Torah, and absolute love—in the Song of Songs.

This is the portrait of the ideal woman of Zion's poets: white or tanned skin, with a tinge of purple; deep, almond-shape eyes, evoking the form of a dove; black hair with long curls that dance on her bosom; even teeth, scarlet lips, strong nose; cheeks and temples transparent to show the blood underneath; long neck; strong chest; long, round, and full thighs; fleshy, warm, and inviting body; an impressive silhouette, a supple but serious gait for sacred dance, fresh as a rose and lily—intoxicating, splendid—madly passionate; worthy of a great king's ransom (Song 1, 8).

The Song of Songs eloquently achieves a goal of prophetic thought: the couple's sexual activity is separated from idolatry. The pagan customs that confused the two were entrenched in the ancient world, where widespread sacred prostitution caused the Prophets to declaim against it,

> because they have forsaken the Lord in not observing his law. Fornication, and wine and drunkenness take away the understanding. My people have consulted their stocks, and their staff hath declared unto them; for the spirit of fornication hath deceived them, and they have committed fornication against their God. They offered sacrifice upon the tops of the mountains, and burnt incense upon the hills: under the oak, and the poplar, and the turpentine tree, because the shadow thereof was good.

Therefore shall your daughters commit fornication, and your spouses shall be adulteresses. I will not visit upon your daughters when they shall commit fornication, and upon your spouses when they shall commit adultery: because themselves conversed with harlots, and offered sacrifice with the effeminate, and the people that doth not understand shall be beaten. . . . They have gone astray by fornication: they that should have protected them have loved to bring shame upon them (Hos. 4:10–19).

This refers to sacred prostitution in which a man, through the hierodule, communes with the idols she serves and pays tribute to her sanctuary. The condemnation is metaphysical more than moral, but the numerous prophetic pronouncements on the subject indicate that the practice was common in the royal period (Hos. 10:5; Jer. 2:20, 5:7, 13:27, 29:23; Ezek. 16:20). There were many sanctuaries for the sexual cult. In periods of decline—under Josiah, for instance—they were even introduced into the Temple as serpent and other nature cults (II Kings 23:7). The principal goal was to win the favor of the gods who controlled the fertility of the fields. In the eyes of the Prophets, the practice was not only impure but futile and sacrilegious. The Law is clear: there must be no cult of man or woman in Israel. A prostitute's money is damned and prostitution in any form is forbidden (Lev. 19:29; Deut. 23:18).

The prophetic stand supports the thought that finds ultimate, and revolutionary, expression in the Song of Songs. Love is restored to its deepest significance, which is to reconstitute the unity of the human being. Woman, made from man's rib, comes back to him in a love that is extended by the mystery of procreation, where a child develops within his mother's body (Gen. 1:27 seqq.; Ps. 139:13). The sexual organs are sacred, an intimate means of expression. The individual and everything that relates to sexual life and the taboos surrounding it are of sacramental importance.

In the love act, man and woman again become one flesh and reflect the face of YHWH, source of all life and fertility. They become a living, primordial unit and recognize each other in the act of love: man *knows* the woman. (The word *yada'* means the vision of nudity, intellectual knowledge, and the sexual act.) The rejection of idolatrous and "natural" cults is the true basis for the sanctification and "intellectualization" of love and the absolute liberation of the couple. This love is conceived in its plenitude in the light and transcendence of YHWH.

Sickness and Death

Body and soul are a living unit. One enjoys life to the extent that one has YHWH's blessing; sickness puts man on the side of death. Healing is above all a spiritual phenomenon that restores the integrity of the being and his free communication with the powers of the creator. The most serious illnesses are cared for in the sanctuaries by the priests and men of God. Excavations have shown that surgery, rarely referred to in the Bible, was skillfully practiced. In addition to many ostraca, the tombs at Lachish contained three skulls showing evidence of major surgery, trepanation. At least one of the patients survived both the illness and the operation—in the ninth century B.C.[14]

Leprosy, or the disease called *tsara'at,* is the subject of long analyses in the sacerdotal code (Lev. 12, 13, 15, 21; Num. 5; II Sam. 12; II Kings 4, 5). The priest is responsible for diagnosis and also for declaring the cure of an illness. Sacrifices and ablutions compete in the purification of the patient and the house that is affected. A demon, who takes possession of the patient weakened by sin, causes sickness. He must be expelled from the tainted body (even from its hair, which is shaved off) and from any objects he may have touched, which are washed and burned. Classical remedies consist of birds, cedar, cochineal dye, hyssop, and running water, and the priest follows a strict ritual. Sacerdotal law codifies the illnesses that make man impure and establishes remedies for purification and cures. Sexual and dermatological problems are most frequently cited in the Bible.

The Bible contains strict regulations for nutrition and sexual hygiene. It aims at safeguarding public health, which takes on greater importance when related to the norms of religious purity and sanctity. The first doctor is God himself (Ex. 15:26). In the royal period, practitioners recommend the traditional treatments, based on the use of medicinal plants. Because they are God's interpreters, Prophets and priests are the best healers. They diagnose illness and treat it by means of their charismatic powers. They cure leprosy, sexual diseases, ulcers, and sometimes even resurrect the dead.

The attitude toward death, *maveth,* as well as love, *ahavah,* is a measure of the originality of the Hebrew civilization, which contradicted the prevailing beliefs in Egypt and Mesopotamia. The mythology of the hereafter that informs the neighboring religions, the details the *Book of the Dead* gives on the judgment of the deceased, the moral or magic rituals necessary to gain the grace of the gods for the salvation of the faithful soul, the excesses of funeral rites, the luxury of tombs, the artifices of the other world, the costly services of the priests devoted to the saving of souls, mummification, the lugubrious (if picturesque) funeral corteges, relations with the dead—this entire array of myths and magic was suppressed, ignored, or reduced to its simplest expression by the Hebrews.

Respect for old age and death is a function of respect for man and life—without explicit reference to an existence in the hereafter. The lawmaker's silence on the conditions of the afterlife and the ambiguity of the Bible on this point attest to a courageous break with the beliefs and customs of antiquity, against which the small, weak Hebrew people stand with conviction. Their attitude toward death, though reasonable, contradicted the fundamental beliefs of the rest of mankind. The soul, obviously, follows the body to the grave. The attention paid the corpse is a duty toward the person who is buried, who goes on being and feeling. This is why the Hebrew can conceive of nothing more horrible than to be deprived of burial (I Kings 14:11; Jer. 16:4; Ezek. 29:5).

The instructions for the last duties toward the dead person are succinct: his eyes are closed (Gen. 46:4), he is buried in the earth itself, without a coffin, wrapped in a shroud or cloak, and with a few personal effects—a sword and shield for a soldier, a mirror for a woman (I Sam. 28:14; II Kings 13:21). Embalming and cremation are not practiced. In this respect, Jacob and Joseph were simply following the Egyptian custom (Gen. 50:23–26).

Mourning is kept at its simplest. Close relatives tear their clothes, cover their beards and faces, throw ashes on their heads, and sit on the ground lamenting. The funeral cortege utters lamentation, the *qinoth,* the most beautiful of which is David's, improvised for Jonathan (II Sam. 1:19–27). Mourners gather with the relatives of the deceased, who is carried on a bier to his burial place for his stay in mysterious Sheol.

Cemeteries and Necropolises

Almost every archeological site reveals tombs, cemeteries, and necropolises. Chalcedonic funeral urns, in the shape of a house or vase, were repositories for the bones of the dead after the decomposition of the flesh. Sukenik in 1934 and Jean Perrot in 1958 discovered a number of them in the funeral caverns of Khoudeirah in the Plain of Sharon and Azor, 6 kilometers from Jaffa, and in Bnei-Braq and Hadera.

At the beginning of the Israelite period, several methods of burial may be noted. Some corpses were interred in tombs hollowed out of the earth or rock, their heads pointing east and their bodies, bent at the waist, pointing south (twelfth and eleventh centuries), with pottery and sometimes bronze mirrors. Burial may also be in huge pottery urns (eleventh and tenth centuries), or in brick coffins covered with tiles, or in common graves, sometimes 3 by 2 meters and 1 meter deep, where the dead were placed one over the other (these were probably for the poor). There is also rare evidence of cremation in this period (the second half of the eleventh century)—charred bones are preserved in pottery at Tel Qasile and Azor. Cemeteries for both man and animals (horses) are rare, but in Beth-shean the ancient necropolises contain anthropoids' funeral urns of Philistine origin.

The necropolises of Achzib (ninth to sixth centuries) indicate the custom of burying the dead in a kind of subterranean city, which became a highly complex development in Beit Shearim in the postbiblical era. Numerous objects are placed around the corpses and benches line the walls.

In Jerusalem, archeologists have tried to find the tombs of the Kings of Judah, and several have been identified. One of them, the tomb of Helen of Abidene, consists of a corridor measuring 16 by 2.5 meters and varying in height from 4 to 1.8 meters.

A burial place from the royal period was discovered in Siloam on the banks of the Kidron and has been named the Tomb of the Daughter of Pharaoh. It is a cube carved out of rock (5 by 5 and 8 by 4 meters) and is topped by a pyramid 4.5 meters high. The tomb, which resembles an Egyptian-style chapel, opens onto a corridor and a chamber with a vaulted ceiling. Several mortuary chambers of the same style, hollowed out of rock, have been found on the banks of the Kidron. The tomb of the "Overseer of the King's Palace" is inside the village. This man must have been a shrewd administrator, for the entrance to his tomb bears an inscription warning thieves that there is nothing valuable near the remains and cursing anyone who violates his place of burial, which seems to date from the seventh century. Outside the city of David, only two burial places of the royal period have been found, on Mamila Street; they contained pottery from the period of the Kings of Judah. The so-called Tombs of Absalom, of the house of Hasir and Zechariah, date from the period of the second Temple. Day by day the inventory of the excavations grows, and archeologists still hope to find the royal tombs in the depths of Jerusalem. Monumental mortuary chambers, erected in the ninth century in sumptuous Phoenician style in the Valley of the Cheese Makers, have been discovered recently. They were used for the important people of Israel, and perhaps for members of the royal family.

Sheol

As we have seen, Hebrew thought discourages necromancy and occult practices and speculation on the hereafter is very limited. Nonetheless, the dead continue their existence in Sheol. It is located underground, in the deepest abysses of the cosmic ocean, under the roots of the mountains, or in that beyond where the sun plunges each evening to bring darkness. It is the site for the final assembly of the living, a dark and chaotic domain of silence. Never is it a hell where the accounts of life are weighed. This idea appears much later, in the Hellenistic period, probably due to influences from Persia.

The Fourth Gate The Daily and the Eternal

The Past Is a Mental State

The past is completely in the mind, Paul Valéry taught, stressing the weight of historical disagreement. In order for an event to take on meaning, he wrote, it requires belief.[1] The Hebrew would have been able to accept this idea, but only by pushing it to the extreme where all history is contemporary and every event exists only in relation to the power of the word that explains it, the idea and speech. The first verse of Genesis has the skies, earth, waters, light, darkness, and time coming from the word of God: "There was night and there was morning, one day"—*Yom ehad*—absolutely *one,* in whose darkness and light the universe continues forever.

Time is an abstraction which originates in the government of the sun and moon; it has no reality of its own. Isaiah prophesies the time when the sun will no longer light the world during the day, nor will the moon at night—when YHWH alone will be the light of the universe. The tense of the Hebraic verb clearly expresses the Hebrew's notion of time's duration. Unlike the Western languages, it has no past, present, or future. The Hebraic phrase depicts situations and each of its words projects an image like a film, where every letter of the text, every accent, every breath, every pause is an essential element. There is no concern for formal logic. Reasoning by *analogy* eclipses inductive or deductive thought. Reflection is totally controlled by direct vision, and by an overwhelming power of synthesis reaches all levels of consciousness. The *time* of the action, which is essential to the Westerner, is not even secondary; it is never explicit for the Hebrew.

The present does not exist in Hebrew, or in the other Semitic languages. An action has taken place and it belongs to the preterit; or it has not taken place or been completed, in which case it is expressed in the aorist. Between past and future there is *nothing.* The date of an event is a function of its nature or character. The Hebrew conception of duration is global and specific. His realism surrounds the fact in its ramifications and consequences. It is so inevitable that everything is seen in God, *sub specie aeternitatis.* The past and the future meet in the totality of reality, from which they originate and where they blend, and to a certain extent disappear in the transcendence which founds them. Such is the basis for the *realism* of Ecclesiastes, who has been mistakenly labeled skeptical or pessimistic: "Vanity of vanities, everything is vanity" (Eccl. 1:1). The word *hevel,* traditionally translated *vanity,* means *vapor, breath,* etymologically. Indeed, Ecclesiastes states the quiddity of duration, a vapor, a breath, and sees how the daily event arises from a universe beyond the mental, from a *totality* which must involve God's universe and eternity. Thought, *mahashavah,* in the sequence of the facts of duration, is a *calculation,* a reflection on the concrete, or, to translate the word in relation to its etymological meaning, an *evaluation.* "A word which sets one to dreaming," Valéry used to say. Certainly—and the Hebrews affirm it: "There are many thoughts in the heart of a man: but the will of the Lord shall stand firm" (Prov. 19:21). These evaluations of the heart of man are his thoughts, the manner by which he receives God's counsel, in the dailiness of its duration. The other verbs for thinking refer to a conception of reality: *zamam* indicates the premeditation of an act, *imagined* (damah) before being accomplished, and thus passing from the power to the act.

Etymologically, the verb which indicates the deepest meditative thought, *hagah,* means to murmur, to grunt, to divulge, to speak, and then to meditate and to dream. Man must therefore contemplate the Torah of YHWH day and night (Ps. 1). That is to say, he must put himself in a state of contemplative receptivity before the global universe, which transcends duration, and then receive it in himself to the point of being transformed by it. A man who follows God's order becomes one with the word he receives. He identifies himself with eternal life, which dwells within him forever. There, again, thought is not discursive. Man has only to be silent internally to *listen* to YHWH, his Elohim, in order to unite with his light and be transformed into his love, which is the instrument of unitive knowledge. Meditation allows one to transcend the daily universe, and the power of prayer introduces man into the holiness of YHWH. This change allows the rebirth of man in God and sweeps his duration and dailiness into the eternity of universal life. The normal passage of the Hebrew's duration is commanded by the perfection of the Covenant which unites him to YHWH, to heaven and earth, to water, to the animal kingdom, as well as to the surrounding nations. Reality is a huge, living organism which can be understood only within its fullness or totality. Its totality is a living soul which requires the perfect functioning of each part. Should one part falter, the life of the world is in danger.

Man's daily living, then, depends on his acts, which come from his thoughts. If these are proper—that is, in conformity with YHWH's order—man will be blessed. Should they be in contradiction to the divine will, man, and whatever has been contaminated by him, will be accursed.

As Pedersen clearly understood, man's time is one with his acts; or, to express it differently, it is one with the quiddity of his effective thought.[2] His days will be what he makes of them—forever, from beginning to end; his past will determine the quality of his future. It is in this sense, and in this sense only, that time has reality: in the contents of the acts of man. That is why YHWH must protect the days of the undefiled (Ps. 37:18). Benediction and malediction come from them. The abstract measure of time into hours, minutes, and seconds is foreign to the Hebrew. The day is a function of the visible course of the sun. The moon governs the sequence of days in the month; the sun and the seasons control the sequence of months in the year. We are in the presence of a concrete duration which is at the extreme poles of the notion called "dead time." The life of duration is animated by a succession of "meetings," *mo'adim*—the days, Sabbaths, and holy days—where the sacred enlightens the profane, where the eternal informs the daily, illuminating and transforming it in the density and fullness of its transcendence.

"Eternal" is the overtaking of duration and time, the overtaking of the succession of days and generations, refound in YHWH, in the omnipotence of their reality, which is the basis of the life of man, the history of nations, the future and salvation of the universe.

The Unity and Dichotomy of Reality

Like the God who gave it being, the universe is one. It is God who, by the power of his word, draws it from the chaos of diversity and gives it its unity, just as he draws Adam out of the sleep of matter by breathing a living soul, *nephesh,* into him. The Hebrew sees man and the universe not in their physical components but as a living soul. The most current term for man is *nephesh;* before anything else, he is a soul, upon which depends the destiny of man and the world. The Aristotelian definition "the soul is the form of the body" suits the Hebraic conception, which is manifest in all of man's thoughts, acts, and interests. It is a living entity that defines the personality and will of man, for the soul cannot be distinguished from the heart or the mind. The body is dependent on the will and the health of the soul. If the latter falters, the body will suffer; if it dies, so will the body. What is true of man is true for all creation, whose soul includes man's soul and, to a large measure, is dependent on it. The Semite's consciousness of reality is global and is informed more by the powers of direct intuition, of vision, than by abstract thought.

Yet abstract thought is carefully put into play when it becomes a question of distinguishing the opposites that animate the internal dynamism of the universe. Here the Semitic view rejects the nuances of its general vision to abruptly introduce a fundamental dichotomy in the created order. It is striking how the people responsible for monotheism "covers" itself for disclosing the apparent dichotomy in the universality of reality. Just as Noah fills his ark with pairs of every animal, YHWH operates in the same manner toward the universe. Everything is in two's. God's unity, as soon as he begins to function, gives rise to complementary and contrasting realities.

On the first day he creates the heavens, which are the divine abode, and the earth, which is defined as chaotic and deserted: the sea and the desert, darkness and light, night and day. From its inception, the earth is divided in two, and this division becomes greater when Adam and Eve are cast out of Paradise for having committed the sin of pride and tasted the fruit of the knowledge of good and evil.

Good and evil introduce a host of contradictory notions into Hebraic symbolism: life and death, love and hate, justice and iniquity, purity and impurity, the sacred and the profane, anguish and joy, happiness and misfortune. The distinction between heaven and earth is reinforced: on the one hand there is the primordial chaos, darkness on the face of the abyss; on the other, the light and spirit of God hovers over the waters. This distinction constitutes the black-and-white harmony of the first day. It allows war, anguish, and death; but man's earth excludes indifference. Every soul must choose between the only two ways which divide the totality of reality: the path of good and that of evil. The choice is inescapable; it is the requirement that risks a break in the original unity. Hebrew thought, be it political or moral, cosmogonic or metaphysical, is based on this axiom: The way of darkness and the way of light share the universality of reality. On the narrow line which separates them is the endless confrontation of the just and the defiled, the good and the evil: it is a life-and-death struggle from start to finish. On this battlefield, horror attacks and destroys joy mercilessly. This is the natural world as it is, condemned to live in this manner until its total transformation, at the hour of light's final triumph over darkness, of good over evil, of peace over war, of life over death. On this path, Hebrew thought rejects the conclusions of Manichean dualism. God is one, like the totality of reality.

Conflict between Nature and the Spirit

In spite of the contradictions of nature, man, the family, the people, mankind, and all creation have the vocation of unity. This confers the *historic* character on the religion and thought of the Hebrews, in contrast to the natural religions of antiquity generally.

The universe has a beginning. A supreme will, YHWH's, gives life to it and directs its future toward clearly defined ends: the haven of salvation that will be reached at the time of the Messiah's triumph. In the interim, the organization of daily Hebrew life aims for maximum effectiveness, for a total sanctification of man, the family, and the people in view of the victory of good over evil, for the coming of the kingdom of God on earth.

All Israel's past, its laws, its traditions, and its customs are reinterpreted as a function of an ideal goal, set in the messianic future: its establishment will crown the history of mankind and the mission with which YHWH has charged Israel. In the messianic era, the spirit will have effected the transformation of nature: the daily and the eternal will be one, as will the lion and the lamb. Humanity will have become a huge, pacified family living on a new earth, under new skies. Death itself will be conquered: a miracle will permit the supreme change in creation and its joyful submission to the order of justice, love, and peace as desired by YHWH. The duty of the Hebrew is to prepare the coming of God's kingdom by subordinating his entire life to the fulfillment of the Torah, the vehicle of the divine will within reality.

The Arms of Victory

In the contradiction between light and darkness, good and evil, man is called to take a stand to assure YHWH's victory. The Hebrews put all their interest in life here below and erase from their minds the Mesopotamian and Egyptian myths of the hereafter. They push their love for life so far that they declare death *impure,* as they await its disappearance. Not only will man know eternal life, but the just will be resurrected. This apparently insane belief is part of the deepest logic of Hebrew thought, inspired by an all-powerful love of life. Is not YHWH's name the living eternal?

Between the two opposing currents in the religious history of mankind—that of the natural religions, which favor the unleashing of instincts, and that which denies the realities of the baser world—the Hebrews opt for a sanctification of the routine realties, directed toward the triumph of life over death and of the history of man over nature.

The Covenant, which celebrates the marriage of YHWH and his creation with mankind—with his priests, his people, and their Kings

—is a "war machine" introduced into nature to change its course and to prepare its revolution and rebirth in the new conformity with the transcendence of the divine will.

The Torah, the law that comes from the Covenant, defines not only a theoretically good morality but the moral transformation to which the chosen people must submit if they wish to attain the objectives YHWH assigns to its destiny. Such is the profound meaning of the Hebraic election. Because mankind was cast out of Paradise, and because it is destined to messianic regeneration and the road is long, difficult, and uncertain, a people must be chosen to keep God's trust and fight the battle which will assure the triumph of the eternal. The concepts of the family and the people, tribal solidarity, patriarchal predominance, legal purity, and voluntary segregation consented to for the fulfillment of the divine will must be understood in the context of the historic dynamism of Israel. Its religion was not a philosophy but a leaven introduced into history to assure, more than revolutionary changes, a global transformation. Thus the Hebrews must preserve the integrity of the divine message by an incredible withdrawal into their original sources, which oblige them to oppose the entire body of mankind's beliefs and practices. "They are Hebrews against the other men," Saint Paul will say later (I Thess. 2:15). How could they be otherwise, if the nucleus of their message was to denounce as illusory, insane, or criminal the beliefs and practices of all mankind, including the wanderings of their own people?

The weapons of the prophetic combat will be essentially spiritual. The Hebrew is not charged to crusade against the nations. How can he do it in his apparent weakness? His mission consists of effectuating a human community that practices the justice of the one God and establishes his order on man's earth so as to force the nations to operate in relation to this center of holy incandescence, YHWH.

The Law, Transformation, and Life

The Hebrews' absolute adhesion to life definitively directs them to practice a very strict moral transformation, destined to free them from the impurity of the fallen world and to re-create them in the light of the God of life. The biblical Law is a vast municipal ruling expanded to the dimensions of an entire people, in the hope of eventually including the universe—at least in its basic ordinances. Law and moral transformation become one: its domain is the totality of man, not only his social relations but his personal life, thoughts, feelings, sexual relations, and, what is more, his purification and sanctification in the eyes of God. The religious character of the Law, affirmed by all antiquity, is rigorously expressed. God is the unique source of right. He is the master of life, which he normalizes for his glory. Man's juridical activity is none other than his religious activity, his moral transformation. In God's unity the Hebrew sees all barriers fall, and finally man, freed from his idolatrous illusions, finds his roots, his heritage, his meaning, and his liberty. The idea of social dependence, which all law expresses, is herewith authoritatively fulfilled by the rebirth it provokes in the supernatural order of God. The Law, by the moral transformation it imposes on man, changes his days: it becomes teacher, truth, life, and the instrument of true liberty. It deploys its transcendence in the supreme dignity that places its beginning and its end in God himself.

In addition, Hebraic Law, which holds a central position in the Pentateuch, is of prime importance for the society that originated it. The Hebrew laws during the patriarchal period are only indirectly known, but tradition assumes its character in the Mosaic period, when it adapts itself to the necessities of the land of Canaan. It continues to grow, thanks to the contributions of prophetic teaching and the royal administration, for the King in Israel, as in all the ancient East, is the guardian of the law and the supreme judge. He is the protector of the widow, the orphan, the indigent, and the foreigner. He must judge fairly. The Hebrews, like Easterners generally, are unaware of the juridical formalism that characterizes Roman law. The Law is essentially oral. Even when it is codified— *the law which is written*—it is always paralleled with an oral tradition—*the law which is on the lips*—which clarifies and specifies the meaning. This oral tradition, carried in the memory of the Hebrews from the beginnings of their history, is known to us only through the rather late codifications of the Mishnah, the Talmuds, and the principal monuments of rabbinical literature. It is very difficult to date these different contributions with any precision, but the whole juridical corpus of the Hebrews has great internal coherence. Although it is impossible to distinguish its different stages with scientific precision, the Law is a major historic source for the study of the Hebraic society.

The juridical tradition of the Hebrews differs from that of its neighbors, not only in its definition of transgressions and penalties but in the very spirit of the laws. The Law always falls back on the fact that it is the Law of YHWH, revealed to Moses, who is but the herald and organ of the divine will. In Israel, the Law once handed down on Sinai no longer depends on the will of men, who are forever bound to its precepts.

The Law, of divine origin, imposes itself on man as a consequence of the Covenant—*Berith*—he has concluded with God. It is a *social contract* of divine essence and ontological nature, whose validity is renewed in different eras—after the flood, at the foot of Sinai, at the time of Joshua, in the period of Josiah—by the public adhesion of the entire people, who solemnly accept the obligations that descend from the past. The historic character of the Hebrew religion gives the Law one of its most surprising aspects: it is not presented in the form of a code, as it is everywhere else. It is inserted in the book of the history of Israel, where one finds, helter-skelter, not only the relation of Israel's past since the creation of the world but also civil, criminal, and municipal laws of procedure, which blend with theological considerations, moral commandments, and cultural and sacrificial ordinances, which combine regulations for public administration or rules of international rights—in a desperate quest for purity, holiness, and justice—which may lead to the establishment of God's kingdom on earth. The most technical laws of the Hebrews are accompanied by moving discourses, and sometimes pathetic adjurations, with the view of persuading the people to obey the commandments. The Torah is not distinct from daily life; it commands the nature and content of daily life by dispensing benediction or malediction.

The ancient peoples distinguished clearly between the *jus* and the *fas,* between civil and criminal, moral and religious law. In Israel, it is almost impossible to define the civil law and extract such articles in the aggregate of the religious, moral, and mystical commandments. Since we have no period documents on the practice of Hebraic tribunals, no reasons adduced from any judgment or contract, it is almost impossible to make a clear distinction in the juridical activities of the city. They were hidden in the unity of a life completely oriented toward the fulfillment of the will of the living God. So David, who has committed adultery with Bathsheba, and who has rid himself of the inconvenient husband by sending him to die on the battlefield, is conscious of "having sinned against YHWH alone."

The basis of such a disorder and this apparent confusion is found in Hebrew thought, which is committed to "seeing everything in God." Yet the Law is severe; on every page it reflects the ancient "Eye for an eye, a tooth for a tooth." Biblical legislation is that of a poor society of farmers and shepherds. The superior activities of a rich society, of doctors or architects, are not regulated, as they were, for example, in Mesopotamia. It is the Law of the period of conquest—which the royal period will develop by adapting it to the new state of Hebraic society. The duties of the father, the absolute master of the patriarchal family, are limited. A father cannot punish his children as he likes (Deut. 21:20); he cannot adopt a stranger and, at his whim, change the natural order of succession, which always operates in relation to blood ties and only on the father's side. It essentially concerns the transmission of lands, which are the basis for the stability of families and tribes.

The law establishes sanctions for offenders, whom it turns over to the judges. But supreme sanctions are always left in the hands of YHWH, the source and guardian of the law. In numerous cases, notably civic obligations, the sanctions are given solely in deference to God's will. The prohibition of lending at interest and the condemnation of usury; the order to "open your hand to your needy and poor brother, who lives in your land" (Deut. 15:11); the duty of defending the widow, the orphan, and the foreigner; the prohibition of all corruption; reserving the corners of the fields or the harvest of the seventh year (Ex. 23:11); and the second tithe, every three years, for the poor (Deut. 14:28) are legal obligations without juridical sanctions: offenders will be punished directly by God. Again, distinction between the daily and the eternal is denied.

Once more the concern of the lawmaker is directed to the priests and strangers, explicitly to better inform the daily by the eternal. The Levites have cities, pasture lands, and fixed revenues (Lev.

27:30; Num. 18:21, 35:1; Deut. 18:1). The foreigner must be especially protected by the society which receives him: he must not be persecuted or be made the victim of injustice; he must be helped as though he were one of YHWH's poor; he must be loved and shall be ruled by the same laws as the citizen, even in religious matters (Ex. 22:20, 23:9; Deut. 10:18, 14:29, 16:11, 24:14, 27:19; Lev. 16, 17, 19, 22). Nonetheless, it would be a curse for "the foreigner to be first and the Hebrew to be last in line" (Deut. 28:43). Liberalism is in conflict with the requirement of maintaining the supremacy of YHWH's people.

One must distinguish the alien, *ger,* from the foreigner, *nochri.* One may charge the latter interest (Deut. 23:21); one may make him pay a debt even after the year of remission (Deut. 15:3). Being outside the Hebraic city, he does not bear its obligations and consequently does not enjoy its advantages.

Civil law directs itself to two other kinds of members of the community whom it particularly protects: the hired man and the slave. This concern to protect the lowly proceeds from the great principle which inspired the formative ancient societies: they were hierarchically organized, but counterbalancing the hierarchical principle was the concern to maintain equality within the city. This regime may be defined as an *egalitarian hierarchy.*

The same theological and moral concerns are present in other rules, which gives Hebraic society its particular imprint. The laws that determine civil responsibility in cases of injury by neglect inform the life of the peasants and farmers. The man who has not covered his well is punished for the damages his negligence causes others (Ex. 21:33). The peasant is responsible if his animals graze in the field of another (Ex. 22:4), or if they injure people or other animals (Ex. 21:35). He must return, even to his enemy, the stray animal (Ex. 23:4) and help ease the animal's burden if it is falling under it (Ex. 23:5).

Thus the human will is the law of the parties: no formality accompanies a contract. But a recurring theme is the warning not to make false claims (Ex. 22:1), not to cheat on weights and measures (Lev. 19:35; Deut. 25:13), not to lie, not to sway in one's honesty in cases of trust or loans (Ex. 22:6).

The religious character of Hebraic Law appears even more forcefully in criminal matters, where responsibility falls on both man and beast. Contrary to the secular law of the other Eastern peoples, the animal that kills or wounds a man incurs a direct penal responsibility. It is God, the supreme master of the Covenant, the basis of universal harmony, who punishes it for having violated the obligations set up for it, as well as for other creatures of the Covenant (Gen. 9:5). A bull that kills a person must be stoned, and his impure meat may not be eaten (Ex. 21:28). An animal that has served to assuage a man or a woman's sexual appetite must be put to death (Lev. 20:15). Thus the Law does not operate according to the principle of moral responsibility but as a factor for the elimination of all sins or obstacles that may hinder the positive functioning of the Covenant.

In criminal matters the Law establishes the principle of individual responsibility. Collective or hereditary responsibility is condemned by legislation. "Fathers will not be put to death for their sons, nor the sons for their fathers" (Deut. 24:16). It is after a long effort that the principle of individual culpability finally emerges, with all its exigencies, in the juridical thought of the Hebrews. The texts give some indication of a period when "God avenges the sins of the fathers unto the third and fourth generations" (Num. 14:18; Lev. 26:39). At a later period, the principle of collective responsibility operates in particularly odious cases—for example, in offering Molech one's children in holocaust, for which God will punish both the doer of the deed and his family (Lev. 20:2). In special cases, also, society administers a collective punishment, which the Law restores to God's hands (Josh. 7; II Kings 9:26, 21:1). But nowhere do the tribunals apply the principle of collective or hereditary responsibility. They limit themselves strictly to the personal culpability of the offender, one of their most significant contributions.

Observing the line between the daily and the eternal so closely that it disturbs our modern logic, the law distinguishes the penalty decreed by the tribunal of men and the one that God will apply directly. "He who addresses himself to magicians and soothsayers and prostitutes himself by following them" will be destroyed from the midst of God's people (Lev. 20:6). And if the crime of offering one's children to Molech is not punished by the tribunal, it will be avenged by YHWH "destroying the guilty soul" (Lev. 20:3, 17:4,

14, 19:7, 30). Thus to the different methods of capital punishment —stoning, hanging, slaughtering, and burning—is added one of celestial origin: the destruction of the soul of the guilty. In a general way this punishment sanctions the cultural obligations of man or his duties of sanctity and purity (Ex. 12; Lev. 17, 22; Num. 9, 19). Sacrilege, too, is punished by the "destruction" of the offender (Lev. 24:15). The ordeal of the adulteress proves the extraordinary power the permanent intrusion of the eternal into the daily has in the Hebrew conscience (Num. 5); God's judgment is directly solicited to prove the transgression.

The crimes whose punishment is in the hands of YHWH can be expiated, in certain cases, by the offering of sacrifices (Lev. 4:5, 5:3 seqq.). The witness who shirked his duty to give testimony can expiate by confessing before a priest and offering sacrifice, or perhaps he made up for his lapse beforehand (Lev. 5:1). A religious sanction often is used to punish a penal offense (Lev. 19:22, 21:22). Conversely, penal law sanctions often apply to gross religious offenses, such as the profanation of the Sabbath, use of God's name in vain, false prophecy, recourse to magic or necromancy, and the worship of idols (Deut. 18:10; Ex. 22:17). These reprehensible acts are "abominations in the eyes of YHWH"—as are the sexual offenses of adultery, incest, homosexuality, sodomy, and bestiality. Not only must God and men punish these "horrors," but the earth itself will "vomit its inhabitants" because of these crimes (Lev. 18:25). The earth plays an active role in penal repression: it does not forgive the spilling of blood until it has drunk the blood of the criminal (Num. 35:33). If the murderer cannot be found, the inhabitants of the nearest city must offer the earth a heifer as a sacrifice of expiation. The intention is to "make all loss of innocent blood disappear, if you want to do what is just in the eyes of YHWH." Again, the juridical technique is inextricably tied to specifically religious considerations. The same is true for children who have struck or cursed their parents: in either case the penalty is death (Ex. 21:15, 17; Lev. 20; Deut. 5:16), as a consequence of the divine commandment handed down on Sinai in the Mosaic decalogue: "Honor thy father and mother" (Ex. 20:12; Deut. 5:16).

This explains the essential importance of intent in determining the gravity of an act. Murder is always punished by death because it is never involuntary. This is also true in the case of wounds inflicted on a slave: if he dies, the master is put to death; if he survives a few days before dying, the death penalty is replaced by a fine (Ex. 21:12; Num. 35:16; Deut. 19:1–5). Legislation concerning brawls, blows, and wounds is highly developed: if a man beats a pregnant woman and she aborts, he is fined; if the woman dies, the penalty is death (Ex. 21:22).

These considerations of intent as a factor in the seriousness of penal responsibility lighten the consequences of the ancient law of the talon, which will progressively be interpreted symbolically. "An eye for an eye" (Ex. 21:22) will evolve into a monetary fine which corresponds to the cost of the damages inflicted. Sometimes Hebraic law establishes penalties which to us seem out of proportion to the sin: "If two men are fighting and the wife of one comes to help her husband by seizing the other by the testicles, you will cut off her hand without any pity in her regard" (Deut. 25:11). It is obvious, however, that the lawmaker saw this case as a sexual crime whose penalty is independent of the damage—another direct reference to the internal universe of the Hebrews.

The Law is designated by eleven synonyms in Hebrew, showing the central importance of these ordinances in daily life. As we have seen, there is no distinction between personal moral transformation, the life of the community, and juridical activities. The Law, whose basis is found in YHWH and in the order of the Covenant, must allow the accomplishment and fulfillment in God of the life of man, the family, the people and, finally, mankind. The Law is the condition and the vehicle for the last ends of humanity, which lie in the order of salvation.

The Teaching of the Torah

In the period of this study, the "people of the Book" have not reached the same level of organization in the area of instruction that is found among their important neighbors. The Bible does not mention school at all—the very word is absent from its terminology. The child receives his earliest education from his mother and then from his father; girls learn everything they know from their mother; and the children of the wealthy have preceptors. The fundamentals are transmitted orally and not through books. (Modern minds can only marvel at these powers.) It is to the memory of the children that traditional learning is entrusted. Books, in scrolls or tablet form, are rare. The elders, priests, Levites, and scribes help the parents in the important religious and social obligation of educating the children.

The art of writing, as has long been the tradition in the East, is a technical specialization which is not necessary for learning. One can be very cultured without knowing how to write, just as today one may be highly educated without knowing how to use the typewriter. The Kings, Prophets, and prominent men have scribes, whose training must have been as thorough and exact as in the neighboring empires that made an ample contribution in this field (II Sam. 8:17). Instead of a signature, the Hebrew marks the end of a document with a cross or, better, his seal (I Kings 21:8). Diggings have uncovered hundreds of seals, some engraved in rare stones. In Lachish, a seal was found belonging to "Gedaliahu, House Intendent," who may have been the governor appointed by the Babylonians after the destruction in 586. During this period seals are affixed to documents written on papyrus, which have not survived because of the climate, explaining the lack of documentation for secular life. At that time papyrus was imported from Egypt, or perhaps was made in northern Israel. Jeremiah dictated his prophecies to his secretary, who wrote them in ink on sheets of papyrus about 15 by 15 centimeters in size. Bound, they formed scrolls measuring up to 9 meters in length. It was such a book that King Jehoiakim burned to erase the vestiges of Jeremiah's prophecy (Jer. 26). A more noble material was parchment and wooden tablets (Isaiah 8:1, 30:8), or ostraca, found by the hundreds from the royal period. It is likely that the prophetic texts were first written by the disciples on pottery, as later the Koran will be written on pieces of leather, fig leaves, or bones. The scribes used a pen cut from reeds and black ink so well made that it was used for tens of centuries without any alterations.

There is not much information on the scribes, their training, and their techniques, but it is certain that the transmission of the spiritual, cultural, and historic patrimony of the Hebrews depended largely on them. Future discoveries may provide a portrait of the scribes of Israel in the period of the Kings.

Music and Ecstasy

Contemporary research has shown a close relationship between the spiritual life, popular myths, magic, the symbolism of numbers, and musical instruments. Music has always held a central position in the life of the nation. Genesis tells us that after the creation of the world, mankind exercised three occupations: animal husbandry, the working of bronze and iron, and music (invented by Yuval) (Gen. 4: 20–22). Singing, the playing of musical instruments, and chorusing are expressed by a series of synonyms almost impossible to translate, so rich are they in meaning and so subtle in nuance. Every event— birth, marriage, death, coronations, and especially sacred liturgies and processions—are accompanied by instrumental, orchestral, and choral music. Music, like words and thought, is a powerful means of communication with heaven, with man, and with all creation. It modifies reality, and when well executed has exceptional powers of enchantment. It acts on men's minds, on their psyches, as well as on supernatural and preternatural powers.

The oldest instruments (connected with Yuval's memory) are the prerogatives of the priests and sacred liturgies: horns, trumpets, *yovel, shophar, hatsotsrah.* String instruments are entrusted to the Levites: the lyre (*kinnor*), the cithara and the harp (*nebel*), and similar instruments: the *'asor, minnim, sambukha, santerin.* There were also woodwind-type instruments: the *'ugab,* a sort of reed flute, made of cane, wood, bone, and later of metal: the *halil, abud, mashroqita.*

Percussion instruments, of brass or other metals, complement the orchestra: drums, timpani, the *tsiltselim, pa'amonim, metsiltayim*— cymbals, gongs, and bells. Thirty-six of these bells, skillfully made, decorate the high priest's robe and play a cleverly composed melody as he walks.

There is a complete body of symbolism for sacerdotal instruments, of which the most classic are the *yovel* and the *shophar,* an animal's horn. The sound man makes with it has a sacred value and ritualistic powers. The *shophar* appears in the Temple liturgies, in the theophanies, and also on the battlefield, where Gideon played it to trick the Midianites. It has not only surprise effect, but the sound of the *shophar* is a weapon in itself, with magic powers capable of driving the enemy away.

Though musicologists can reconstruct the Hebrew chants in the period of the first Temple, the orchestral music of the royal period remains unknown. The Temple orchestra is impressive, with 120 sacerdotal trumpets accompanying the melody of the harps and lyres (II Chr. 5:12). At the moment of the sacrifice, the horns are silent and the silver trumpets, whose mystical powers are greater, are sounded.

Trumpets play a crucial role in combat. They command troop movements, boost morale, and announce the course of battle.

Harps, lyres, and citharas (whose shapes and methods of production evolved considerably during the long period being examined) are the true instruments of Hebraic music. They are part of all feasts, dances, and processions, and the Prophets use them to call the spirit of YHWH upon themselves. The book of Chronicles give details on the often hereditary musical functions, placing the number of Temple musicians—where there was a music school, as in numerous other sanctuaries of the ancient world—at 4,000.

The Hebrews love song, and their hills, cities, and villages echo the Temple symphonies. The art of song and chorusing is an integral part of children's education. Burials are accompanied with music: professional mourners sing their elegies, which musicians (generally flutists) keep time for.[3] Here again, music has a mystical value and fulfills a specific cultural function: man's voice, raised to join God's, allows the deepest spiritual communication. Asaph, Jeduthun, and Heman, "music experts," are advisers to the King (I Chr. 25:1–8), for they are prophets in their way.

Music frees the mystical powers of the soul; it has a therapeutic and liberating value. The Prophets are aware of this and their assemblies are always accompanied with songs and dances to the sound of flutes, drums, and harps (I Sam. 10:5). Saul sends for David to be cured of his "humors" by the powers of music. It is a means by which man may reach a higher state, or ecstasy—where he may see the reality beyond appearances, unravel the secrets of the future, and discover the deepest meaning of the mystery of YHWH.

The Interpretation of Dreams

Dreams, which play an important role in Hebrew life, are considered divine signs which it would be unwise to ignore and fatal to misunderstand. Sleep puts man in contact with God's spirit, and it is crucial to interpret his messages. What is forecast will come to be— Elohim has so decided, and man must take heed (Gen. 40:8, 41: 32). God speaks to man in dreams, as when he spoke to Abimelech, Jacob, and Solomon (Gen. 28–31; I Kings 3:15). When the divine message is unclear, a sage must be called upon to decipher it, as Pharaoh and Nebuchadnezzar had to do (Gen. 37:5, 41:8; Dan. 2). Each dream is a manifestation of God and his message. After a dream, Gideon conquers the Midianites (Judges 7:13). But in these matters, as in prophecy, the wheat must be separated from the chaff. "Dreamers of dreams" are denounced as much as false prophets. Just as the time when God's wisdom will inform all mankind is awaited, the time when the ability of dreaming will be given to everybody is awaited: "I will pour out my spirit upon all flesh: and your sons and your daughters shall prophesy: your old men shall dream dreams and your young men shall see visions (Joel 3:1).

The dream is in the same classification as prophecy and visions. In the best situations it represents a privileged meeting with YHWH. Its interpretation consists in discovering what YHWH has placed in the soul of the dreamer. That is what is in store for him.

Literary Creation

The life of the people, its millennial history, and the revelation of which it feels itself the object result in the development of a rich oral tradition whose essential elements are collected and preserved in writing. The priests and the scribes play a decisive role in this work, whose importance must have been appreciated in the royal period, and especially from the time of Solomon's reign.

Sapiential literature is highly developed in Egypt and Mesopotamia, which the Hebrews know well. In Israel it develops in the spirit of ethical monotheism. Books of wisdom are composed from the ancient popular traditions. Proverbs, the book of Job, and Ecclesiastes illustrate this ancient literary genre.

The priests and Kings give particular importance to the laws whose origins tradition attributes to the divine revelation on Sinai, a consequence of the election and Covenant of YHWH. The Ten Commandments (Ex. 20:2–7; Deut. 5:6–21) and the Code of the Covenant (Ex. 20:22, 23:33) are the most ancient nucleus of Hebraic juridical tradition, which was enriched by texts from the nomadic and semi-nomadic period, and especially by the experience of the people after their settlement in Canaan. The institution of the monarchy accentuates the evolution of Hebraic law, whose orthodoxy is sanctioned by the priests and Prophets. Deuteronomy is the best example of the blending of the juridical current with the teachings of the priests and Prophets, all of which is taught in the name of YHWH.

Historiography develops under royal impetus and scribes are commissioned to write the chronicles of the Kings. The books of Samuel, Kings, and Chronicles are original documents, with no parallel in ancient literature. The saga of the Hebrews is reinterpreted in light of their faith. Historiography aims at the precise transmission of the deeds, discourses, and motivations of their heroes. The simplest details are minutely noted. The writers use the royal archives and are influenced by the oral traditions, which they know perfectly and which they analyze pragmatically in light of their religion. Hence the precision of this large body of literature, which in 160 chapters relates the history of the monarchy from Saul to the exile and whose documentation is confirmed by contemporary criticism (I Sam. 8, 31; II Sam. 1, 31; I Kings; II Kings; I Chr. 10–21; II Chr.). The books of Daniel, Ezra, Esther, Judith, and Nehemiah, and later Maccabees, enrich the patrimony of historic literature.

Along with the Pentateuch and historical books, Hebraic literature has the inexhaustible treasures of the work of the Prophets as it is sketched out in the pre-monarchical period and fully developed under the reign of the Kings of Judah and Israel. Especially esteemed in this literary monument, whose influence continues to grow, are the poetic books, studied not only because they are sacred writings but also because of their artistic value. It is likely that the schools for scribes preserved and taught the rules of Hebraic poetry, which emerges from the masterpieces of the various genres—psalms, victory songs, mourning chants, liturgical poetry and poetry of initiation, riddles, parables, proverbs, oracles, elegies, blessings, curses, epic, lyric and dramatic poems, and songs of love, of which the Song of Songs is an immortal example.

Hebraic poetry may be considered the vehicle of the eternal in daily life, where the people sing the works of their genius in the feasts and liturgies of the Temple. The dividing line between prose and poetry is difficult to determine because the Hebraic phrase lends itself easily to any genre. Daily language is strong and clear, and easily confused with literary prose or poetry. Parallelism, the basis of this poetry, is a means of expression which is found in most popular traditions. In this case it is enriched by the power of the sound, rhythm, and imagery of the language—incredibly opulent when compared to the relative meagerness of its vocabulary. The language in itself is concrete, but the resources of the Hebrew imagination are rich. It speaks only of God, or almost always, and yet has no recourse to the abstractions of the philosophers or—in more modern terms—to the intellectualization of the English "metaphysical" poets of the seventeenth century. The literary world of the Hebrews is none other than the world of everyday reality: earth, rock, desert, water, fire, sun, moon, stars, domestic and wild animals, war and peace, the home, hunger and satiety, life and death. But these realities are contemplated in God—resulting in the transcendental power and the mystery of the language of the Bible, whose subtlety maintains the reader's interest. It seems to hold the secret of all reality: God, the divine, heaven, angels, Satan, the demoniac world, man, all nature, and the nations of Israel, the chosen people united around the city of God, a vessel for the nuptials of its liberation.

Miracles

Daily life depends on thê eternal in a universe where creation comes from and exists only through YHWH (Gen. 1; Ps. 8, 65; Isaiah 40).

159

Every being, every life, and every act is a natural event initiated and maintained by his will, which may be affirmed by a miracle—an impossible, unexpected, salutary event which occurs because of supernatural intervention. The Hebrews live in the memory, in the presence, or in the hope of the "sign," *oth,* of the "wonder," *mophet,* of the extraordinary, *pele,* of the miracle, *nes,* that manifests YHWH's reign and triumph to all men. Storms (Ex. 14), earthquakes (Judges 5), eclipses (Joel 2:10)—all happenings outside the ordinary—are the more readily attributed to YHWH since everything depends on him. Hebrews live their daily life, from birth to death, with undiminished powers of astonishment and wonder in beholding reality and everything that relates to the life of the body and the couple. The accounts of the miraculous birth of Jesus are found in the Bible, which also gives divine intervention direct credit for the birth of Isaac (Gen. 17:15), Rebecca's twins (Gen. 25:21), Joseph, the son of Rachel (Gen. 30:22), Ruth (Ruth 4:13), and Samuel (I Sam. 1:19).

The most outstanding miracles are those which touch upon the history of YHWH's people: the revelation made to Abraham, the flight from Egypt, the crossing of the Red Sea, the conquest of Canaan, the immobilization of the sun and moon by Joshua, the victories of David and the Kings. These events maintain and renew the veneration of the people from generation to generation. YHWH also intervenes to cure the sick, to resurrect the dead, to rescue his people from danger, famine, and destruction. Samson's saga, Jonah's story, Daniel's apocalypse, and the chronicles are filled with miracles. But in the eyes of the Hebrews there is nothing surprising about them, since everything comes from God.

Sacrifices

Daily life is lived within an economy of sacrifice which rules all its activities. The center of the world is not the individual, but God—from whom everything comes, to whom everything is due, and in whom everything is fulfilled. From birth to death the Hebrew lives in conformity to the requirements of the Law by making a permanent offering of his thoughts, time, and possessions to YHWH. This fact culminated in public or private sacrificial rites. The sacrifice is, first of all, an act of allegiance which is expressed by an offering to God (Lev. 23:37; Deut. 16:17; Ex. 29:41, 40:29). To be in his good graces, subjects honor their suzerain in this way. Their sacrifice, *qorban,* is an offering or propitiatory act to bridge the distance which separates the omnipotent King from his humble subjects.

It is also the payment of a tribute which expresses the gratitude of the subject toward a sovereign whose good deeds are incommensurable. The earth belongs to YHWH; it is just, therefore, that the Hebrew, fully conscious of this, should bring the first fruits of his trees, fields, animals, and even his posterity to his God. The firstborn, in principle, belongs to YHWH and must be reclaimed by his father through an offering to God's representative on earth, the priest or Levite (Ex. 13:11, 34:19; Lev. 27:26; Num. 18:15; Deut. 14:23, 15:19). The first fruits participate in the mystery of creation and, as such, belong to the creator. This principle was applied by allotting the tithe to YHWH or his terrestrial representatives (Lev. 27:30; Deut. 12:22 seqq.).

Such is the requirement of the law. But the Hebrew offers additional votive sacrifices, *neder,* when he has received or expects a special favor. The thanksgiving sacrifice confirms the gratitude of the faithful toward YHWH, *todah.* Man, in the joy of a favor granted, may consummate his offering in a sacred banquet where God and his priests are present (Lev. 7:16, 22:21; Num. 6:21, 15:3 seqq., 30:11; Deut. 29:21). Thus in the fervor of his adoration the Hebrew may offer a voluntary sacrifice (Lev. 7:12; Amos 4:5; Deut. 12:17), *nedavah.* All these cases demonstrate the need for communion with God and the concern to give him man's food as a proof of service and adoration. The ancient concern of the human race to feed its gods is evident in the sacrificial law of the Bible.

The perpetual sacrifice, offered twice a day (at dawn and in the afternoon), expresses the bond uniting YHWH and his people. An animal is immolated on the sacrificial altar and consumed in the burnt offering, *'olah,* to YHWH. The sacrifice of a lamb's flesh and blood is accompanied by an offering of grain and a libation, which completes the sacred meal offered as a "perfume of appeasement" by Israel.[4] On the Sabbath, instead of the daily lamb the sacrifice consists of two lambs; at the new moons, the burnt offering is two bulls, a ram, seven lambs, and ample offerings of grain and libations.

On the new moon of the seventh month, on New Year's Day, and ten days later, at the great pardon on the Day of Atonement, the supplementary sacrifice includes a bull, a ram, two goats, and seven lambs. On the major pilgrimages, fourteen young bulls, two rams, and fourteen lambs are sacrificed as burnt offerings. On the eighth day of the pilgrimage of Succoth, the priests sacrifice one bull, one ram, and seven lambs in the Temple. At Passover, the daily sacrifice includes one bull and one ram, in addition to the paschal lamb and the ritual offerings and libations. Ezekiel foresees new practices for the period of the restoration of the Temple after the exile (Ezek. 45, 46).

The sacred meal of meats, cereals, and fermented beverages is accompanied by the "bread of the Presence," *Lehem happanim,* which is exposed on the altar in two rows of six large loaves and serves for the priests' communion on each Sabbath (Lev. 24:5). Sacrificial worship is accompanied by ritual fumigations, with incense rising in the light of the perpetual flame to the sound of sacred music.

The conclusion or renewal of covenants, expiatory rites, rituals of purification for physical or moral impurity, exceptional events of public life (wars, epidemics, mourning, coronations, consecration of the Temple or the priests) or private life (birth, consecration, purification, circumcision, etc.) is accompanied by sacrifices that are strictly controlled by law and tradition.

Sacrifices to the dead (Ps. 106:28) and human sacrifice (Lev. 18:21, 20:2; Deut. 12:31; II Kings 16:3, 23:10; Ps. 106:37; Jer. 7:30, 19:5, 32:35; Ezek. 16:20; Judges 11:30), very common in antiquity, and which mar the Hebraic society in periods of decline, are prohibited and condemned by the Prophets. Orthodox sacrifices refrain from using men or children as victims, but the form is perpetuated in sacrifice of animals whose blood, spilled on the earth, has propitiatory value. Burnt offerings and ordinary sacrifices assure the overflow of the eternal into daily life. Their observance and regulations are adhered to rigorously, for they involve the existence and the future of the nation.

Angels and Demons

The eternal flows into daily life in yet another way, as YHWH's messengers, spirits, and angels who announce God's message, reward the meritorious, and punish the wicked. Three of these messengers announce Isaac's miraculous birth to Abraham (Gen. 18: 10). It is angels who prevent Abraham's sacrifice, explain the nature of the burning bush to Moses, protect the Hebrews during the Red Sea and desert crossings, feed Elijah in the desert, inflict punishment on Israel's enemies, and fight alongside YHWH's soldiers (Gen. 22; Ex. 14, 23:20; I Kings 19:5; II Kings 19:35; Isaiah 37:36; Ps. 35:5). Angels, who appear to man under a human form of divine beauty, enjoy God's omniscience and supernatural powers in the exercise of their mission (I Sam. 29:9; II Sam. 14:17, 19:28; Judges 13:20).

Angels are called sons of God, saints, the holy myriads, and children of the Most High. Formerly, these supernatural beings had been able to marry daughters of the earth, giving birth to a race of heroes and giants. This ancient myth is developed in later periods, as cherubim and seraphim play an increasingly important role in religious and cultural life. Cherubim, armed with double-edge swords, guard the entrance to Paradise, out of which man had been driven; they surround God's throne—as on earth their golden statues stand over the Ark of the Covenant; and they serve as YHWH's vehicle when he moves around the heavens (Gen. 3:24; Isaiah 37: 16; Ex. 25:18–20; I Kings 6:23–28; II Sam. 22:11; Ps. 18:10). Ezekiel describes the angels in detail: they have four wings and four faces, one of man, another of a lion, one of an ox, and another of an eagle; the soles of their feet are like a calf's foot, and they move like lightning on wheels that shine like crystal (Ezek. 1).

Isaiah 6 reports the narration of the vocation of the Prophet, who sees YHWH's throne with six winged seraphim standing upon it. These angels sing "Holy, holy, holy is YHWH Tsevaoth—the world is filled with his glory." One of the seraphim, holding a live coal he had taken with tongs off the altar, burns his lips to take away his sins.

Demons appear in the universe of the Hebrews, however timidly. They personify the forces of evil and darkness that flock around the adversary, Satan. Lilith is the female counterpart of the demon: the anti-Eve, the destructive woman, the bride of the darkness (Isaiah 34:14). Azazel, to whom the emissary goat is sent, is also a demon, who inhabits the howling desert of solitude, the preferred home of Lilith and the powers of evil (Lev. 16:8). The goal of worship, purification, and sanctification is to disarm the demons and eliminate them. Yet it is significant that the Prophets do not authorize any of the magic practices common among neighboring peoples to exorcise the spirit of evil. In the opposing universes of the angels and the demons, critics discern the influence of beliefs current among the peoples of the ancient East, which the Hebrews adopt insofar as they are not absolutely incompatible with their faith in YHWH, the inhabitant of heaven.

After the Babylonian exile, the Hebrews, influenced by ideas of Iranian origin, will assign the malefic forces of nature to demons. Satan, Mastemah, Beliel, Azazel, surrounded by legions of devils rushing from their infernos, will haunt the Jewish conscience from then on, and later the conscience of the Christians and Moslems, thus playing an important role in the development of Western civilization.

The Fifth Gate Heaven

Contemplating his country's sky, which reflects the blue Mediterranean; or noting the contrasts of a subtropical climate and clear desert air; or admiring colors of bright red and deep purple, and pale blue and all the shades of the rainbow, the Hebrew sees the glory of his God and his handiwork (Ps. 19:2). It is to the eternal dialogue with YHWH Elohim that the people direct their genius. Not to philosophy, the arts, or the professions—only to the seductive confrontation with God. The people are conscious that they owe their existence to YHWH's choice. They are not a people who have created their gods; God chose them in his revelation to Abraham, Isaac, Jacob, Moses, and David, whom he made with his own hands for a definite and compelling purpose.

The narrative of Abraham's calling, the formation of the twelve tribes, their nomadic life, then their slavery in Egypt and their miraculous delivery by Moses haunts every conscience and is the subject of fathers' daily teachings to their children and those of teachers to their students. Such is the fundamental vision to which the people relate, such is the power of their calling, forever and ever—that of a God-proclaiming people having partnership with God and with the destiny of mankind. Most other peoples of antiquity were as pretentious in thinking themselves chosen by their gods for an exceptional destiny. What is original with the Hebrews is that they made their transcendental God the almost exclusive focus of their religious and national life and subordinated their fate to his law with inimitable perseverance. In conscience, they knew they were the chosen people and the allies of the creator of the universe.

YHWH is the name of the God of the Hebrews, this self-conscious people who has counted every vowel and consonant, every accent of his Scriptures, without losing a word of it in the course of a 4,000-year history. But add one more paradox to this extraordinary *tour de force:* they have forgotten how their God's name was pronounced.

This ineffable name was not dragged into the streets: it could be pronounced publicly only once a year, in the Holy of Holies in the Temple, by the high priest during the ceremony of the great pardon on the Day of Atonement. Since the destruction of the Temple, the true pronunciation of this name became almost hopelessly lost. The currently accepted *YHWH* is but a hypothesis.

This name, which could have been pronounced Yaho or Yahu, derives from a root meaning *to be.* Subsequently theologians will say: He is the eternal and absolute being; he was, is, and ever shall be; he is being. He reveals himself to Abraham as *El Elyon,* God Most High, and to Moses in these words: "I shall be what I shall be" or "I am what I am": *"Ehyeh asher ehyeh."* So God is the source, the essence, and the becoming. He is also a personal presence. To speak about him, the Hebrews use a variety of anthropomorphisms: God speaks; he comes and goes; ascends and descends; is joyful and is sad; makes plans and regrets; is angered; punishes or rewards; refuses himself, hides; gives himself; and pardons. He creates man in his image, and man does not hesitate to attribute his own gestures, thoughts, and feelings to God. This mysterious resemblance will be the basis of Job's protest, bordering on humanism. God *is* before anything else and he is the creator of all reality. He is the Most High, the God of the Celestial Armies, *Adonai Tsevaoth,* the devouring flame in the angelical hierarchies. He is one, incomparable, holy, and the source of all holiness. Beyond any concept, any thought, any praise, he is the Master of Eternity. *Elohim* is also his name, eternal center of many forces through which he manifests himself in the universe of which he is the inventor, architect, and builder.

Master of the world, he is omniscient, prescient, and omnipresent. Master of history, lord of war and peace, sovereign of all nations. He reveals himself to Abraham, gives his promise to Jacob and his word to Moses. He makes a Covenant with Israel, establishes it as a people, frees it from idolatory, leads it out of Egypt, frees it from its prison, settles it in the Holy Land, protects it from the enemy, and, if he must punish its unfaithfulness, ultimately frees it from death. He crowns Kings and saves the lowly; protects the poor, the widow, strangers, and orphans. He is truly present in the Holy of Holies of the Temple, where his people may talk to him, pray to him, and adore him.

Source of all life and all law, he is Israel's only lawmaker. On Sinai Moses receives God's Law from his own hands, engraved in rock by the divine hand. The Ten Commandments are the charter of the people, the basis for the vast body of Hebraic legislation. The Law is an absolute, derived from divine perennation that commands the world as a function of its source and toward its last ends.

There is no domain outside God's Law. Creator of the whole universe, he judges it with his whole being. Not only does he promulgate the law but he watches over it, rewarding those who observe it and punishing its transgressors. God is the judge of eternity, the one who nourishes, heals, and liberates. He confers on man the divine spark which justifies him and lifts him to the knowledge and contemplation of his mystery, source of all genius, of all truth, of all life. Having delivered Israel from its slavery in Egypt, he brings it back from all its dispersions for he guarantees forever the triumph of the primordial alliance which resolves all conflicts and allows the victory of God, king of all creation, who in his justice and love liberates all living beings.

In essence, Israel's God is transcendent and sovereign. If he rides on clouds, inspects the tower of Babel, and with his own hands disperses those who built it; if he closes the door of the ark behind Noah; if he comes down from his heavenly home to look for Adam in Paradise; if he presses grapes at wine-making time; if he appears as a hero, a bolt of lightning, a relentless judge who weighs all human emotions—joy, sadness, disgust, sorrow, jealousy—it is only in a manner of speaking. The Hebrew knows that his God is beyond this life, in infinity; he is eternity and transcendent being, at the source of the entire universe, which without him is nothing.

"I shall be what I shall be." These, the key words of the Mosaic theophany, underline one of the deepest and most persistent dialectics of the Bible: the God of the Hebrews is the god of the word. He creates the universe by his word, which shapes and forms it. He speaks to man to counsel, guide, reprimand, and save him; he communicates with him. And Moses spoke to God as a man speaks to his neighbor. This permanent dialogue moves the internal dynamism of Hebrew history and Scripture, for the creator is also the master, lord, king, father, and friend. These titles, in the form of images, translate the interior life of his God for the Hebrew. He is also the "rock of Israel," a metaphor that tends to become a substantive rather than a figure of speech.

God is invisible, yet omnipresent in a reality that is essential to all life and all creation. God is one. "There is only one God and none other is like him." This cardinal principle of biblical thought disputes the beliefs of all peoples and ages of antiquity.

The Hebrews stress the unique quality of the visitation of their God. They feel his presence as an *absolute* revelation which leaves no room for doubt. This irresistible revelation is as obvious to them as the sun in the skies: God is omnipresent, omniscient, omnipotent. Every manifestation of God makes such an impression on those who experience it that the effect is reflected in the people from generation to generation. God preserves his people because he lives in their conscience as a marvelous, miraculous, and holy presence.

The national conscience is overwhelmed by the God of Abraham, known and acknowledged as an absolute being, free of all dependence on matter or the laws of destiny. He is pure freedom. In his freedom, this transcendent God steps into creation to speak to man, as he did to Abraham when, as a test, he ordered him to sacrifice his son, or to Moses amid the thunder and lightning on Sinai. He also acts through intermediaries and messengers, the angels. But Moses has the tremendous privilege of seeing him face to face, of speaking to him as friend to friend in the Tent of the Assignation. In varying degrees, God's mystery shows itself to those who love and seek him. His glory appears to his worshipers as a blazing column to lead them through the desert night, as a miraculous flame in the burning bush, as a "light voice of silence" speaking to the heart of Elijah.

The original notion of a single, transcendent God is not the result of a logical process of learning about the world and the chain of being. For the Hebrews, Pascal's words could have been the key: "The God of Abraham is not the God of the philosophers." It is a vision which imposed itself on Israel, whether it likes it or not, and which defines and develops itself. A new religious intuition, felt as an objective revelation, places all creation, the totality of being, in the dependence of the absolute will of one God in the highest.

Israel's monotheism does not emerge after an effort of concentration on nature or from abstract meditation on the essence of God. It imposes itself as an observed and experienced fact. This is the manner in which the Prophets and the people, who believed themselves to be the object of an incredible revelation, understood and proclaimed it. It explains the aggressiveness of the new faith in a God whose will has no limit and whose all-powerful governance is exercised over the universe, conceived in its totality as a created unit. It is easy to abandon a theory derived from a meditative process. It is not possible, however, to turn from astonishment before a God who reveals himself to man and dictates his Law to him. Israel's thought, born of the vision, will not be expressed by philosophical concepts but by images, signs, allegories, symbols, and real situations. Therefore the narrative of biblical revelation marks the rigorous theological, metaphysical, and political construction in which, according to the Prophets, the most secret plan of creation must be read.

"Elohim Created the Heavens and the Earth"

Myths of creation existed in Mesopotamia, in Canaan, and among most of the important civilizations of antiquity. Biblical texts differ from them in that they base the existence of the universe on the order of a transcendent God and that they place man, conceived in the image and likeness of God, at the summit of it all. Cosmogony is subordinated to anthropogony, and the ensemble is intended to bring to light the secret of the human condition. The notion of creation intrinsically tied to God's revelation is a pinnacle of Hebraic thought; it is absolutely an innovation in the history of human thought, freed of the bonds of idolatry. Everything that heretofore had appeared to be divine, incontestable, precious, and worthy of adoration is henceforth "wood and stone," a phantasmagoria of which humanity has to be cleansed.

The Hebraic revolution renews man's awareness of the universe.

From now on, a spring is a spring and a tree is a tree—not divinities to be feared and appeased. Taboos, totems, ageless restrictions, and astral divinities lose their undisputed dignity and man is freed from the throne where Egyptian kings were worshiped as gods. The absolute being of the God of Israel is the unique, the only divinity worthy of being served—not any created thing, man or matter—affirm the Prophets.

This God is the most surprising, the most unexpected, the most incredible of all the divinities adored by antiquity. If the Hebrews had decided to propose a god who would have the least chance of acceptance, they would have probably invented something resembling this Elohim, who is intangible, invisible, unknowable, terrible and jealous, omnipresent, beyond conception—who is not born, does not grow, does not die, but reigns alone in the fullness of his glory and holiness, which is fundamentally related to his unity and transcendence. God is holy because he escapes the contingencies of the tangible world and because he rules forever in his eternal kingdom, where the life and death of every creature is determined. For the Hebrews, holiness is the equivalent of the Greeks' philosophical abstraction. This mysterious God requires holiness from all his faithful, and thus a new scale of values is defined by the Prophets and lawmakers.

These values, pitted against all man's instincts and inclinations, require him to be holy, though he may be torn by conflicting forces. He must be just even when faced with iniquity; he must not kill, he must not steal, though he may be the victim of theft and murder. He must not covet, though he is made of desire. He can overcome his condition only through election and grace. Yes, a jealous God, who asks man to be the opposite of what his nature makes him, who demands not progress but a revolution of his being, which is saved by the new possibility of grace and election.

The God of the Hebrews is also a God of grace, love, and peace. There is no contradiction in the interior life of the divinity who is sovereign omnipotence, pure will, and the plenitude of unity. Israel's thought excludes the mythologies of the war of the gods. The factors which condition man's life are not decided on Olympus but on earth, where men, not gods, affect their own lives. The struggle is no longer among enemy gods; it becomes man's affair and is related to the grandiose plan of all mankind's evolution. Hebraic meditation's primary object is man in his relations with the absolute and in his historical act of becoming.

An Environment of Highly Developed Culture

It took several centuries for the Hebrews to complete the Bible, which demonstrates an impressive uniformity of style and context in this collection of books that has been the vehicle of Israel's thought, from century to century, throughout the world. One is obviously faced with a new language of humanity and with a concept that will never lose its originality, and that chooses unexplored and incomparable ways for human communication. The thinking of Israel's elite is devoted entirely to the definition, preservation, and transmission of God's message.

The elders, the Levites, and the scribes assure the continuity of the oral and written tradition of the nation. The Semitic memory is developed to an extreme limit, which accomplishes the continuous transmission of the texts and teachings of the ancients. Memory, incomparably dependable, trained and strengthened by continual exercise and ascetic requirements, is the surest vehicle of Israel's wisdom. It is the conservator and universal guarantor of the survival of the nation and its spiritual patrimony. The object of this conscientious exercise is the Torah, the vehicle of God's will. The Hebraic language becomes a prodigious instrument for the definition and elaboration of thought. Two millennia later the biblical texts have lost nothing of their depth, luster, or fascination. The language is as rich as it is forceful. It transmits a thought whose vitality and rhythmic elaborations continue to attract and arouse a following, not through philosophy but through the immediate communication of a mystery whose origins are known. Clearly, the written tradition supports a wide body of oral teaching. And both require the fidelity of men who are capable of hearing, understanding, preserving, and transmitting them.

From age to age the Prophets inveigh against Israel, stressing its crimes, its infidelities, its sins and its betrayals. On page after page they curse weaknesses and detail the consequences of evil, fulfilling their role as they envisage it. It must also be said that this same people accepts the criticism of its inspired censors, who subordinate everything to the preservation of their religious teachings.

A Bossuet or a Shakespeare is inconceivable in an ignorant society, one incapable of understanding their work, which presupposes a public that is equal to and understands their deepest meaning. Such is the case with the Bible. The complexity of its meaning and implications, the depth of its concepts, the richness of its vocabulary, and the elaborateness of its language are difficult to conceive without a vast public attuned to its teaching. In the last century there was a tendency to describe the Hebrews as a primitive people who lived out their nomadic or semi-nomadic lives in destitution or in the poverty of their ever-jeopardized settlement in Canaan. But this destitution and poverty did not prevent the development and blossoming of an exceptional series of geniuses who enlightened the world.

The Priests and Levites

In each generation the establishment of a highly intellectual social milieu was the work of thousands of persons dedicated to teaching and preaching: the Prophets, priests, and Levites. Prophetic preaching and the Law assured the basis of this institution, which develops and plays an unparalleled role during the entire monarchical period, and especially after the reforms of Solomon. The priests and Levites, organized into a perfectly defined body, endowed with cities and ample resources, are the masters of the ideas of the people. Not only in the Temple, but in each tribe, city, and village they assure the mediation between God and his message and the people who are charged with its command. For them the will of God is the fountain of all knowledge. First of all they must teach and pass on national traditions. They back the family's educative role. Apparently, during the entire monarchical period education reached a large portion of the population. The agricultural calendar of Gezer proves that in the ninth century young peasants were taught to read and write. Shepherds and farmers reach the heights of human expression without eliciting surprise or misunderstanding in their immediate circles. That, too, is an aspect of the daily life of the Hebrews.

The priests and Levites teach what is known about astronomy, medicine, geography, history and, above all, law. But their teaching functions were not exclusive, as they were for the sacerdotal caste of Egypt or India. Priests and Levites are not a separate caste. They may marry the lowliest virgins of Israel. In addition, teaching is open to whoever is willing and capable. The functions of the priests and Levites are not an exclusive privilege or monopoly but a vocation.

In the Temple the Levites' role is that of servant and guardian, auxiliaries to the priests. In Moses' time theirs is a one-time consecration by lustration, by sacrifice, and by the laying on of hands, which assures the transmission of spiritual powers whose source is God, Moses, and Aaron. Their authority is hereditary and they serve between the ages of thirty and fifty (Num. 4, 8). Their training period lasts at least five years. Their tribe has the right to occupy forty-eight cities throughout the country. The tithes the Hebrews offer to God provide for their needs. The livestock is counted and every tenth animal, good or bad, is given to the Levites. If an owner tries to substitute a bad one for a good one, both are taken from him (Lev. 27:33; Num. 18:21). The Levites, in turn, owe a tenth of their revenues to the priests, who also receive their share of the additional tithe in the form of sacrifices offered in the Temple during the annual pilgrimages. Their income is considerable, but so is their role in the education of the people.

The Priests

The Levites of the family of Aaron are consecrated to the priesthood specifically. They alone have the right to enter the sanctuary. To exercise their vocation, they must be free from any infirmity, bodily handicap, or vice. Their marriage is strictly controlled. They must protect themselves from all contact with corpses and any other source of impurity. While exercising their duties they must abstain from wine and other alcoholic drink (Lev. 10:9). Beyond their sacrificial and liturgical functions, they are responsible for the administration of the Temple, sanctuary control, visits to lepers, and the appraisal of goods consecrated by vows. They have juridical powers in difficult cases and teach the Levites and the people the laws relating to Temple life. In the later period the priests are divided into twenty-four classes, with the high priest, the successor and descendant of Aaron, at the top of the hierarchy.

In the daily life of Israel the sacred corps of priests and Levites creates and maintains the cultural and religious level that makes the thrust of Hebraic prophetism possible. It was because of them that the prophetic message was formulated, accepted, and transmitted.

The Prophet-Apostle

The Prophets do not discover God through a long search marked by syllogisms. They are ignorant of all the philosophic elaboration or metaphysical speculation that informs the religious life of the Hindus or the Greeks. They are unaware of all theological constructions. They stand at the threshold of the contemplation of a pure vision which elevates their conscience to the supreme realities that engross and inspire them. If they speak, it is because God has spoken; if they raise their voices, it is because God has commanded it; if they judge, it is because God has legislated. Prophetic preaching is a phenomenon with no parallel in history.

The monotheistic adventure begins with a man, Abraham, who hears voices, believes them, and obeys them to the point where "madness" makes him accept the idea of sacrificing his son to God. The impassioned dialogue and his total obedience make Abraham the knight of the new faith that will mark the beginning of a historical cycle that still encompasses us.

According to the Bible, the origins of Hebraic prophecy go back to Moses, and more precisely to the theophany of Sinai. The God of Israel comes to the mountain where Moses has been for forty days. He appears to the people midst thunder and lightning and promulgates the Ten Commandments. Moses' prophetic mission is crowned with divine glory. It is a new beginning in Israel's history. Its authority is founded not on the discursive value of the message but on its divine source. The theophany initiates the prophecy. The unfolding of history—and sometimes its miracles—proves its authenticity. In the eyes of the Hebrews, only the Messiah will be greater than Moses, the greatest of men.

The Prophet and the Magician

Differing from Zoroaster, Buddha, or Apollonius of Tyana, the Prophet of Israel does not operate by virtue of a divine power he incarnates. Essentially, he is the spectator, the vessel, and the messenger of God—not a magus or magician, a common type throughout the 2,000 years preceding the Christian era among all the Eastern peoples. The magician and the sorcerer were the only recourse these peoples thought they had against the cruelty of the gods, idols, and hostile forces of nature. The sorcerer was the central pillar of ancient societies; his amulets appear at the very origins of mankind. When prophecy appears in Israel, all the nations of the world are in the grip of mysterious natural forces that sorcerers and magicians, magi and wizards, oracles and witches attempt to ward off or invoke. Only magic can deter the fatality controlling man. Magic rites are the tools of the priests and sorcerers in the service of idols. They devote their lives to the occult sciences, upon which the well-being of a city depends. Their monopoly over the occult liturgy and secrets ensures their power. It takes years of practice for the magician to be able to dominate the magical forces, to conjure up fate, to read the future by various means—mirrors, birds, stones thrown into water, incense fumes, animal entrails, the lines of the hand, lots, fumigations, cups filled with oil, dreams, incantations, sacrifices, communications with the gods, the spirits and the dead, and all kinds of signs and omens.

Magic is not unknown in Israel. The texts mention the clairvoyant, the *hozeh;* the seer, *ro'eh;* the man of god, *Ish ha Elohim;* and the prophet, *navi.* At first these four terms were not used with precision and it is difficult to know whether the early clairvoyants of Israel used the same techniques as the magicians. The fundamentalist school, represented by Kaufman, states that such methods were never used by the Hebrew seers. Moses, however, competed with the Egyptian magicians and Elias confounded the idolatrous prophets by besting them at their own game, putting similar, but superior, forces to work against them.

The seer of Israel is aware of being in direct communication with God, either by the power of his intuition or in the oracles he issues with the help of mysterious means for interrogating God, the *urim* and *tummim*. He condemns all implementation of supernatural powers except with God's intercession. All forms of magic, sorcery, divination, and spiritism are, in principle, punishable by death. King Saul renewed the old Mosaic condemnation and forbade necromancy; nonetheless, when pitted against misfortune he resorted to the sorceress of Endor. Disguised, he asks her to consult a ghost, and a specter rises out of the earth. It is Samuel, torn from his eternal rest, who answers the sorceress: Saul, his dynasty, and the Israelite army are doomed. They will join Samuel in the place of the dead the next day—the day of Saul's defeat and suicide.

Necromancy is neither unknown nor disputed but it is forbidden and illicit. And like Saul at Endor, the Hebrews address themselves to sorcerers and magicians, attracting the anathema of the Prophets and, on rare occasion, the repression of the law. Magic processes, sorcery, and necromancy, although separated from their polytheistic context, are integrated into popular religion.

The Seer

The seer and the priest have equal prestige in Israel, as in Babylonia. In the period of the Judges, Micah, the seer, has a private sanctuary consecrated to God in which he erects a sculpture and a silver idol —an *ephod* and *teraphim*. A Levite is in Micah's service. Both predict the future so well that the Danites take them and their idol, dedicated to the God of Israel, to install them in the sanctuary of Shiloh (Judges 17–18).

Samuel is a seer, a man of God, and a Prophet; but he is also a Judge and a priest, like his master Eli. Like him, he is dressed in linen, carries the *ephod,* offers sacrifices, directs the people, makes their decisions, and, even after death, predicts the future and performs miracles.

It is difficult to distinguish clearly between seer, Levite, priest, and Prophet. In an ecstatic state, the seer is inspired by God. Like the dervish, he prepares his ecstasy with tried techniques. He sings, dances, makes frenetic gestures, and fall into trances in which the spirit of God takes possession of him and leads him to the brink of madness. Saul meets a troupe of these seers near the sanctuary of Gibeon; they dance to the harp, tambourine, flute, and cithara to the point of delirium. Saul, with them, is possessed by God, who henceforth is in him, inspires him, and guides his path (I Sam. 10: 5 seqq.). Asaph, Heman, and Jeduthun, David's Levites, like the King himself, accompany their ecstatic prayer with the lyre, cithara, and cymbals (I Chr. 25; cf. I Kings 22:5). The prophets of Baal also dance themselves into delirium, and in addition, according to customs that have not completely disappeared, slash their bodies with spears and swords until blood flows (I Kings 18:26–28). Elisha, who uses more subtle means, calls for a lyre player, whose music allows him to achieve spiritual inspiration (II Kings 3:15). Elijah, his master, escapes to the wilderness, where he crouches with his head between his knees or keeps watch at the entrances to caves to hear God's command, which inspires him and makes him master of the elements—able to resurrect the dead, multiply flour and oil, or make the fire of heaven descend upon his sacrifices.[1]

Whereas seers and priests were common in antiquity, the Prophet is an original contribution of Israel, but together the Hebraic Prophets and seers bear the yoke of the one God of Abraham, Isaac, and Jacob: to spread his faith among the people. They are inspired by that heaven whose sole inhabitant is the creator of the universe. Both speak in the name of the same divinity and share the same faith. Through different means and at different levels they spread their revolutionary religion.

Internal strife may appear among the seers and Prophets. Sometimes it is even bloody. Each party accuses the other of being "prophets of the lie"—which is to say orators lacking grace and divine inspiration, deprived of all authenticity, servants of idols, and profaners of the Covenant. Behind these accusations the historian may note the political, social, and economic causes feeding the conflicts.

In the period of the Judges, the priests and the seers had another function, which was to become fundamental in the order of prophecy: that of chroniclers of the monarchy. Samuel, Nathan, Iddo, Gad, Ahijah, and Shemaiah write the chronicles of the reigns of Saul, David, Solomon, Rehoboam, Abijam, and Jeroboam. Following this, the official chronicler is attached to the royal court. The seer, who continues to function in the sanctuaries, generally belongs to the religious order in which he received his training. He is considered a son of Prophets. His order provides him with his discipline and the techniques of his vocation: learning how to offer sacrifices, interpret dreams, predict the future, operate wonders, and master the powers and the techniques of contemplation, as well as the ways of ecstasy, the incantations that prepare for it, the power of tongues, and the fervid prophecies that allow revelation of the oracles of God. Leading each group of seers is a chief, who is assisted by deputies who are eligible to inherit his powers and succeed him. Unlike the Prophets, priests and seers are paid for their services.

The role of the priest-seer was considerable in the daily life of the Hebraic society. He is recognized as the man of God in immediate communication with him. Without any intermediary, he may influence the divinity. He is the spiritual head and political guide of large groups of people. (Elijah plays a primary role on the political plane.) When the priest-seer is the head of a sanctuary or a religious order, his spiritual, political, social, and even economic role may be considerable. He is the director of the conscience of the people among whom he exercises his talents. In Shiloh, for example, the priest-seers are so important that they are the only unifying and centralizing force in the tribes of Israel. It is the man of God who foreshadows, prepares, and ultimately decides upon the establishment and the fate of the monarchy. His power, though essentially spiritual, is such that he may make or unmake Kings. One may deduce that the Christian canonists based their theory of the relationship of spiritual authority and temporal power in the theocratic society on this example.

As the monarchy became stronger and established its central organs in Jerusalem and Samaria, the political influence of the seer declined. His voice is no longer so powerful as to be heard by the

King, who has assumed the powers and prestige of the priest-seer. David and especially Solomon are political *and* spiritual leaders. They receive their power and authority from God himself, who inspires them. The priest-seer is relegated to secondary rank. Only the Prophets, to whom we must return, are powerful enough to censure the Kings and lead the people.

Madmen of God

Abraham and Moses have always been the two perfect models who inspired Hebraic prophetism. Both were the chosen missionaries of God. They began the great and incomparable tradition of prophetism: a man comes to the fore among his own people to make the message of Israel's God heard. The Prophet received God's revelation as an instrument of his will in his historic incarnation.

Abraham and Moses represent the two extremes of Hebraic prophetism. The former, who announces it, is the first knight of the faith, blindly believing the voice that inspires him, though it may require his permanent exile or the sacrifice of his only son. He does not try to oppose the will of YHWH, except to intercede for Sodom. He personifies certitude, fidelity, abandon, and love, even when it means isolation and failure—poor madman of God.

Moses is the Prophet of historic fulfillment. In his grandeur he is the mediator between his people and God; man of the great dialogue and its supreme interpretation, alone whether he is facing God, his tribes, or his enemies; prophet of an incomparable obsession, from which he tried to escape but of which he is prisoner. He must accept the divine will and realize his destiny, plagued by doubt, denial, fear and trepidation. He is also the man of sorrow and revolt, preparing the exodus from Egypt, the crossing of the desert, and the bestowal of the Law of Sinai. His mission is ended just as his people are about to be settled in the Promised Land. Both of them, Abraham and Moses, are *Hebrews,* men on the march, with their people, toward that which is beyond the promise, guided by a transcendent voice that inspires their undertaking and the outcome of their mystical struggle.

The Writer-Prophets

Abraham, Moses, and all of Israel's charismatic leaders draw their power from the spirit of YHWH, who controls man's destiny. The spirit breathes where it will. God's choice falls upon a sterile couple and a people emerges; on a man who stammers, Moses, and makes him his "defense lawyer"; on a woman, Deborah, and she is transformed into a military leader; on an outlaw, Jephthah, to make him a Judge of his people; on shepherds, Saul and David, to make Kings of them.

A man of God is not chosen with his consent; it is a unilateral act. Samson is vowed to the Nazarite by his mother; Samuel is of miraculous birth, as are the Patriarchs Isaac and Jacob; Moses is saved from the waters; Jeremiah knows he is chosen while he is still in his mother's womb: "Before I formed thee in the bowels of thy mother, I knew thee and before thou camest forth out of the womb, I sanctified thee, and made thee a prophet unto the nations" (Jer. 1:5).

The Prophet is invested with a supreme mission: to orient the course of history in the direction God wishes. He has the power to overthrow and demolish, to build and plant. Elijah and Elisha, in the extraordinary cycle of legends their actions inspired, moved prophetism in the direction of political activity. The strongly theocratic monarchy had replaced the priests' and seers' control of spiritual authority by centralizing worship and making a bureaucracy of the priesthood. After Elijah and Elisha, the writer-Prophet alone —and often against everyone else—fulfills the functions of the spiritual censor. The fundamental change in prophecy began in the middle of the eighth century, the high royal period, and continued to the end of the sixth century and the two national catastrophes in 722 and 586. The prophetic message is delivered in its purest form against the extreme threat of Assyria and Babylon.

The Prophet thinks, preaches, and acts in the daily life of his people. One day he hears a voice, sees a burning bush filled with God's glory, meets an angel. He is enlightened; he is suddenly transformed into the creator's agent and advocate.

The lion shall roar, who will not fear? The Lord God hath spoken, who shall not prophesy? (Amos 3:8)

Frequently the Prophet tries to evade his election: from Moses to Jonah, the normal reflex was to flee the place where God manifested himself and to shed the feelings with which he was filled. Only Abraham and Isaiah submit to their destiny without revolt or resistance. The others know what terrible days and suffering lie ahead for them as YHWH's heralds.

Since the Prophet carries out his mission in the political atmosphere, he stands guard at the city gates to warn the people of misfortunes and, if possible, exorcise them. The Prophet speaks, acts, threatens, and promises in the presence of his listeners. In a sense he is a political being, but not in the sense that the term is used in modern times. His "party" is God and his only "platform" is the justice and peace that will result from the coming of the kingdom of God and his new order. The Prophet is inspired, but his contemporaries see him as a psychopath who shows no concern for decency, favor, logic, or human respect (II Kings 9:11; Jer. 29:26; Hos. 9:7). He is possessed by a presence that dictates his behavior and his words. He is the object of a visitation, and the power he embodies, initiated by revelation, is absolute in its determination. He himself is nothing; his personal spirit has no reality except by the grace of God, who reveals his secrets to him in direct speech. The Prophet is in dialogue with the creator of heaven and earth, with the master of history, who leads his people to death or salvation, who scatters or unites them, who destroys or saves them, according only to his will. It is impossible to comprehend or conceive of the Prophets outside their historical context. But even within it, the paradox and mystery of prophetic preaching remains.

The Prophet is neither priest nor head of state. He is a man of YHWH and he proves his quality by the truth and power of his words or actions, which often take on a symbolic character. They are designed to stand out. Hosea marries a prostitute as a symbol of Israel's infidelity. Isaiah goes about naked for three years to announce the misfortunes of his people (Isaiah 20:2, 3) and he gives symbolic names to his children. Jeremiah puts a yoke around his neck. Ezekiel has his bread baked on cow dung and human excrement; he eats a parchment; goes through periods of muteness and immobility tied to his bed (Ezek. 3:22 seqq.); he loses his beloved wife and ostensibly does not mourn her (Ezek. 24:15 seqq.); he shaves his beard and head, burning a third of his hair in public, cutting another third with his sword, and with the remainder signifying the source of the fire that will burn Jerusalem (Ezek. 5:1 seqq.). In his ecstasy, the Prophet is often delirious: glossolalia is one of the signs and expressions that denotes the possession on which his power is based (Isaiah 28:10).

The Powers of the Prophet

Prophets are endowed with supernatural powers. Their political theology is based on the certitude that divine intervention can force destiny's hand to implement the impossible. (A miracle is a realization of the impossible by the intervention of a superior power, for which the man of God intercedes.) Armies are routed, sieges are broken, famines are overcome, the dead are revived, the sick are healed, bread is multiplied, waters are parted, and punishments and rewards are unexpectedly meted out—all with the personal intervention of the Prophet's acting on God's orders, who commands the elements. Celestial legions move to conquer Israel's enemies. Thus miracles are God's normal instrument for effecting historical changes. The people, taught by the Levites, priests, seers, and Prophets, live with both memory of and hope for miraculous delivery from their evils. Though we have the written works of some twenty Prophets between the reigns of David and Josiah, hundreds of others, known and unknown, performed their office. The Prophet is an orator and sometimes a writer, but his power comes from his vision and the divine voice that inspires and authenticates his mission. In the ecstatic state, he sees beyond appearances and the present. Reality in all its fullness is revealed to him. He sees even hidden things that happen afar, and he knows the future. He can detect donkeys that have gone astray and tell the outcome of a battle yet to be fought. Like Ezekiel, he can levitate. And like Moses on Sinai or in the Tent of the Meeting, he can see and speak to YHWH face to face. He understands the depths of men's souls and directs them to do his will, which is none other than that of the heavenly master. Clothed with hides or linen, he awaits the inspiration of the spirit of God and ecstatic surrender to the mystery of the union. So great are his powers that he retains them even after death: a corpse is resuscitated after being placed in contact with Elisha's bones (II Kings 13:21).

The Prophet does not always share the earthly destiny of other mortals. Like Elijah at the end of his career, he may be taken up into heaven in a whirlwind and a chariot of fire (II Kings 2:1 seqq.).

The Kings and people look to him as a director of conscience, a judge, a doctor, a counselor, and sometimes a strategist. He is the conscience and heart of the nation; its share of heaven—and its consolation. The very act of approaching a man of God fortifies the ordinary mortal and puts him in contact with the divine powers that inhabit such a man (II Kings 4:23 seqq.). The Prophet sanctifies his people and directs his Kings. Inspired men are always part of the King's entourage: Gad and Nathan attend David, Shemaiah attends Rehoboam, Ahijah attends Jeroboam, and Amos attends Jeroboam II. They serve as counselors and censors. Nathan's audacity in criticizing David indicates the measure of their courage (I Kings 20:35; II Kings 8:7; Neh. 6:7 seqq.; II Sam. 12:1–15).

A Universal Dispute

With the appearance of a new type of man, the writer-*navi,* prophetism changes in nature. Its exterior characteristics lose importance in relation to the contents of its message, which are defined with unsurpassable clarity from the eighth century forward. Animal hides, ecstasy, sacrifice, and glossolalia become secondary. Henceforth its preoccupation is preaching and political action for the promotion and triumph of the essential Mosaic ideals.

Amos is the first of the new Prophets: a shepherd from Tekoah who lived during the reign of Jeroboam II (782–753). Possessed by God and torn from his flocks, he immediately rose to the heights of political courage and poetical expression. Twenty-eight centuries separate us from him yet his message is still meaningful. He denounces the crimes of his King, his people, and the neighboring nations. He condemns hypocrisy and luxury, injustice and war, corruption and vice. The clergy and the rulers band against him and he is expelled from Bethel. His message is that of a thinker and a brilliant poet. For him, Israel—elected by YHWH and dedicated to the fulfillment of the sanctifying will of its Lord—plays a unique role in the economy of universal salvation. But first God requires a just and holy life: the sacrifices and liturgies of the sanctuaries are despicable if they mask injustice and sin (Amos 5:25).

This Prophet makes the triumph of justice and the great spiritual, moral, and social ideals the condition for national survival. Indeed, he introduces a revolution in values and gives primary importance not to man's worship of God but to justice and respect for human values, to the protection of the weak and the poor. Israel will be judged and sentenced "for having sold the just man for silver, and the poor man for a pair of shoes" (Amos 2:6). The rich, the powerful, the notables, the Kings, and the priests are nailed to the pillory and severely scourged for their crimes against the poor, against justice, and against peace. There is no specific magical or mythical value to worship; salvation depends on God's grace and man's justice. If Israel is punished for its crimes, it will be restored in the joy of the final liberation. His eschatology begins with terrifying perspectives: waves of invaders will initiate the catastrophic end of the world, described as the invasion of an army of locusts. He denounces the cruelty of the world, which is destined to death. Consequently, other Prophets develop this theme of the destruction of the world in an apocalyptic tone that intensifies from Hosea to Joel, from Isaiah to Micah and Habakkuk, reaching its apogee in the outbursts of the incomparable Prophets of doom: Jeremiah, Ezekiel, and later Daniel.

Jeremiah remains unmarried so as not to have children. His neighbors in Anathoth find him so unbearable that they try to assassinate him. Later he is arrested for disturbing the peace, thrown into prison, beaten, freed, and arrested again, and this time he is condemned to death. Saved by some officers, he resumes his criticism. His secretary, Baruch, publicly reads his works on the Temple grounds, whereupon King Jehoiakim orders the seditious texts burned and instigates a new arrest of the Prophet, who goes into hiding. In the reign of Zedekiah, Jeremiah at first enjoys the favor of the King, whom he advises. Then he breaks with him and denounces the royal policy, which he considers catastrophic. When the nation is attacked by Nebuchadnezzar, he preaches unconditional capitulation, restitution, and desertion. Again, the King condemns him to death but organizes his escape behind the scenes. Babylon, the victor, frees the reimprisoned Prophet, who exiles himself to Egypt. There he censures the idolatry of the Jews, before disappearing under suspicious circumstances. This is the sad career of one of Israel's most inspired men. He cursed his world and his times, condemned Kings, censured priests and powerful men, preached rebellion and encouraged treachery, but escaped death because of the great mystical respect surrounding the man of YHWH.

Thus the Prophet bears witness to an absolute requirement that he presents in the creator's name. He defends neither an idea, doctrine, or theory, nor the interests of a group, class, or nation. His claim is of a divine nature, metaphysical and universal. This explains his extreme stands.

The point of departure of the prophetic movement, put into motion by the vision and the voice of God, is an open revolt against the established order, against man's nature and the nature of things. The ultimate goal of the prophetic claim is the total change of reality and its rebirth in the supernatural order of justice, unity, and love.

Separated from their community, the Prophets engage in running disputes with the city, its social structure, its gods, its beliefs, its ambitions, its luxury, its hypocrisy, lies, and injustices. Hosea, Amos, Isaiah, and all the other Prophets are unmerciful toward the life style of the royal period. They reproach the people for abandoning the purity of former times, for serving pagan idols, exploiting the poor, living in overly sumptuous luxury, for eating, drinking, and dressing too well, for perfuming themselves excessively, for living in frivolity, for fornicating, and for enriching themselves at the expense of the poor—all this contrary to God's Law, whose definition they had influenced.

The protest goes further, condemning man's enslavement to his labor and demanding the respite of the Sabbath even for the foreigner, animals, and nature. This thinking culminates in the idea of a perpetual Sabbath, that is, a civilization of leisure where man will be freed from the curse of work.

Addressing their challenge to the city, the Prophets spared neither King nor priest nor notable—it may be said that these were their preferred target. Just as Samuel objected to the institution of the monarchy, which was supposed to represent a radical change in the history of Israel, the Prophets criticize the effects of the regime: the lax observance of the Law and ancient customs, the power and high-handedness of important personages, and the exploitation of the poor, whose "flesh they have eaten and whose skin they have plucked from them" (Mic. 3:3–5). Most severely attacked are men in high places, "the enemies of good and the friends of evil" (Mic. 3:2). In so doing they operate not only in the spiritual and moral order but also in the political and social sphere. Sometimes their attacks on royal policy are so vehement that they are imprisoned or condemned to death. Not one of them is indifferent to the temporal order because of his love of God. Quite the contrary: everything belongs to God, even the King.

The protest does not end at the national frontiers; it encompasses the idolatry and crimes of all nations. Today the diatribes against idolatry seem unexceptional but at the time they were revolutionary and bold. To state that the gods of all the other nations were nothing but "stone and wood" was to undermine the fundamental structure of universal order and, what is worse, add sacrilege to rebellion. Despite their weak and precarious condition, the Hebrews dared to denounce the evils of Egypt, Assyria, and Babylon.

But the revolutionary claims of the Prophets went even further, to attack the nature of man and the world. Physical man, dominated by his instincts and desires, his hate and violence, must be transformed into a new being who will have repudiated his nature and become similar to the ideal image of the just person created in God's image. He will live by the law of love and refrain from evil. Not only will nations be transformed but the animal kingdom also: the wolf and the lamb will live together in peace. Liberated man will live on a new land and under new skies in an absolute and definitive revolution of the natural order. The prophetic vision, fulfilled, will have become history. God's justice will no longer differ from man's. It will rule heaven and earth and end the Hebrew's quarrel with the creator's justice.

There remained one more step for the prophetic movement to take, a last barrier to overcome: the one separating life from death. At the end of the monarchical period a last hope pervaded the Hebrews: death itself would be conquered; the dead will rise again on the day of the triumph of the God of life. Injustice and sorrow, therefore, are transitory entities on man's long road to deliverance.

Love, the Basis for Ethical Monotheism

In the course of the five centuries of the monarchy, the Prophets, proceeding from the traditions and conditions of patriarchal life and the period of the Judges, developed a conceptual structure whose richness has not been exhausted by centuries of meditation. It is not a rational dialectic but a body of broad affirmations that aim at translating the powers of the vision and attuning man to the realities of his divine vocation.

The basis of their ethic is love. The ancient commandment "You will love your neighbor as yourself," identical in essence to the other: "You will love YHWH your Elohim with all your heart, with all your soul and all your strength," expresses one of the ontological bases of the Hebrew universe and defines the real order that must assure man's normal relations. Since the individual is part of the social body, he is a creature who conditions the harmony of the universe and must, consequently, bend to its law. Love is not a relative sentiment, to be taken lightly. It is the reality and the source of all life and all peace. When the "counsel of peace" obtains between two people, love develops between them because their wills become one (Zech. 6:13). The union of wills is the miracle that makes love, the source of all life, possible.

Peace and blessing, like love and life, are so closely linked that it is impossible to dissociate them. They are two facets of the same plenitude of strength and life. Peace is to evil what light is to darkness (Isaiah 45:7; Jer. 29:11). He who has peace has everything; he is blessed with the fullness of life, salvation and deliverance, liberty and light, joy, fecundity, and love. Peace accompanies the one who is blessed: he is at peace with his household, his posterity, his friends, and his goods. Everything flows from a single source, the perfection of his soul and his life in God. Peace is a supernatural and all-powerful reality that defies all risk and danger. He who is blessed is saved from every evil by his God. Death, famine, affliction, anguish, war, calumny, slander, drought, frost, wild beasts, and illness cannot touch him, for God is his salvation (Job 5:19; Ezek. 34:25–30). Peace comes with the victory of God's kingdom and the rule of his Law, a concept that leads to hope for the abolition of war and an era when warfare will be forgotten (Zech. 9:9–10; Isaiah 9:1–6, 11:10–14, 65:25).

The Hebraic dream thrives on the expectation of a renewal of the realities of the terrestrial paradise at the hour of the triumph of God and his Messiah. The Prophets provide the major theses of the messianic theory, which will not fully develop until the return from the exile. Later, it will take on the impact that today we recognize in Judaism and, to an even greater degree, in Christianity.

God Lives among His People

The intervention of God in history, because he is its master, assures the victory of the innocent over the wicked, of good over evil, and prepares the ultimate happiness of the coming of the Messiah.

Sin bears its own penalties. God's judgment is timeless and concerns every living being. One central idea rules the metaphysics of God's judgment: man is what he desires to be. He identifies with what he loves, and his answer to the essential question—to be or not to be? to live in God or disappear into nothingness?—comes freely from himself and is eternally recorded. What develops is the notion of the judgment of God, of the "day of the Lord" that will be effected for Israel and for all nations. All creation will be judged on the day of the messianic birth of the new heavens and new earth. Nations that resist God or his Messiah will be destroyed. Kings who attack Zion will flee in panic and be swallowed up in the same apocalypse as Gog of Magog. The victory of Israel's God will result in the conversion of nations. All the families of the earth will bow down before him and will follow his law of justice and love. The pride of the mighty will be broken. The just man who has suffered and his people, formerly prisoners of their humiliation, will become the keystone of a reconciled and redeemed humanity. God's victory allows the return of the exiled, the rebirth of Zion, and the rebuilding of Jerusalem. Once again the Temple will become the place of the real presence of the God of Abraham, the source of universal and eternal salvation. The vision sharpens and enlarges: from the ends of the earth, all nations and peoples will bring offerings to the God of Israel. His Messiah rules forever in glory. The rest of Israel is saved; the exiled have been freed from their misfortune, pacified, and converted. Henceforth their hearts are filled with God's Law and they risk no relapse—they are pure, just, prosperous, and strong. Peace reigns forever over the earth. Banished forever are war, misery, injustice, hunger, sickness, ignorance, hate, and sin. This revolution is possible because the earth will be filled with the knowledge of God. Man will be transformed in love, pardon, and peace. The victory of the Messiah will be marked by the birth of a perfect humanity. Death itself will be vanquished. "And many of those that sleep in the dust of the earth, shall awake: some unto life everlasting, and others unto reproach, to see it always. But they that are learned shall shine as the brightness of the firmament: and they that instruct many to justice, as stars for all eternity" (Dan. 12:2–3). The realities of divine justice will be absolute and their effect will be retroactive, in the ultimate fulfillment of the promise.

Liberty, Joy, and the Hope of Israel

The myth upon which the nation's existence rests, and is all the more entrenched because of its historical reality, is the exodus from Egypt and liberation. Passover, the principal Hebraic feast, is a reminder of the harshness of slavery and Pharaoh's hold, of Moses' greatness and YHWH's miracle, of the liberating God and the benefits of liberty. Never has the ideal of deliverance been so deeply experienced as by the Hebrews. Significant and all-encompassing, Passover commemorates the passage from slavery to freedom, from anguish to joy, from darkness to light. It also spells the defeat of Pharaoh and his people before Moses and the Hebrew slaves. It shows the triumph of YHWH over the gods. Passover is celebrated each year as if it were a contemporary event because each generation must free itself of its pharaoh and relive the miracle. Each individual feels himself directly engaged in this major event, which is the precursor of absolute deliverance, the final messianic Passover.

The Hebrew knows he is free by the grace of God. He was delivered from the pagan myths and mysteries, the pagan temples and gods. He also feels freed from nature, which he no longer considers a blind or fatal power. Nature, too, is God's creation and is no longer a threat. Man, created in the image and likeness of God, is called upon to control and cultivate it. Yet he must not become a slave to his own work. The seventh day of rest guarantees that. The Law guards against the temptation of capitalistic hoarding, forbids the charging of interest, and demands a periodic check on boundaries and subdivisions of land. The Hebrew's faith has delivered him from hate and fear. He lives in the sublime and divine presence. He does not fear death, for it, too, will be overcome. His total reconciliation to his condition explains his joyful life.

Never has joy been so enthusiastically proclaimed. The book of Psalms is an ever-current collection of the songs of the soul's felicity. The joy is deep, lasting, and informed by the assurance of primary knowledge and a precise vision. In the worst moments of history or life, the Hebrew knows that man's fate is interconnected with three basic facts of reality: night and evil are the province of the devil; the just man must confront them, at the cost of martyrdom if necessary; at the end of night comes YHWH's judgment, which marks the inevitable defeat of evil and the victory of that which is good. Dawn finally replaces darkness and proclaims the glory of the messianic reign. When misfortune strikes, the Hebrew knows how to wait for the hour of joy.

The daily life of these men is dedicated to the joy of their union with YHWH and their days are accomplished in the happiness of the Covenant that their poets celebrate in an endless liturgy. They sing of the transcendent and immanent God whom they love and serve, and they praise all creation, the work of his hands. An extreme familiarity attaches the Hebrews to the land, sun, stars, moon, and animals. Tirelessly he praises creation and its masterpiece, man —body, soul, and mind. He sings of the love that fills his household. The Song of Songs, a poem written to the love between two human beings, is in some respects a national anthem of the Hebrews.

Their joy is not blind. They know the price of flesh and blood, its limitations and tragic condition, while maintaining their hope. Man must trust in God until the moment of complete deliverance. To show man's hope, various (five) synonyms reappear as a lietmotiv in the Bible. YHWH is the real name of hope, which is why, even in the face of death, hope is not in vain. Hope is a living link between God and the deliverance of Israel—the expectation of the eschatological realities by which the real order of the world will be reestablished forever, in the truth of love and the plenitude of peace.

Epilogue

Eschatology and Messianism

The internal dynamism of the biblical people springs from two thoughts: the memory of the lost Paradise and the expectation of its restoration, when Israel's and mankind's destiny will be accomplished. The strength of these two myths explains the perseverance and strength of the Hebrews in preserving their faith, language, and culture from the threats of time.

The remembrance of a lost Eden is renewed by admiration of Israel's past glories, of its patriarchal election and partnership with God, in whose image it was created. The power of tradition gives the nation courage when it must fight for its survival, which is all the more important since, in the Hebrew conscience, Israel's future is linked to that of all mankind, for whom it validates the promise in the grace of God. Awaiting its ultimate fulfillment, the nation is certain of its past and is inspired by the notion that YHWH, creator of the world and Israel's ally, will lead Israel and all nations to their salvation. The present condition of the world, Israel's misfortunes, the reality of evil, war, hate, the success of the infidel, and the arrogance of the iniquitous are transitory, a nightmare which is forgotten the next morning. One may rest assured, for YHWH is coming to create a new heaven and a new earth in keeping with the fullness of his promise and his Covenant.

God's decisive manifestation is the nucleus of Israel's eschatology and messianism. Once more history is the essential expression of the religious thinking of the Hebrews. The Prophets describe the day of YHWH in the same terms as the ancient theophanies—Abraham's, for instance, or the exodus from Egypt, the gift of the Torah, the war of the conquest, the Covenant with David (Isaiah 10:24, 11:15, 43:16, 48:21, 51:10, 52:11; Hos. 2:14; Ezek. 37:26). YHWH will appear to judge the world: to condemn the unjust, to save the innocent, to reestablish Israel and punish the unfaithful nations. Their revolt and the wars they unleash will occasion their punishment and their conversion. The nations that defy God or his Messiah will be crushed; the kings who attack Zion will be driven away. YHWH, himself, will defend his heritage and crush his enemies to assure Zion's eternal victory.

The more precarious the country's position, the stronger its hopes. Salvation is linked to the judgment of a merciful and just God. He will conquer his enemies universally, and this cosmic victory, obtained with the help of his allies, will be manifest in the history of Israel and the nations (Isaiah 27:1). His victory will not be blind. Its result will be the destruction of evil, which stands in the way of love. It will conquer the false gods, the powers of evil (Jer. 25:15; Ezek. 25, 32), and the iniquity of Israel as well (Hos. 4:1–2; Mic. 6:1; Jer. 11:21, 20:1–6). Punishment will come in the form of the sword, famine and pestilence, fire and earthquakes, or the horrors of war (Jer. 5:15, 14:12; Ezek. 6:11; Amos 1:11, 2:13, 5:3 seqq.; Isaiah 5:26). The day of YHWH will necessarily be a prelude to the triumph of God on earth because the punishment of evil must precede the absolute reign of justice.

The day of YHWH precedes Israel's restoration to Eden's splendors:

> The Lord therefore will comfort Zion, and will comfort all the ruins thereof: and he will make her desert as a place of pleasure, and her wilderness as the garden of the Lord. Joy and gladness shall be found therein, thanksgiving, and the voice of praise (Isaiah 51:3).

Peace will reign on earth, even among the animals; infant mortality will cease; the human life span will increase so that death at one hundred will be premature (Isaiah 65:20). The day of YHWH, the living God, will mark the victory of life over death. This idea becomes increasingly accepted through the centuries. The myth of Paradise regained crystallizes in the expectation of the Promised Land. Once the latter is won, hope is directed toward that time when it will be delivered from evil on the day of its final redemption. Amos, the first of the great writer-Prophets, stresses the catastrophes that will accompany the day of YHWH (Amos 7, 8, 9), which will consist of darkness and not light (Amos 5:18–20, 8:9). Salvation will include only those who love God. They alone will be protected from the apocalyptic catastrophes made inevitable by the world's misdeeds. For them, the kingdom of David will be restored to its ancient glory (Amos 9:11–12) in the new era of peace and happiness that will survive YHWS's judgment. Hosea also accentuates Israel's central place in eschatology. It will be delivered in spite of its sins, thanks to YHWH's love, and restored to its original strength. Isaiah and Micah expand their vision to encompass the universe. God's salvation will concern not only Israel and the nations but nature itself; the skies and the earth will be renewed on the day of YHWH.

Zephaniah combines the destiny of the nation with the fulfillment of mankind's last ends. The iniquity of Judah and Israel will not be judged less severely than that of others, who will be purified in the fire of God's anger. In the bloodshed that closes the history of the kingdoms of Judah and Israel, Jeremiah, Nahum, Habakkuk, Ezekiel, Haggai, and Zechariah find the incomparable accents of the eschatological lyricism that reaches its zenith in some of the psalms and especially in the last chapters (40–55) of the book of Isaiah. Deutero-Isaiah is the most complete doctrinal resumé of Israel's messianic eschatology.

The day of YHWH has brought its punishment. The new era of redemption rules. In his grace and mercy, YHWH delivers his people. A new Passover marks the rebirth of Zion, which is filled with the survivors of the apocalypse. Jerusalem and the Temple are rebuilt (Isaiah 44:28). YHWH reigns in Zion over his people, who have been redeemed and freed from their enemies forever.

Israel's salvation precedes the redemption of the nations. It is the servant of peace, light, truth, and love. The blind shall see, the deaf shall hear, the captives will be freed from their dark cells. It will be the light of nations, and because of Israel the salvation of YHWH will cover the universe, transformed into a new and incredible reality of goodness and love, justice and peace. The exile of Israel and Judah accentuates the promise of a universal salvation that conquers death and renders justice to man's suffering: the resurrection of the dead. Ezekiel and Daniel push the Hebraic eschatology to its ultimate revelation. The way is opened to the apocalyptical symbols that will forever maintain their grasp on the nation and on a large segment of mankind after the triumph of Christianity.

Apocryphal and pseudo-epigraphical literature will prepare the way for the teachings of Jesus and the New Testament. Henceforth the claims of the triumph of life, justice, and love will be universal in their essence and finality. The entire earth is dedicated to the exigencies of the kingdom of God and its deliverances. At the end comes the announcement of the Messiah, who will bring the deliverance the world awaits. The Messiah is YHWH's anointed one, *Mashiah*. Chosen by him, he is conceived of and hoped for as a King and ideal priest (Lev. 4:3; I Sam. 24:6), in and through whom all the promises of the Covenant will be realized. Peace and blessings will reign after he has defeated all his enemies. His power comes from YHWH whose son he is, the eldest, the beloved.[1]

Isaiah and Micah, in the spirit of the ancient tradition, foresee an extraordinary and mysterious birth for this person:

> Out of thee shall he come forth unto me that is to be the ruler in Israel: and his going forth is from the beginning, from the days of eternity . . . till the time wherein she that travaileth shall bring forth . . . And he shall stand, and feed in the strength of the Lord . . . and they shall be converted, for now shall he be magnified even to the ends of the earth (Mic. 5:2 seqq.).

Isaiah goes into a detailed description of the heavenly peace this descendant of the line of Jesse will bring:

> The wolf shall dwell with the lamb: and the leopard shall lie down with the kid: the calf and the lion, and the sheep shall abide together, and a little child shall lead them . . . And the sucking child shall play on the hole of the asp: and the weaned child shall thrust his hand into the den of the basilisk. They shall not hurt, nor shall they kill in all my holy mountains, for

195

the earth is filled with the knowledge of the Lord, as the covering waters of the sea (Isaiah 11:6 seqq.).

The ancient dream that has informed the nation since the time of the promise made to Abraham—that of Israel's becoming a world power by the supernatural victory of YHWH, not by the power of armaments but by the powers of his divine omnipotence—is confirmed by prayer and hope and provides refuge in times of adversity. Israel's mission is not to assure the victory of one nation over the others but YHWH's over all of them, through a supernatural reconciliation of man and nature with the word. Again, the domination of the King of Israel is conceived of as from "sea to sea, and to the extremities of the earth," and within the framework of general disarmament:

I will destroy the chariot out of Ephraim, and the horse out of Jerusalem, and the bow for war shall be broken: and he shall speak peace to the Gentiles (Zech. 9:10).

On that day man's heart of stone will be circumcised and replaced by a heart of flesh. YHWH's Law will be engraved upon it (Jer. 31:31–33). The blind shall see and the deaf shall hear. Eternal salvation will come to Israel, home from exile, when peace and happiness will fill mankind (Isaiah 45, 52, 60, 66). Isaiah develops his best style in describing YHWH's triumph.

The day of YHWH will be the triumph of his holy spirit and the coming of the Messiah, who is the representative, the witness, and the instrument of the creator of all things. That day will implement a revolution in man, in Israel and among all nations, reconciled and at peace on a new earth under new skies. Hence the urgency of the messianic hope for each Hebrew from time immemorial (Gen. 49:8–12; Num. 24:15). This expectation has changed in form and in conceptual expression, yet it is the most original and most routinely found characteristic in the life of Judah and Israel. Isaiah, Micah, Jeremiah, Ezekiel, Haggai and Zechariah, deutero-Isaiah and deutero-Zechariah all have a different vision—which leads to numerous interpretations—but all await the hour of deliverance, the metamorphosis of the realities of national, international, and universal life in the renewal of creation.

History and Utopia

Such revolutionary courage and lack of realism are not entirely expected of a mountain people who are characterized by ascetic precision and purity of expression. Quite suddenly they follow a new direction, which will profoundly affect mankind, as they dream about the great day and foresee a much more radical upheaval than will be proposed in the course of political history, a revolution infinitely more global than its successors, including (in our own time) Marxism, Leninism, Trotskyism, and Maoism. Rereading the prophetic texts so many centuries later, one would be mistaken to see a "utopia" in them.

The Prophets forecast a "social" revolution in creation, not in the name of a social, moral, or philosophical ideal but as a consequence of their knowledge of YHWH. Their God had identified himself to Moses: *"Ehyeh asher ehyeh";* "I shall be what I shall be" (Ex. 3:14). It is because YHWH *is what he is* that universal history has a beginning, a direction, and an end. It is not absurd, in spite of the cruel course it takes. Nor is it a blind succession of closed cycles in which man is the eternal victim. From its origin, history orients itself toward that end when humanity will witness YHWH's triumph. It must not be concluded, however, that the Hebrews have a philosophy of history—they have not a philosophy but a knowledge, *sub specie aeternitatis,* of the past, the present, and the future of their people and of nations that are led by the omnipotence of YHWH toward the haven of eternal salvation. The doctrine of the Prophets is not a dream of a utopia but a vision and a prediction. Social justice, peace, and the metamorphosis of mankind and nature will come about because YHWH has willed it. In his kingdom the rich and the poor, the carnivorous and the herbivorous, Israel and the nations, will ultimately coexist in peace.

For five centuries the Hebrews receive the message from their Prophets and assume their unusual destiny: guardians and witnesses of a Torah that will give rise to three monotheistic religions: Judaism, Christianity, and Islam. Generation after generation they receive, preserve, and transmit teachings that will influence mankind's destiny by renewing its thinking, its aspirations, and its languages.

A Greek visiting the Near East in the time of Solomon, Isaiah, and Ezekiel, for example, would have seen few differences between the country of the Hebrews and those of the Assyrians, Babylonians, Syrians, Phoenicians, or Egyptians. The same habitat, eating habits, style of dress; the same monarchical regime, the same techniques for working metals, for temple construction, for warfare, for tilling and harvesting. On the physical level, it would have been difficult for the traveler to see any essential difference between the Hebraic city and the others.

On the political and social levels, differentiation becomes easier. The relationships between individuals—between King and subjects, rich and poor, citizens and aliens, employers and employees, masters and slaves—the notion of property and its control, of man and woman's private life, and the role of moral aspirations in social life give the Hebraic city, in spite of certain similarities, a distinct quality in the ancient world.

The unique innovation, however, is the Hebrews' conception of YHWH and their vision of mankind's future. Their God is a unique, transcendent, and jealous God. This simple affirmation will ultimately weaken the foundations of all the ancient societies, whose divinities are henceforth denounced as worthless, untrue, and dead. The Hebrews—and they alone—initiate this revolution in the history of universal thought, putting an end to the reign of idols, their myths, and their mysteries.

This basic stand is accompanied by a denunciation of natural man—by unconditional condemnation of murder, theft, injustice, hate, war, bestiality, untruth, and even desire. Unheard of aspirations toward holiness and justice, together with the stringent requirements YHWH's Law imposes on man, engross him and make him wonder about another human nature, a spiritual one, that would allow the cosmic reconciliation announced by the Prophets.

Finally, a messianic vision inspires the internal dynamism of Hebrew history, presenting mankind with an ideal of justice, love, and peace. The Hebrews proclaim the truth of their belief and predict its imminent fulfillment. In this way, too, the centuries just described mark a decisive point in the history of civilizations, exemplified in the birth of Judaism and Christianity. The dream of universal redemption becomes more precise and widespread. Utopia has a new possibility of becoming history and inspiring humanity's difficult trek on the road to true unity.

The concrete Hebraic ideal of the time of the Patriarchs, the Judges, and the incipient monarchy is later universalized and systematized. In some texts of Isaiah, Jeremiah, Zechariah, and Ezekiel it becomes a vision of supernatural essence that denies life and nature, such as they are, to proclaim their change: the creation of a new world and a perfect man whose soul is freed from all vice, making his fall inconceivable and impossible.

God, creator of the world, is also the sovereign master of the fate of man and the course of history. The latter is looked at in its totality: it has one goal, the establishment of the kingdom of God. All the events of sacred history—the election of Abraham, the exodus from Egypt, the Covenant, the gift of the Law and prophecy—are but steps toward the supreme end. Thus the choice of Israel and its destiny, in the biblical perspective, does not diminish God within the framework of a tribe but is a necessary act in the process of universal salvation. The people of the Covenant must become the instrument for the Covenant of all peoples, the bearers of the salvation that has been promised.

God has chosen Israel so that its people and their Prophets, apostles, saints, and ordinary men may transmit the revelation received on Sinai: the history of mankind is the most universal category of biblical thought. Creation has meaning, and mankind, betrayed by its own misdeeds, must ally itself with God in order to permit the fulfillment of the works of creation. It is not by chance that the Bible has been called a holy history (very few of its books fall outside the historical genre), but the obvious goal of all its books is the accomplishment of God's plans for his people and all his creatures. History is the central focus of creation: it has a beginning and directs itself, though through thousands of reversals, toward an end. In the conscience of the Prophets, it is a sacred rite whose stage is the universe and whose stakes are man's fulfillment and liberation.

Salvation, redemption, and liberation are positive in content: not only will they deliver man from evil, they will assure the complete victory of goodness. Justice and truth are the foundation of life.

Without them neither love nor the Covenant can endure. Justice, in all its aspects, is an essential trait of the Covenant. Originally Israel's philosophers did not distinguish between the notions of right and duty, which were confused within the revelation of the divine will, the Covenant, and the Law. The notion of justice is at the center of Hebraic thought from its outset to Job's dramatic account, which challenges God and contests his reality in the name of justice. For the Hebrews, justice is the main problem of life, and they keep returning to the definition of God's justice and man's.

This subject is debated throughout the centuries in Israel and Judah. The acceptable ideas are expressed by Job's friends: man must be just so as to merit God's blessing. In any case, he must accept whatever comes to him and have faith in the divine decree. Those who rebel will be swallowed up in Sheol, whereas the peace-makers will inherit the earth on the day of the Lord. The just man's submission to the will of God becomes a major theme in Job, the Psalms, and the Prophets. The automatic relationship between justice and benediction is challenged: the mystery of God's justice exists and man can reach it only through faith and submission. "Trust in the Lord, and do good, and dwell in the land, and thou shalt be fed with its riches" (Ps. 37:1–5).

But the demands of social justice increase and the Prophets continue to inveigh against the rich and the mighty, who are in power in Jerusalem, Bethel, and Samaria, and against the empires of Egypt, Damascus, and Mesopotamia, which wage war and cause destruction. They are relentless in their condemnation of the powerful, whose lives are dedicated to luxury, sensuality, and exploitation of the starving poor. The lowly are always right because they are defenseless, and their cause is just; the rich man is always wrong because he breaks the law of the Covenant and injures his people and the animals and plants around him. Indeed, his transgressions are absurd because everyone eventually suffers from them, and he will be the ultimate victim. Justice will triumph and will erase the most serious contradiction within the Hebraic universe, the contradiction between the domination of evil and iniquity and God's justice. The Prophets apparently were not interested in any of the other metaphysical and moral problems that concerned the ancients. Justice alone engrosses them, and the obvious contradiction that Job condemns remains a mystery for them, unrevealed until the day of God's triumph (Jer. 12:1–4; Job 21:21; Ezek. 3:20, 14:14–20).

Prophetic meditation deals with the mystery of evil and directs itself toward a new hope that becomes most forceful after the return from the exile: in the heart of the two religions that rise from the wealth of the Bible—Judaism and Christianity.

Appendix One From the Origin
to the Conquest of Canaan

Babylonia	Assyria	Syria-Canaan

Dynasty of Akkad
  Sargon ca. 2673
  Naram-Sin
  ca. 2557
1st Babylonian
  Dynasty
  ca. 2057–1758
  Hammurabi
  ca. 1955–1913
Dynasty of the
  "Country of the Sea"
Kassite Dynasty
  ca. 1746–1170
	Period of submission
	  to Babylonia
	
	Samsi-Adad II
	  ca. 1716–1687
	Period of submission
	  to the Mitanni	

	Ashur-uballit ca. 1386–1369	Period of El-Amarna

	Adadnirari I
	  ca. 1305–1277
	Shalmaneser I
	  ca. 1276–1257
	Tukulti-Ninib
	  ca. 1256–1233
	Decadent period
		Height of Hittite
		power
		Hattusilish
		  ca. 1289–1255

Egypt [1]	Biblical Facts
IVth Dynasty (Memphis) ca. 3100–2965	

Vth Dynasty ca. 2965–2825

. . . .

XIIth Dynasty (Thebes)
ca. 2212–2000 (Sesostris)

XIIIth Dynasty (Thebes) ca. 2000–1750 Hyksos invasion and domination ca. 1800–1580	Abraham's call and travels (XXth century) Jacob's entry into Egypt ca. 1740

XVth and XVIth Dynasties

XVIIIth Dynasty ca. 1530–1315
Ahmose I   1580–1558
Amenophis I ⎫
Thutmose I   ⎬ 1557–1501
Thutmose II ⎫
Hatshepsut   ⎬ 1501–1447
Thutmose III ⎭
Amenophis II   1447–1420
Thutmose IV   1420–1412
Amenophis III   1412–1375   Exodus, according to the
Amenophis IV   1375–1358   "long" chronology
   (Ikhnaton)

. . . .

Tut-ankh-amen   1358–1350

. . . .

Harmhab   1350–1315

XIXth Dynasty   1315–1205
Ramses I   1315–1314
Seti I   1314–1292
Ramses II   1292–1225
Menephtah   1225–1215   Exodus, according to the
Amenmoses ⎫   "short" chronology
Siptah   ⎬ 1215–1205
Seti II   ⎭

1. All dates for the history of Egypt are calculated by the hypothesis of the "short" chronology.

203

Appendix Two From the Conquest of Canaan to the Fall of the Kingdom of Judah

Assyria	Babylonia	Egypt
	Assyrian hegemony	XXth Dynasty
Tiglath-Pileser I	IVth Dynasty of	ca. 1200–1090
ca. 1115–1102	Pasha	Setnekht ca. 1200–1198
	1170–1038	Ramses III
	(Nebuchadnezzar I)	ca. 1198–1167
	Vth Dynasty of the	Ramses IV to XII
	Country of the Sea	(consecutively)
	VIth Dynasty	1167 . . . 1090
	of Basu	XXIst Dynasty (Theban)
		ca. 1090–947
		Siamon ca. 970–950
	. . . .	
Adadnirari II		XXIInd Dynasty
911–889		(Bubastite)
Ashurnasirpal II		ca. 947–702
884–859		Shishak
Shalmaneser III		ca. 947–925
859–824		Osorkon I
		ca. 925–889
Samsi-Adad V		XXIIIrd Dynasty
824–811		(Thebes)
Adadnirari III		ca. (860) 838–740
811–782	IXth Dynasty	XXIVth Dynasty (Saïte)
	(Assyrian)	726–712
		XXVth Dynasty (745–)
Tiglath-Pileser III		721–663
(Pulu) 745–727		
Shalmaneser V	Uprisings of	XXVIth Dynasty
(Ululai)	Merodach Baladan	663–525
727–722	721–710;	Psammetichus I
	703; 700	663–609
Sargon 721–705		
Sennacherib		
705–681		
Esar-Haddon	Xth Dynasty	Necho II 609–593
681–669	Nebopolassar	Psammetichus II
Assurbanipal	ca. 625–605	593–588
-669–626		Apries 588–566
	Nebuchadnezzar II	
	605–562	

Israel

Entry into Canaan ca. 1360, 1200
Period of Judges
Saul 1031–1011   Samuel
David 1011-·971   Nathan-Gad
Solomon 971–931   Shemaiah, man of God
                        Ahijah of Shiloh

Kings of Judah		Prophets	Kings of Israel	
Rehoboam	931–913		JEROBOAM [1]	931–910
Abijam	913–911			
Asa	911–870	Hananiah the Seer	Nadab	910–909
		Azariah ben Oded	BAASA	909–886
Jehoshaphat	870–848	Oded the Prophet	Ela	886–885
			ZIMRI	885
Joram	848–842	Jehu ben Hananiah	OMRI	885–874
Ahaziah	841	Nathan	Ahab	874–853
Athaliah	841–835	Elisha	Ahaziah	853–852
Joash	835–797	Micah ben Imlah	Jehoram	852–841
Amaziah	797–768			
Azariah	768–739	Amos		
			JEHU	841–814
Jotham	739–735	Hosea	Jehoahaz	814–798
			Jehoash	798–782
Ahaz	735–717	Isaiah-Micah	Jeroboam II	782–753
			Zechariah	753–752
Hezekiah	717–687		SHALLUM	752
			MENAHEM	752–742
Manasseh	687–642		Pekahiah	742–740
			PEKAH	740–732
Amon	642–639		Hoshea	732
Josiah	639–609		Fall of Samaria: end of	
Jehoachaz	609		the Kingdom of Israel	
Jehoiakim	608–597	Jeremiah-Ezekiel		
Jehoiachin	597	Haggai		
Zedekiah	597			

Fall of Jerusalem:
   end of the Kingdom   Malachi   ca. 500
   of Judah, 11 Ab (15   Esdras   (458)
   August) 586   Nehemiah (445)

1. In the Kings of Israel column, founders of dynasties are in capital letters.

Notes

First Gate

1. Cf. episode concerning Vespasian related by Flavius Josephus, *The War of the Jews,* 4, pp. 8–4.
2. The reader may refer to the works in this La Vie Quotidienne collection by Georges Contenau: *La Vie quotidienne à Babylone et en Assyrie;* and by Pierre Montet: *La Vie quotidienne en Égypte au temps des Ramsès.*
3. M. Burrows, *What Mean These Stones?* pp. 99–140.
4. Deut. 1:15; II Sam. 24:9; II Chr. 14:8, 17:14, 25:5, 26:11. There is an obvious exaggeration in the estimates of the numbers of troops. These estimates are more symbolic than statistical in value.

Second Gate

1. J. A. Knudtzon, *El-Armana—Tafeln,* 2, p. 877, no. 290.
2. M. Burrows, *What Mean These Stones?* pp. 90, 140 seqq.
3. Cf. G. A. Danell, *Studies in the Name of Israel in the Old Testament.*
4. Daniel-Rops, *La Vie quotidienne en Palestine,* p. 46.
5. The oldest alphabetic document was found in the necropolis of Byblos, the sarcophagus of Ahiran, which dates from the time of Ramses II (1292–1225).
6. The latter in eastern Aramaic like Manichean and Mandaean literature.
7. Aramaic is spoken in Mosul and its environs as well as in two villages of Lebanon. Syriac has survived as the liturgical language of the Syriac church.
8. The tribe of Judah is not included, no doubt because of its fiscal and other privileges.
9. Athaliah was the daughter of Jezebel and Ahab, or of Omri according to another tradition.
10. I. Mendelsohn, *Slavery in the Ancient East,* pp. 23 seqq.

11. The urban regrouping of the rural population was necessary to the security of the farmer, who went to the fields in the morning, returned home to his city or village each night, and stayed in the fields under his tents only during the harvest and the Feast of Tabernacles.

12. Cf. Roland de Vaux, *Les Institutions de l'Ancien Testament,* p. 121.

13. Num. 31:15–18; cf. Deut. 20:10–18. Archaic legislation for the conquest of cities and the fate of their populations. If the conquered city beyond the limits of the Holy Land surrendered voluntarily, the population had statutory labor imposed on it. If it put up a fight, the men were killed, the women and children were counted as booty.

14. II Kings 15:19–20 allows the conclusion that in ca. 738 there were in Israel some 60,000 heads of comfortable families, representing a population of about one million inhabitants for the entire country.

15. For example, the *Annals* of Sennacherib. Cf. de Vaux.

Third Gate

1. Cf. the scenes represented at Beni-Hassan, ca. 1892 B.C.

2. To make up for it, he identified the fortress of Tell el-Foul, which dates from the Maccabees, as a work of the crusades.

3. A. Parrot, *Le Musée du Louvre et la Bible* (Cahiers d'archéologie biblique, no. 9, Paris, 1957), p. 82, n. 2; cf. I Kings 7:23 seqq.

4. Ex. 23:19, 34:26; Deut. 14:21. Also, eating the thigh of a four-legged animal before removing the nerve is forbidden. Cf. Gen. 32:32. These laws would be elaborated upon infinitely during the post-exilic period and would ultimately constitute an important aspect of Judaism.

5. A. Barrois, *Manuel d'archéologie biblique,* 2, pp. 251–52.

6. A. Barrois, op. cit., p. 257.

7. Num. 23:5 seqq. Shinouer Document, twentieth century B.C.

8. El Amarna 73.7; 13.8; 37.52; 15.226; 8.255. Gen. 37:25; cf. I Kings 5:1–26.

9. I Kings 5:25; Ezek. 27:7; Neh. 13:16; J. B. Pritchard, *Ancient Near Eastern Texts Relating to the Old Testament* (Princeton, 1955), p. 487.

10. Cf. "la tablette calcaire de Guézer," in de Vaux, op. cit., 1, pp. 279 seqq.

11. The entire Psalter is based on a rite of passage from sorrow to joy; cf. A.C., *Le Cantique des Cantiques suivi des Psaumes,* P.U.F., 1970.

12. Cf. Fené Voeltsel, *Le Rire du Seigneur* (Strasbourg, 1955).

13. Gen. 38:8. Biblical onanism designates only *coïtus interruptus* and not, as generally accepted today, masturbation. The Bible does not say a single word about the latter.

14. Cf. *Encyclopédie des fouilles archéologiques en Israel* (Jerusalem, 1970), t. 1, p. 297; *The Interpreter's Dictionary of the Bible,* t. I, p. 848.

Notes

Fourth Gate

1. Paul Valéry, *Variété IV* (Gallimard, 1939), pp. 129 seqq.
2. Pedersen, 1, p. 488.
3. Meshnah Ketuboth v, 4.
4. Ex. 29:38; Lev. 6:13; Num. 28:3. Chapters 28 and 29 of Numbers give the details of daily sacrifices.

Fifth Gate

1. I Kings 17 seqq. Refer to the Elijah cycle, which is one of the most admirable documents of Hebraic antiquity.

Epilogue

1. Ps. 2, 20, 21, 72, among the numerous messianic psalms; cf. Paul Vuillaud, *Les Psaumes messianiques*.

Bibliography

The Bible is the primary source for any knowledge of Israel from its origin to the time of the exile. We have read it in the original and supplemented it with innumerable traditional or scientific sources published in Hebrew. The French reader may refer to the *Bible* of E. Dhorme (Pléïade collection), the *Bible de Jérusalem* (Cerf, 1958), or *La Sainte Bible* (Pirot et Clamer, éd.).

J. Bonsirven's *En marge de la Bible hébraïque* (Paris, 1953) makes the Apocrypha accessible.

The Talmud may not be used authoritatively for the period concerning this study. Yet, it has been useful for the examination of the great currents of Hebraic thought. In English one may consult the recent translations of important Jewish post-biblical literature: the Talmud and the Cabala, which are extremely accurate. Unfortunately this vast body of literature is unavailable to the French reader. Maurice Schwab's edition (reprinted in 1960) or the attempt at a synthesis presented by A. Cohen (*Le Talmud,* Paris, 1958) gives only a small indication of the inexhaustible wealth of the original text. E. Lévinas (*Quatre leçons de Talmud,* éditions de Minuit, 1968) points the way to a dialectic essential to a correct interpretation of the major currents of Hebraic thought.

Biblical encyclopedias are indispensable for a greater understanding of the material used in our study. The reader may refer to Vigouroux's five-volume *Dictionnaire de la Bible* (1895–1912) or preferably to the subsequently published supplements. These publications are old and fragmentary. A more up-to-date biblical study is available in English: *The Interpreter's Dictionary of the Bible* (4 vols., New York: Abingdon Press, 1962), very useful for its concise and complete information. In Hebrew the *Encyclopedia Mikraït* (6 vols., Jerusalem, ed. Bialik) is definitive for current knowledge on Hebraic antiquity.

Archeology is the second means of access to Hebrew life in biblical times. There are excellent French manuals for biblical archeology: A. G. Barrois, *Manuel d'archéologie biblique* (Paris, 1953); M. du Buit, *Archéologie du peuple d'Israël* (Paris, 1958); and especially W. P. Albright, *L'Archéologie de la Palestine* (Paris, 1958).

In Hebrew a new contribution in this area, *Encyclopedia of Archaeological Excavations in Israel* (Jerusalem, 1970), is the most complete and authoritative reference work. Translations of it would be highly desirable.

For information about neighboring civilizations works in this same Librairie Hachette collection are useful: *La Vie quotidienne en Égypte au temps des Ramsès* by Pierre Montet, and *La Vie quotidienne à Babylone et en Assyrie* by Georges Contenau, and the bibliographies of these works. To the books listed there we add the excellent work by W. P. Albright, *YHWH and the Gods of Canaan.*

The *Histoires d'Israël* are indispensable. Several have been published in French. The most complete and precise one recommended is the *Histoire d'Israël: vie sociale et religieuse* (vols. 1–5, Paris: Presses Universitaires de France, 1957, 1964), by S. W. Baron. This authoritative work includes a very thorough bibliography. The text makes use of information from hundreds of books and thousands of articles in several languages. This study has no substitute. Unfortunately the treatment of the period with which we are concerned is too brief (I, 1:3–181).

The best syntheses published on the life of the Hebrews in biblical times are those of Pedersen and de Vaux. Johs-Pedersen has written *Israël: Its Life and Culture* (I, II, III, IV—2 vols., Oxford University Press, 1926–40). The two volumes of the Danish scholar are timeless.

The two-volume *Les Institutions de l'Ancien Testament* (Paris, éd. du Cerf, 1961–66) by Roland de Vaux, O.P., is the current basic work in our area. The information it contains is accurate and complete and has been an inspiration for our publication. Its forty-page bibliography includes thorough references to reviews and books which have enriched the domain of biblical studies in German, English, Hebrew, and French. This is a highly recommended tool of research for the reader.

It is significant that the recent Hebrew translation of de Vaux's work has been entitled *The Daily Life of the Hebrews in Biblical Times.* In fact the attempts at a synthesis and reconstruction of Hebrew daily life in the time of the prophets are rare, incomplete, or out of date. In English the few works in this category are for Sunday-school classes and do not rise above the conscientious popular approach of E. W. Heaton's *Everyday Life in Biblical Time* (London, 1956).

For a thorough synthesis of the daily realities of the Bible one must refer to *Palestine: Description géographique, historique et archéologique,* by Salomon Munk, employed in the manuscript department of the Bibliothèque royale (Paris: Firmin Didot frères éditeurs, 1845). The work consists of 704 pages, in double columns and small print. Two maps and sixty-eight plates enhance the text, an incomparable source of accurate information published over one hundred years ago that is still current. One last comment—Salomon Munk lost his sight at the end of his long research into Hebraic antiquity.

Reference is made to two recent books in Hebrew: *History of Israel,* by A. Malamat, H. Tadmor, M. Stern, S. Saffrai, and H. H. Ben-Sasson (Devir,

Tel-Aviv, 1969); and the *History of the People of Israel,* vols. 1 and 2, *The Patriarchs and the Judges,* published under the direction of Benjamin Mazar (Tel-Aviv, 1967). These works renew our knowledge of the Hebrew past and have been an important source of inspiration.

Finally, the various encyclopedias devoted to the history of work, science, technology, and economic life in antiquity are indispensable tools of research into biblical antiquity. In French we cite volume 1 of the *Histoire générale du travail* under the direction of Louis-Henri Parias, Paris, 1959.